Group Work With
American Youth

Group Work With American Youth

A GUIDE TO
THE PRACTICE OF LEADERSHIP

GRACE LONGWELL COYLE

PROFESSOR OF GROUP WORK,
SCHOOL OF APPLIED SOCIAL SCIENCES,
WESTERN RESERVE UNIVERSITY

HARPER & BROTHERS PUBLISHERS

GROUP WORK WITH AMERICAN YOUTH

M-K

CONTENTS

P R E F A C E

THIS BOOK IS ADDRESSED TO THOSE
who have undertaken to work as leaders with leisure-time groups
of youth. It is written in the belief that within such groups lie
potentialities for enriching experience and stimulating growth which
can be of great value to the individuals involved. Within them also,
if society knows how to use them, lie the means to direct the expanding energies of youth into responsible citizenship and the acceptance of their place in maintaining and developing an increasingly
democratic society.

The community's concern for its youth is demonstrated in the
support it gives to the organizations, public and private, set up to
provide leisure-time services. It is not enough, however, to set up
committees or to build facilities. More important still is the provision
of a leadership that has skill, understanding, integrity and conviction.
The art of leadership in such groups must lie in the capacity to
understand with humor and sympathy the enjoyments and aspirations,
the struggles and tribulations of youth. It must act as stimulant and
assistance along the road to individual maturity and social responsibility. Good intentions alone do not produce such leadership, nor is
it enough to know the recreation activities that youth may demand.
It requires beyond that an insight into the deeper meaning of life as
it unfolds within these groups and a disciplined ability to use that
insight to enable people as they can to develop their powers and serve
their generation. It is to those who are undertaking such leadership
as professional group workers, as teachers of informal classes, or as
club advisers that this book is dedicated.

In limiting the scope of this book to the direct leadership of youth
groups I am, of course, not confining the use of group work either
to this age group or to the types of groups described here. Leadership
based upon the understanding of group relations has its place with

all ages and with many types of groups, administrative as well as recreational.

This book is written primarily for the professional worker employed in an organization offering recreation or education activities, or for those in training for such positions. I am, of course, aware that many groups are led by volunteers and part-time workers and it is hoped that this book may be of help to them also either directly or indirectly through the assistance in leadership they receive from the professional workers. I have not included here any material on supervision or administration, with which many professional workers are largely occupied. This omission is due to no lack of recognition of its importance but only to a considered decision to concentrate here on the direct problems of group leadership. It is, moreover, my belief that the best supervision and administration must rest on a concrete and sound understanding of the firsthand practice itself to which it is hoped the following pages may contribute. In accepting these limitations I have hoped that within the narrower furrow here defined I might dig deeper into the rich soil of human experience available within these groups and from such concentrated attention might better bring to fruition that unity between intuition, knowledge and action upon which the art of leadership must rest.

I wish here to express my thanks to the agencies that gave permission for the use of the illustrative material contained in this book. This material is drawn from records and studies written by graduate students majoring in group work in the School of Applied Social Sciences of Western Reserve University and doing field work in a wide variety of agencies. I am especially indebted for the use of their material to Maree Brower, Dorothy Dye, Julia Esty, Robert Ludwig, Robert Perlman, Howard Robbins, Elma Stuckman and Florence Tupper.

I wish also to express my thanks to my colleagues who have read the manuscript in its first draft. Their thoughtful criticism and concrete suggestions proved of great assistance. Finally I wish to express my thanks to Miss Lois Winters, whose skill and co-operation in preparing the manuscript did much to hasten it on its way.

G. L. C.

Group Work With
American Youth

Recreation and Voluntary Education
as Community Services

THE GROWTH OF COMMUNITY
services is one of the major characteristics of modern industrialized
society. It is an essential expression of that concern for the individual
which lies at the root of what we mean by democracy. As our conception of what is essential to a full and satisfying life is expanded
with the slowly rising standard of living, our democratic creed—
feeble though it often may be in practice—has been potent enough
to give birth to a constantly expanding effort to bring such essentials
within the reach not only of a privileged few but of the entire population. We have seen such efforts in one line after another produce
our system of public education, our responsibility for public assistance and social security, our expansion of public health, our development of public libraries, public employment offices and public parks.
Many of these programs have emerged first as movements originated
by private citizens and have after they have gained acceptance become government functions. Others by the very nature of their function remain permanently the responsibility of private groups. This
book will deal with one aspect of such services—namely, the provision of recreation and voluntary education or, as they are sometimes
called, the leisure-time services. Such services are increasingly regarded—no matter how they are financed—not as charity by a few
for others but as our common effort for our common good. With
the slowly rising tide of democratic respect for each we must come,
as the late Dr. James Plant once said, to feel "not I am my brother's
keeper but I *am* my brother." This sense of identification of each of
us with all frees the community services from the taint of philan-
thropy and places them all upon the self-respecting basis of collective

enterprises in which as citizens we all are both providers and participants. The recreation and voluntary education services need therefore to be seen as a part of this larger circle of the community services which out of the three hundred years of our life upon this continent have with great effort won their place in American society.

AMERICA'S USE OF LEISURE

Every community has developed certain ways of spending its leisure, but within the past century major social changes have precipitated in our society new needs and new ways of meeting them.[1]

The ingenuity and creativeness of man when released from the demands of work and when provided with any means to make life more interesting seem to be limitless. Not all of such expression obviously is either valuable to the individuals or fruitful to society. Some of it is vicious, some antisocial, some trivial. But it is a testimony to the vitality and wholesome capacities of the citizens of a democratic society that our expanding leisure and our higher standard of living have combined to produce so much that is socially productive and individually enriching. The intricate and kaleidoscopic variety of such activities defies description or classification. For the purposes of this book, however, it seems valuable to point to three strands of purpose which one can trace through the maze and which are significant for those who work at the provision for others' leisure.

There is in the first place the search for enjoyment—the chance to experience those consummations of life for which money is earned and work is done. To say that people in their leisure are seeking enjoyment answers no questions. One test of both an individual and a society lies at the point of the choice of enjoyment. What does one enjoy when freed to pursue the ends of life for which the means are made? What does our society sanction and honor? What does it reject and condemn among the sources of enjoyment? The capacity to select the sources of enjoyment that bring growth to oneself and value to the community is of increasing importance in our kind of social order. There is no escape from the necessity for such choice. This question of the anatomy of enjoyment will run through the following pages, but it should be clear at the start that for those who work at the provision of others' leisure activities this predominant factor must be kept in mind. Such activities must first of all yield enjoyment.

A second strand evident in America's use of its spare time is the desire for learning. This involves not only the adult education movement but the response of children and youth who are still in school to opportunities to learn more and different things "for fun." The expansion of demand for supplementary education is a witness to the traditional American support of education. It is more than that, however. It is the proof that growth involving the expansion of one's powers and horizons, and the development of skill and knowledge, is a widespread end in itself which people seek voluntarily when provided with time and resources. The more formal education people have the more the appetite has been developed for continuation of learning after required or formal education is over.[2] With the rising levels of public school and university education this gives promise of a steadily rising demand for more voluntary education.

A third major strand of motivation which can be seen at work in our communities is the American habit of organizing voluntary associations for all kinds of civic and social purposes. This tendency to organize for social ends is no accident. It is inherent in a democratic society where citizen opinion and action are free to express themselves in collective forms. The right to organize as well as the right to assembly is an essential element in a democratic society. One has only to remember the suppression of these rights in the totalitarian countries to realize their significance. However we may complain at times about the multiplication of such organizations, their number and vitality are evidences of civic consciousness and a welcome testimony to the basic freedom on which intelligent citizenship must rest.

To search for enjoyment in recreation activities, to pursue learning, to take part in public concerns through voluntary organization—these are among the major habits of our communities. Upon these motivations, already well established in our cultural pattern, the organized services which the community establishes under public and private auspices can build their programs.

In our American communities we have at present a mixed system which combines several methods of satisfying such needs. Obviously much of our leisure is served by commercial amusements in which vast private enterprises have arisen. A large proportion of our recreational life is provided for also on a kind of co-operative basis by the great variety of voluntary associations in which people organize for their own enjoyment or edification as well as for various kinds of civic and social action. A third development in our American communities consists of private organizations and agencies in which recreation and education activities are provided for specified parts of the population and subsidized by those interested in such programs. Finally we have the systems of public recreation and free voluntary education supplied by governmental bodies. Since this book is addressed primarily to professional workers employed in such private and public agencies we will at this point turn our attention to the developments in those two areas, recognizing always, of course, that these need to be seen in relation to the commercial and self-organized activities as well.

The Development of the Leisure-Time Services

The community services providing recreation and voluntary education today represent approximately a century of growth. In typical American fashion this has been a growth of independently organized agencies and movements, created by social pioneers and interested groups of citizens and groping their way toward their goals by trial and error. Many have grown up without contact with each other and have clung fiercely to their unique and independent status. Traditions have accumulated in the course of a century, alignments and rivalries have become established. Methods of work have been wrought out of experience. The professional worker in one or another of the agencies today steps into a network of accumulated traditions and relationships, of established objectives and methods, as soon as he accepts his job. From whatever agency window he surveys the field it is well for him to understand something of its structure and the flow of social history of which he is a part.

It is not important here to disentangle the web of traditions, aims and methods that is found in this congeries of organizations. Nor is it feasible to evaluate their accomplishments. It is well in terms of purpose of this book to provide as an introduction a kind of map of the field as defined by the major functions of the organizations within it.

One of the factors common to all these organizations at the present moment is the increasing acceptance by the public of the essential character of constructive leisure-time activities for individual health and for society's well-being. Our urban communities and our shorter hours of work have been with us long enough to make evident the necessity for community provision of some kind for the better use of that hard-won leisure. Our higher standard of living has expressed itself not only in better food, clothing and shelter but increasingly as we rise above the margin of subsistence in expanding demands for more and better opportunities for recreation and informal education. The vast commercial industries are one indication of this demand. In addition we are increasingly expecting our communities to provide us either by tax or by privately supported agencies with such facilities.

The war speeded this demand in many ways. It was obvious that the armed services must have an extensive system of recreation and education services and the public response to the USO and Red Cross appeals as well as the government-supplied services provide a measure of the acceptance of the need. In home communities the demand for youth canteens represented the same realization of the essential character of such opportunity. Industry and labor alike give evidence of the same recognition. The war-impacted communities by their very lack of the customary facilities gave a vivid demonstration of how important a part they had become of the expectations of our population. All of this development can be summarized by saying not only that we consider these opportunities essential but that we have come to think that they should be accessible to all.

An aspect of our present situation which affects our future usefulness is the state of co-ordination between the organizations. On the local level some co-ordination has been achieved largely as a result of common financial need. There still remains, however, considerable intense individualism in certain organizations and some competition. Differences in philosophy and tradition separate public and private agencies in some places. Slowly the instruments for evaluation and joint planning are being produced. Here and there new methods of co-ordination promise a more effective use of the very limited resources available.

Beyond the local level similar moves toward co-ordination are evidence of the trend. Several newly organized state recreation commissions are acting to bring together all these organizations and others with related interests, with results yet to be seen. At the national level the clusters of large private agencies multiply in permanent and temporary bodies—such as the Education Recreation Council of the Social Welfare Assembly. Efforts for the co-ordination of the several federal agencies with recreation functions are also under way and moves under federal auspices for the better correlation of public and private bodies show considerable promise. If they can overcome structural problems and organization egotisms, we may in time move toward mutual understanding and the best use of our combined resources.

We shall here limit ourselves to those agencies and organizations customarily included within the scope of Councils or Federations of Social Agencies. These at present seem to fall into four major subdivisions: (1) programs which provide primarily recreation or education activities; (2) programs combining such activities with a social purpose or ideology aimed at affecting individual behavior or social attitudes along with or by means of the recreation and education programs; (3) recreational and educational activities developed as secondary functions of organizations with other central purposes; and (4) recreation and education activities used as a part of treatment of physical, mental or emotional difficulties.

The first type includes those activities, public and private, devoted exclusively to providing recreation or education activities.[3] Most, although not all, such programs are publicly supported. They include our public recreation departments, local, state and federal, our adult education programs in libraries, schools and the extension services of universities, and the community activities of housing estates. Within many private agencies, boys' clubs, settlements, camps, youth canteens, Y.M.C.A.'s and Y.W.C.A.'s and other private institutions, recreation and education activities are available whose essential character does not differ in purpose from those offered under public auspices.

This great growth of recreation and voluntary education arising in the second half of the nineteenth century has grown steadily in extent and variety during the past hundred years. Beginning with the establishment of the first children's playground in 1866 and developing into an extensive playground movement, nationally organized in 1885, the acceptance of the value of recreation has spread geographically over the country into large and small cities. The simultaneous rise of the physical education movement during this same period and the steadily increasing interest in sports gave it further impetus. The concept of recreation extended with this experience. It was gradually accepted as essential not only for children and youth but for all ages. It was expanded to include not only sports and physical activities but the recreational arts—music, drama, dancing, crafts, and many types of informal education hardly distinguishable from play. It won its way not only as a requirement for so-called underprivileged groups but as an essential common need for all economic and social levels. This steadily growing recognition of the value of recreation underlies all such programs but the philosophy of recreation has been most clearly defined perhaps by the public recreation departments, the National Recreation Association, and the National Society of Recreation Workers. Out of these organizations especially has come the administrative experience essential to effective running of large public services. They have also contributed greatly by their constant enrichment of the number and types of program activities which have proved acceptable as recreation to the American public. Further than that, they have built into the thinking of the community the realization of the value of recreation to individuals. Such organizations are guided by a philosophy which stresses the inherent values in recreation as an end in itself. A closer examination of this philosophy reveals that these inherent values actually include a wide range from physical fitness to citizenship, from the attainment of skill to the improvement of taste.[4]

During the same half century that saw the birth of the recreation movement, a similar development was occurring in the field of adult education.[5] After an abortive attempt in the lyceum movement of the early 1830's, the modern adult education movement began to sprout in the 1870's and 1880's. The movement for free public libraries, the organization of the Chautauqua Institution, the expansion of educational services in museums, and the development of the university extension movement all got underway in those decades. In the period immediately following World War I there emerged newer branches out of the same root. The programs to abolish adult illiteracy and to provide education for the foregn born, the expanding interest in adult education in churches, women's clubs and similar organizations, and a growing movement for workers' education[6] all gave evidence of the same trend to turn to voluntary education as the period of leisure lengthened. By 1926 these scattered efforts were focused through the organization of the Adult Education Association. Many of the organizations affiliated with councils of social agencies have been a part of both these related movements for the provision of recreation and voluntary education.

In addition to these organizations, public and private, which provide recreation-education activities, we have in the field a great variety of programs in which an ideological purpose is combined with or propagated through recreation and education activities. The growth of such agencies demonstrates the variety and freedom of a rich culture manifesting itself in numerous and intertwining objectives. No one organization is likely to express a single purpose only. It is not possible therefore to describe these organizations in airtight compartments because they have in fact greatly influenced each other. It may help to clarify the multiplicity with which we deal to see rather several of the strands of purpose that combine in differing proportions in various organization programs.

One of the most prominent of such strands is that related to the maintenance or in some cases the reconstruction of neighborhood relations as important both to vital social contacts for the individual and to sound community self-government. While this emphasis upon the neighborhood is the traditional focus of the settlement movement[7] as it originated in the 1890's, it is not now confined to the settlements.

The significance of this concept and its rise into social consciousness is the result no doubt both of our urban growth and of the geographical and social mobility characteristic of our communities. In smaller communities and in stable populations the network of relations which we call a neighborhood grows spontaneously. It is no accident that the settlements came into being at a period in our history when city life and the migration of rural populations both from abroad and from our own rural areas had created the depersonalized jungle of the urban slum. Their emphasis upon the conscious and planned creation of the neighborhood as a functioning unit does in fact go far beyond their own neighborhood activities. As Lewis Mumford has pointed out, "The colonization of the slums by means of the Settlement House was an important event; not merely did it give the slum dweller himself his first glimpse of art, literature, drama, music, play; not merely did it provide a place for clubs and social groups to meet. Something else happened. The success of the Settlement House called attention to the fact that more prosperous neighborhoods were in fact equally devoid of the elementary organs of association; civically speaking every middle class neighborhood was a nonentity too. It was, then, precisely out of the most degrading poverty and the most disorganized environment that the new conception of an organized urban neighborhood with a central building adapted to a varied round of communal activities took shape. The conception . . . will probably remain even though the name disappear and the institution be modified the most fundamental cultural contribution to the metropolis of the new order."[8]

Starting from these beginnings in the settlement movement, the new concepts of community organization on a neighborhood level have made their way increasingly into other related organizations. The development of area and community councils, the opening of public schools as community centers, the decentralized programs of Y.M.C.A.'s and Y.W.C.A.'s and the Jewish centers, the development of community activities as a part of public housing,[9] the provision for community organization in such artificial communities as the camps for migratory workers—all these are extensions of the concept of neighborhood making into new situations. While such neighborhood activity under community auspices often includes more than leisure-time services, it is significant for our purposes here that one of the dominant concerns of neighborhood organizations is more adequate recreation and voluntary education through its local schools, its public recreation bodies, or its private agencies. It is also true that vital community feeling necessary to such organization is stimulated by recreation activities and expresses itself naturally through recreation and education programs. This strand of neighborhood making therefore is likely to be a permanent part of the total community effort for recreation and education services.

A second strand evident in the activities of organizations in this field is the accent on youth as such. This has taken two different but related forms—the development of adolescent programs appealing chiefly to nine- to sixteen-year-olds and mixing their recreation and education with "character-building" activities and the development of youth organizations for older youth from eighteen to twenty-five with a variety of purposes often tied up with religious or national cultural values or with socio-economic viewpoints. While most of the youth programs have been under private auspices, this is not always the case. The 4-H Clubs, for example, represent a public program of activities for rural youth and during the war the Office of Civilian Defense developed temporarily a war-service program for young people.

The common characteristics of all these diverse agencies are their concentration on the need of constructive activities for youth and their provision of a program combining recreation with some set of social values.

Obviously we, like all societies, rely largely on the family to perform many of the essential functions in the nurture of the younger generation. Within our American traditions we have always put our faith in the school and the church as the major instrumentalities outside the home for these purposes. Within the past century, however, we have invented an additional institution. This new organ is our familiar set of organizations of, for, and by youth.

These activities and the organizations that promote them represent in fact a variety of social invention whose full potentialities we are only beginning to understand. It is a significant fact that the same or similar organizations made their appearance in many European countries[10] during the past century and that most of the organizations have had, except during wartime, international connections covering Europe, America, and parts of the Orient. The taking over and perversion of such activities under Nazi and Fascist auspices have served to point up their educational potentialities.[11] It seems apparent that we have in our hands a new and significant social institution now rooted in the conditions of Western culture and developed to meet certain needs of an industralized urban society. Like most social institutions this development has come about unintentionally without much awareness of its full meaning.

Two related but independent developments have served to throw into new focus the potential significance of the voluntary leisure-time activities of youth. On the one hand, the concern for all the conditions of youth has been increasingly evidenced by many events. The outstanding work of the American Youth Commission of the American Council on Education[12] has served through its studies and the recommendations proceeding from them to high-light both present conditions and proposed ways of meeting them. The Report of the White House Conference on Children in a Democracy in 1940 gave further direction to unmet needs.[13] Officially the federal government's program for youth in the depression through its provision of the CCC and the NYA marked a new assumption of governmental responsibility. Within the past few years eighteen state organizations of various types have been appointed to consider youth needs and innumerable local communities have set up similar bodies. All of these are symptomatic of a new awareness of the needs of youth in our society and of an accumulating resolve to do something about those needs.

Concurrently with this concern there has been developing here the new realization of the influence that the use of leisure inevitably has upon developing youth. The confluence of these two streams of public concern gives to the youth organizations providing recreation and informal education an increasing significance. We are beginning to see that among the means at hand for the creation of the bridge between childhood and adulthood youth activities have an essential part.

As adaptive instruments by which our society is attempting to mold its young, it is significant to observe the varying emphases that have appeared at different times in our development of youth programs. The earliest and still one of the most extensive elements in such youth programs is that which combines religious influence with the meeting of recreational needs. The early Y.M.C.A. and Y.W.C.A., started approximately a century ago, represented the first attempt to extend the protection of the church around the youth of the period who were confronted with the dangers of urban life and employment. Some similar need to strengthen religious interest no doubt accounts for the fact that within the twenty years between 1875 and 1895 every large Protestant denomination organized a youth program of its own. There can be little doubt that the Epworth Leagues, the King's Daughters, the Baptist Young People's Unions, and more recently organized youth bodies have served not only to unite youth with the church. They have also provided much-needed recreation for youth of both sexes. Catholic programs for youth are traditionally a part of the life of the church, but in the period since 1915 a group of new organizations for Catholic young people have come into existence and the organization of the National Catholic Youth Council in 1937 has focused attention and planning on such activities. Approximately the same period has seen the birth of a large number of Jewish youth groups representing in some cases affiliation with temples and synagogues and in others various ideological interests. This development of youth organizations by all three religious bodies would seem to indicate both an awareness of youth and a new sense of the need to provide leisure-time activities under church auspices.[14]

With this earlier experience in mind it is interesting to speculate on the social factors that produced in the decade between 1910 and 1920 a new youth-forming device—our now familiar "character-building" programs—the Boy Scouts, Girl Scouts, Camp Fire Girls, 4-H Clubs, and similar smaller organizations. Although there are some differences in emphasis between these they present a remarkably similar pattern. They are geared to and are successful with youth in the preadolescent and early adolescent period. They are all one-sex organizations and serve to create bonds between those of the same sex in the period just before heterosexual interests develop. The values carried through their programs represent a kind of secular ethics centering around such personal virtues as honesty, loyalty and integrity, with some obvious distinctions between the masculine and feminine virtues. They rely commonly on competition and ritual to motivate the program, although of course their appeal rests also on the intense pleasures of the recreation activities with which the ideology is blended. In a social period when economic conditions and educational requirements commonly necessitate postponement of marriage at least ten years after puberty, it seems quite possible that such programs serve to delay the psychosexual maturing process somewhat and to sublimate those needs into activities and loyalties sanctioned by the community as appropriate to early adolescence. The fact that these programs seem to have their greatest success with middle-class youth may also indicate that this retarding and sublimating process and the social values of the ideology presented fit especially into their needs.

A further strand of ideology evident in our youth programs today is that related to ethnic or cultural values. This emphasis seems at present to be on the increase. In its older forms it had appeared in the programs of the early settlements during the period when their neighborhoods were filled with recently arrived immigrant groups and in some other organizations, such as the International Institutes of the Y.W.C.A., which had encouraged groups based on nationality and cultural interests. In its first form these activities represented an attempt to create appreciation of immigrant cultures among the American population, to preserve the self-respect and cultural pride of the immigrant groups, and to achieve an integration of the values of the Old and the New World.

Within recent years, however, this emphasis has reappeared in two quite different forms within the recreation-education agencies. On the one hand, there is among Jewish agencies an increased trend toward the inculcation of Jewish cultural values throughout the activities of Jewish centers.[15] This is no doubt a reflection of the war experience of European Jewry and the rise of the interest in Zionism in this country. How extensive and persistent this trend will be only the future can reveal.

Simultaneous with this, there is a greatly enhanced concern in many agencies for interracial and intercultural understanding between Negro and white, between Christians and Jews, and between various nationality groups within the membership of the organizations. This concern is a part of the widespread interest in ethnic relations and the realization that within the recreation and education agencies lie both occasions of friction and opportunities for experience in better understanding.

These two trends arising at the same time within co-operating agencies seem to represent diverse approaches. They both have their roots in the current enhanced consciousness of racial and nationality identification. The cultivation of awareness and pride in cultural roots is certainly a right of any group within a democratic society. The necessity, however, for working out mutual appreciation and methods of co-operation is also in our present society an urgent problem with which agencies with recreation programs are especially equipped to deal.

The heightened awareness of the democratic values produced by the demonstration of the meaning of fascism and the issues pointed up by the war have led to a rethinking of such policies on the part of some agencies. Along with educational bodies, churches, and other social agencies public and private these agencies in recent years have come to a new awareness of the need to express our democratic values in our social practices. The major outcome in the recreation-education field has come at two points. The first of these is the development of race relations committees and interracial codes by Councils of Social Agencies. Beginning with Detroit following the riot of 1943, a considerable number of Councils now have such codes.

In the second place, some individual agencies have redefined their policies into new codes of interracial practices.[16] Both these developments indicate the dawn of a new policy within the ideology of such groups. Moreover, they are being followed by a new concern for methods by which such practices can be achieved.[17]

Another strand is evident in the ideologies of these organizations dealing with youth, that which deals with relations of individuals to the community and to various social conditions. As might be expected, these strands reflect all the shades of current social and political opinion. Among a number of organizations the social emphasis consists of a training in community participation. This is interjected through social service projects especially for adolescents below voting age, registration and voting at elections for older members or participation in social action to improve social conditions. In addition to such civic concerns some of the agencies also reflect and promote social points of view that are more controversial. These run all the way from the promotion of the ideology of business enterprise, for example, through the Junior Achievement program to the endorsement of more adequate medical care, better housing, the prevention of child labor, or the promotion of fair employment practices which are included in the Social Action Programs of various agencies such as the National Federation of Settlements and the National Board of the Y.W.C.A.

The ideology of any one of these agencies which combine social purpose with recreational and educational activities is likely in fact to contain its own unique blend of these strands. Combinations of religious emphasis and personal ethics, of racial and cultural interest with neighborhood creation, of personal ethics and political coloration, these and many more find their way into the various organization objectives which select, guide and permeate the recreation and education programs that the agencies offer to their clientele. Even under the auspices of agencies bearing the same name and branches of the same national organization the ideological flavoring will differ. The strength and vigor with which such stated purposes of the whole organization actually penetrate into every club, swimming pool, team or class show great variation. In fact, as mentioned above, some of the activities promoted under the auspices of these organizations are in practice untouched by any ideological flavoring and offer the participants only the satisfactions to be gained from the activity itself. In understanding the relationships and functions of the various agencies public and private it is well to keep in mind, however, these differences in agency objectives which serve to clarify their unique functions and the place each can serve in planning for the community's leisure.

A third major division in the recreation and education programs in our communities consists of those developments which have grown up around organizations with other purposes. These include the recreation programs of industrial plants and of the unions, the use of recreation in churches, in political parties, and in politically oriented organizations. In some cases such activities appear because the members, having organized for one purpose, begin to develop social relations which express themselves in such activities. In other cases the recreation program is definitely used to attract and hold people to the organization by strengthening the ties that bind them. Such activities provide the means occasionally for direct inculcation of the organization's main educational purpose but more often serve indirectly to strengthen the attachments and to prevent distraction of interest by competing attractions offered elsewhere.

One particularly significant type of such activity for our purposes here consists of the organization of youth movements by sponsoring adult groups advocating social, economic or political programs. The only extensive development of a youth movement of this sort in the United States was seen in the brief life of the American Youth Congress during the 1930's. In that movement several of the youth-serving agencies participated by representation from their groups. More recently signs of the organization of international youth movements have begun to appear. Smaller and less influential movements of youth around political ideologies or around specific social objectives are found in many of our communities. These are occasionally self-organized but more often are organized and directed by sponsoring adult groups. Their local units appear at times within social agencies or in local youth councils. While these movements are not extensive at present, they are significant to all who work with youth as indications of opinion among youth and as influences with which groups within the social agencies may be in contact.

The final division among the leisure-time agencies is that which uses these interests and activities for definitely therapeutic purposes. This is the most recent and perhaps the most rapidly expanding of the strands evident within this field. Included here are such agencies as the camps for diabetic or cardiac patients or for emotionally disturbed children, hospital recreation programs, treatment groups affiliated with psychiatric clinics and outpatient departments of hospitals, recreation activities in children's institutions for the emotionally disturbed, mentally retarded or delinquent. In their earlier form, such activities focused on the use of recreation activities as a part of treatment with the emphasis primarily on the results of the activity —music, drama, dance, craft or game. This type of therapy has been carried on for approximately thirty years and has been used in many hospitals and clinics. More recently, increasing recognition has been given to the conscious use of group relations for treatment. These efforts now go under a variety of names and auspices. Of these group therapy and group psychotherapy are the most commonly used. The experience of psychiatrists dealing with war-produced mental illness has given enormous impetus to the already promising beginnings in group therapy. Because these two streams had in some cases separate origins and are rooted in different approaches to treatment itself, we do not yet have a complete blending of these two lines of effort. Some of these activities, especially psychotherapy or at times so-called group therapy, are carried on by psychiatrists and lie in the area of medical practice. Some of it is carried by recreation therapists or specially trained group workers working with doctors. Some has become a part of the practice of social agencies.[18]

These highly significant developments show promise of extensive growth in the immediate future and are likely to give rise to specialized methods and personnel. Since we are in this book focusing our attention on recreational and educational services rather than on the predominantly therapeutic, we shall not include these more specialized activities. The line between therapy and education is as thin and wavering as that between the abnormal and the normal. As later chapters will show, our recreation agencies contain many individuals who need and find therapy in its nontechnical sense through their activities. This is inevitable and desirable. The specialized programs of recreational or group therapy, however, whose major purpose is treatment we shall not attempt to include within this volume.

PLANNING THE LEISURE-TIME SERVICES

In concluding this introductory chapter it is well to point out that the map of agency purposes presented here in no way indicates that in reality the communities are now getting adequate services in this field. In both extent and coverage of need, in the co-ordination of services and often in the quality of the programs offered, there is much to be desired. The past century has established the public concern for such leisure-time services, it has given birth to experiments of various kinds, it has produced the first sprouts from which adequate services may in time flower. To bring these beginnings to maturity requires constant and expanding effort.

One of the most important needs today is for a clarification of the function of leisure-time agencies in relation to each other. The freedom to organize so essential to democratic social development requires also a clarity and restraint among organizations if confusion, duplication, obsolescence and rivalry are to be avoided. It is the job of agency executives and professional workers, working, of course, with their governing bodies, to keep the particular functions clearly defined in relation not only to the tradition of each organization but to current needs and to the similarly evolving functions of other agencies. The relation of public and private recreation agencies, of settlements and adolescent youth agencies, of religious to non-sectarian organizations—these and many more illustrate the necessity for clear thinking against a background of broad community knowledge. More than that, wise planning requires the capacity to evaluate both community needs and the capacities of each agency to meet them in its own way but always in relation to others.

Inevitably the methods of organization adopted by the agencies have their effect on the community pattern of larger group relations. What are the methods of organization now in use doing to racial attitudes, class distinctions, or religious loyalties? What attachments are being strengthened? What opportunities for bridging social chasms are offered through programs? At present too much of this is done inadvertently or incidentally. It needs to become a part of the conscious planning of agency policies. This will involve both a definition of those to whom membership is open or offered, an intake policy, in other words, and a defined basis of organization for clubs, interest groups, canteens, councils and mass activities.

At the present time planning for leisure-time services seems to be entering a period in which a new concept of coverage is slowly gaining acceptance. Planning groups are beginning to think in terms of the amount of service needed in a total community. For some years estimates have been used effectively in the municipal recreation systems of the amount of park land, of play lots and playgrounds required for the total population and for various age groups within it. While in terms of physical equipment these concrete standards are useful, in terms of the less tangible elements of kinds of programs needed, personnel required and agencies best qualified to provide services, planning for leisure is still in a stage of patchy, vague and incomplete thinking. This often leads to agency competition and to gaps and surpluses in service. Within Councils or Federations of Social Agencies where planning is occurring there is evidence of the slow development of a concept of coverage of the entire community with at least a minimum of essential recreation services.

In addition to coverage with an essential minimum for all there should be also a recognition that certain groups in the population need special attention and a special type of planning as to both amount and kind of services. There are obviously the special problems of the socially disadvantaged areas. The correlation between inadequate recreation facilities and poverty, bad housing, poor health, delinquency, and often racial segregation is too well established to need argument. It is now clear that these constitute a complex of factors all contributory to each other. It is socially naïve to assume that any one of them can be cured by a simple application of a single remedy. The claim, for example, that more recreation facilities alone will prevent delinquency no longer gains credence among those planning for such services. It is true, however, that the extension of recreation facilities *along with* efforts to raise wages, provide adequate housing, improve public health measures, abolish segregation and provide psychiatric services is an important part of a community-wide approach. The attack needs to be a co-ordinated one in which the recreation and education agencies play their part. It seems clear that such areas need a greater concentration of service than will be needed in middle-class areas with back yards and play space in the homes.

Another type of coverage which is only beginning to be seen is related to the special needs of disadvantaged individuals who cannot take part in regular programs but who need such experience as much as or more than the average. At present these developments are in the stage where one can find in a hit-or-miss fashion certain communities with one sort of specialized program and in another a different type. There is little co-ordinated effort to consider and plan for them all in order of their importance. Among the specialized needs now recognized are provision for physically handicapped persons, camping for diabetic or cardiac children, hospital recreation for convalescent patients, or protected group experience for emotionally disturbed youth. These are merely illustrative of the need to pick up the valid but scattered experience of today to weave into a consistent well-planned coverage for tomorrow.

A further necessity in community planning is the correction of certain established patterns which represent vested interest rather than sound planning. Every study reveals certain underserviced groups. In terms of youth, for example, there is common agreement that there are three glaring inequalities in the present recreation services.[19] They are the underserved rural areas, the provisions made for minority groups, and smaller opportunities available to girls as compared to boys. It is only necessary to examine the budgets and the buildings in any American community to have visual proof of this. The present apportionment is a measure of the value placed upon various parts of the population in our earlier, competitive periods of development. It is essential to apply to the distribution of such services the yardstick of human need and the democratic right of each regardless of race, creed, sex or age to the opportunities now considered essential for the privileged few.

Any planning raises not only questions of amount of coverage but the further question: coverage with what? The previous analysis of types of programs reveals the diversity now developed. If planning is to progress not on a basis of vested interests or power politics among agencies, there must be developed an understanding of the contribution which each program has to make and a willingness to reach by free discussion in planning groups the decision of the amount and distribution of services on the basis of the best interests —not of the agencies, but of those to be served. This requires professional restraint of the vested interests in each agency and a statesmanlike approach to the common good. Communities are obviously a long way from attaining any such program of adequate community services in this field. The professional worker must assume responsibility along with his lay boards both in planning and in bringing such plans to fruition through social action.

CHAPTER II

The Basic Assumptions
of Group Work

AS THE AGENCIES AND
organizations described in the preceding chapter have matured into
well-established parts of the community services, the differentiation
of function has produced staff with various types of skills. There
are obviously the executives whose major skills lie in the area of
community organization and administration. There are certain spe-
cialists with particular program skills including the teachers of
physical education, dramatics, music, current events or other recreational and educational content. In many agencies there are part-
time workers, paid or volunteer. There are in certain agencies
counselors with case work or other specialized training whose function it is to provide individualized service on personal and family
problems or vocational testing and advice. However, the largest
group of staff in such agencies are those to whom this book is
addressed. Although titles differ between agencies, an increasing
agreement is being reached as to the functions involved. Several
recent studies have served to define more accurately the job specifica-
tions and responsibilities for these positions.[1] They are positions
whose central function is the organization and leadership or the
supervision of leadership of recreational and educational program
in various types of groups, large and small, clubs, classes, interest
groups, canteens, committees and councils.

It is among practitioners filling these positions in the field that
there has been the development of interest in method. This has led
to the gradual emergence of group work as an approach with defined
purposes and techniques.[2]

The first realization of the educational possibilities within such groups was stimulated among professional workers in the field by the philosophy of John Dewey and William Heard Kilpatrick and its application to formal education.[3] The emphasis upon interest as the necessary foundation for learning, upon creative rather than imitative or repetitive experience, and upon the developing of social attitudes illuminated informal as well as formal education. In fact more opportunity to develop along these lines is often available within the greater freedom of the leisure-time setting.

Simultaneously a growing contact with other aspects of social work and increasingly with psychiatry has brought to bear upon the situations presented by leisure-time groups a new understanding of the bases for human behavior.

The fields of sociology and of psychology have also provided in their growing interest in face-to-face groups and in interpersonal relations a third source of increasingly scientific material which has contributed to a more penetrating analysis of the group behavior with which group leaders are dealing.

Out of these diverse but related developments there has emerged an approach to the leadership of groups already somewhat defined and clarified in the term "group work."

The very nature of the functions to be performed set the problems that the developing body of practitioners had to solve. Their first problem centered around the questions as to what people wanted to do for recreation or what they wanted to learn in their spare time. It was out of these first questions that there developed the extensive experience with program activities. As the concept of recreation to be offered broadened from athletics or physical exercise to the cultural arts—music, drama, crafts, dancing—as the obvious need for social contacts led to the growth of clubs and the provision of large social recreation occasions, so the experience with education proved the almost limitless extent of the curiosity of people let loose to learn for pleasure. One conscientious student has carefully classified all the discoverable recreation activities[4] but it is doubtful if any tabulating machine can keep up with the ingenuity of mankind when it finds itself with "free" time.

As programs developed it became clear that most of it went on in groups which provided continuous face-to-face contact for their members. It is true that some pursuits are solitary—the hobby enthusiast, the reader in the library, the solitary hiker, the withdrawn child who is alone even in the hubbub of a game room in full swing, the hospital patient with his specialized needs. On the other hand, some recreation and education is carried on in large discontinuous groups. This is somewhat inaccurately called, regardless of size, mass recreation or education. Its characteristic is plain, however. Whatever the size or type of the group, we know there are occasions where people can dance, swim, play games, listen to speakers, or otherwise amuse themselves with no continuous or meaningful relation with the other participants. In such situations the social relations, while they may be present between small groups within the mass, do not embrace the whole.

The great bulk of recreation and education activities, however, goes on in groups small and continuous enough so that people know each other and establish interpersonal relations of varying degrees of intimacy. Leaders, therefore, working with such groups, clubs, interest groups, committees, councils or canteens began to be aware that it was not enough to offer program alone in the form of recreation or education activities. They began to realize in one organization after another that the social relations meant as much to the people as did the program activities themselves. They recognized that their leadership involved understanding and dealing with these relationships. It was out of this realization that group work as a method emerged.

Since group work has had a considerable period to achieve coherence and direction,[5] it seems desirable here to set forth what for the purposes of this book will be considered the underlying assumptions upon which the following discussion of its concrete problems will be based. These are familiar to present-day practitioners who know by training or contact what is meant by group work. They are stated here only to establish the foundation for the following chapters on the concrete problems that any group leadership involves.

The group worker employed in the leisure-time agencies will need, in the first place, a firm conviction of the value such educational and recreational activities can yield both to the individual and to society. He needs to see that our expanding leisure is both a challenge to us as individuals to use such time for richer personal lives and an opportunity for us collectively to develop a rich and expanding democratic culture. For all of us such activities can and should provide the expansion and development of our powers, the essential satisfactions of companionship, at times the deeper pleasures available in a creative and democratic group experience, and for some at least the means to participate in the vital constructive struggle for a better life for all.

In addition to the recognition of the growth potentialities available to individuals through leisure-time activities, the objectives of the various agencies as described in the previous chapter serve to give focus and direction to such activities within particular agency frameworks. It is through the group leaders that agency purposes can be turned into reality. If the agency's concern for better neighborhood organization, for improved race relations or for greater understanding of economic conditions or cultural background, as the case may be, is to be brought to accomplishment it will come about as the leaders of groups incarnate and interpret such values. No agency or group leader exists in a social vacuum. The agency functions and its defined objectives serve as the framework within which any group leader will work.

If the leader is using the group-work approach he will be aware that such agency objectives, while they may serve to give general direction to his efforts, must be administered in such a way as to leave individuals freedom to choose to participate in them. A group worker is neither a propagandist nor a manipulator. He interprets and makes available the resources of the agency including its outlook on life as expressed in agency objectives. Because his first concern is always the opportunity for self-directed growth, he does not coerce people to accept points of view or teach them indirectly to become subservient to leadership. Free and understanding acceptance of new values and the participation in new learning provide the essential nourishment to growth.

The second basic assumption relates to the insight the group worker brings to his job. The group worker always is aware of two simultaneous streams of activity within his groups. On the one hand, he sees the program activities and their progress, games, discussion, business meeting, dramatics or ceramics, as the case may be. On the other hand, he sees the interplay of social relationships which make up the group. These include the interpersonal reactions between the members and the relation of each to the group-as-a-whole. Affection and hostility, rivalry and submission, loyalty and leadership, he recognizes the process of social relationships of which he is a part.

The awareness of social relationships is obviously not the unique accomplishment of the group worker. He is here sharing in a sharpened sensitivity which has appeared in separate and outstanding form simultaneously in the field of education, in the field of psychiatry and case work, and in the recent developments in personnel management and labor relations. The appearance in all these areas of a similar focus is apparently a proof that there exist underlying causes for this concern. It would seem quite possible that the social dislocations of this period are producing, as Elton Mayo has pointed out in a recent book, a lack of opportunity for many to acquire the social skills in the ordinary course of the maturing process or to find satisfactory personal relations in the usual opportunities that our society affords. As he indicates, in the simpler society of our ancestors there was a stability which has ceased to function in our industrial communities. In earlier communities "every individual understands the various economic activities and social functions and in greater or less degree participates in them. The bonds of family and kinship (real or fictitious) operate to relate every person to every social occasion. The ability to co-operate effectively is at a high level."[6] Within our society, on the other hand, the constant change produced by technology and its accompanying mobility and urbanization has produced a situation in which the social skills of communication and co-operation are not so easily acquired. The results show themselves in an increasing number of unhappy and maladjusted individuals and in the growth of group tensions between conflicting parts of society. Unless this lack in what Dr. Mayo calls the "social skills" can be compensated for, the very survival of industrial civilization is threatened.

It is no doubt because of a sensing of this danger that social relationship has risen to the level of conscious concern in so many places. It is no accident that the most sensitive and progressive of our educators should put the learning of co-operative social relations as a new and urgent element in our educational objectives. The reaction of our larger social dislocations upon the family have led to the development of family case work and to certain other efforts at family counseling. The use of group therapy and the discovery by psychiatrists of the potentialities of treatment not only in but through groups is another indication of the same recognition. The fact that industrial management in certain outstanding instances has come independently to the same awareness of the significance of social relations within the plant is further evidence of the reality of social adjustment problems today.

There is a kind of puzzle with which many of us were familiar in childhood, in which a rose-covered cottage, for example, is presented in a line drawing. Beneath it says "Find the camel in this picture." As one looks long and intently there comes a moment of click in which the outline of the camel stands out of the page. Once seen it is hard to believe that one could ever have overlooked him. The awareness of social relations seems to have come with the click of a revelation in each of these areas within the past twenty years. It is not surprising, therefore, that group workers sharing in the development of both social work and education should have had their eyes opened upon a world to which their predecessors had been blind.

The awareness of social relations for the group worker involves both his capacity to understand the interpersonal relations between members and the sensitivity to the total group process. He must see and feel the collective entity itself and the relation of each to the group-as-a-whole. This includes an understanding of the governmental structure through which authority in the group is created and channeled. It involves an awareness of the ebb and flow of group morale and the variegated attachment of each by which each member contributes to the collective phenomenon.

A third basic assumption of group work is that the program must be seen always in terms of its effect on individuals. This involves, in the first place, keeping his relation to the group person-centered and not activity-centered. Success from the group worker's point of view is seen not in terms of games won, ceramics produced or information learned, but in terms of what the experience means to the participants. This does not mean a neglect of quality or accomplishment, as we shall see in a later chapter, but it means that the participant and not the activity holds the center of the leader's attention. Sometimes a leader's desire to gain credit for successful performance by the group may become the driving motive behind the program. The group worker constantly must ask himself not "How will this program look to outsiders?" or "Who is going to win this game?" but "What is this experience meaning to the people involved?" and "Are they finding in it the enjoyment they came for, the new knowledge they seek, or the satisfactions of mutually enriching personal relations?"

Another test which a group worker uses involves seeing the whole person with whom he works not only the part of him that is obviously involved in his contact with the group. Our earlier programs used to cut people into bits. We presumably gave them physical training in the gymnasium, developed their minds in a classroom, and hopefully produced good citizenship by a ritual, as if we could cut the personality pie into pieces. Group workers are only sharing in a view increasingly accepted by educators, case workers, doctors, psychiatrists and others who work with people—that we must each see the person-as-a-whole.

The close connection of body, mind and emotions has become a commonplace of modern psychology, modern medicine and modern education. To turn this realization into practice is more difficult. It does not mean that every worker—educator, case worker, doctor or group worker—sets out to be all things to any man. It does mean rather that each plays his distinctive part in the light of the man's total life as far as he can do so.

For the group worker in a recreation agency, for example, this means not only that he is aware of the emotional and social as well as the physical and intellectual aspects of the lives of those with whom he works. It also means that he needs to see their leisure-time pursuits related to their work situations, their family relations, their community attitudes. As he fulfills his function in helping them to find the recreation they seek he must be aware of the part this experience plays in their total lives and in the life of the community. His own self-interest in the development of a successful recreation group is therefore controlled by his professional realization that he must seek first the best interests of the participants seen in terms of all their life situations.

Because the group worker does see his program in terms of its effect on individuals he should be able to a considerable extent to provide for the differing interests and needs among the members. This will not be possible on a hundred per cent basis because the needs of each have to be in the nature of the case fitted into each other and into the requirements of the group as a whole. In so far as possible, however, the group worker aims to be aware of each individual as he functions within the group and to help him to find within the activities and the relationships available those experiences which will mean the most to him.

Any group worker who is functioning in terms of the above assumptions is aware of the many opportunities his groups provide for this kind of individual approach. Within any group there are likely to be those who find it hard to participate, who do not know how to enjoy themselves through shyness, or whose aggressive behavior cuts them off from mutual relationships. If the group worker understands the basis of such behavior he is in a better position to help each to use the party, game or discussion to meet his individual needs and to develop creatively his own unique personality.

This leads us to our fifth assumption. If group workers are to help individuals seeking recreation and education to find them in the most fruitful forms they need to understand behavior. To do this they will need to draw upon the underlying social sciences dealing with individual and social development. The later chapters will, we hope, illustrate this point. It is essential here, however, to point out one basic approach to behavior which group workers share with other social workers and with some others whose professions involve dealing with people. The modern approach to dealing with people rests upon the realization that behavior is only symptomatic. Through insight into behavior it is possible with the modern knowledge available to get some understanding of what the behavior *means*. That is the important factor. What is the person actually expressing through his shyness, his aggressiveness, his absorption in his hobby, his pursuit of his interest, his use of his powers as a leader? The group worker must learn not only to see bifocally so that he is aware of both program and social relationship simultaneously, he must learn to see below the surface of both to the meanings they hold *for the participants*. Only then can he actually assist them in their pursuit of enjoyment, of learning, of social participation, of a fuller and more socially constructive use of their powers.

A further assumption needs perhaps to be mentioned here although it too will be illustrated in later chapters. The group worker must learn to function professionally. What concretely does this mean?[7] Briefly it implies, in the first place, that he assumes the obligation of using the best available underlying science relevant to his job. Such knowledge involves the understanding of individual and group behavior and knowledge of broad social developments. "Consecrated ignorance," which relies on good intentions and intuition, is no longer adequate here as it is no longer recognized as adequate in other occupations—teaching, nursing or case work, for example. As the body of the social sciences increases, their application becomes the responsibility of those professions whose practice is the providing of services to people. The separation of the social sciences from their application leads, on the one hand, to futility and sterility for the "pure" scientist and, on the other, to hit-or-miss, superficial and often harmful results to those we deal with. The road to such application requires hard study and long and painstaking effort. In the second place, the professional worker has himself under control and uses his skill for the benefit of those with whom he works. Professional ethics for the group worker are not too clearly defined as yet but it is increasingly recognized that the professional use of skill requires the conscious use of oneself. His awareness of relationship includes not only the interpersonal relations of his group members but the awareness of his own relationship with members and with the group-as-a-whole. Having become aware of them he is more able to use them—not primarily for his own satisfaction but for the benefit of the participants. This conscious use of his relationship is one of the common elements in the approach of all social workers to their clientele.

Group workers are coming to see themselves as members of a profession based on a defined body of knowledge and practicing certain skills in line with the common values and disciplines which they are evolving with other practitioners. The growth of professions of all kinds is a phenomenon of our times as significant as the development of the guilds in the Middle Ages. It is a result of specialization and of the application of science to new fields. The rise of an occupation into a profession is an accomplishment which must be achieved with hard intellectual effort to develop the body of knowledge and disciplined control to use that knowledge for the assistance of those with whom we work. It is the claim of this book that group work as a professional practice within the larger area of social work must achieve that development and discipline.

With these underlying assumptions in mind the group worker undertakes his specific job. He becomes perhaps a club adviser, a teacher of informal classes or interest groups, an executive assistant to committee or council, the staff member in the lounge or a supervisor of others performing these responsibilities. For all these various roles we shall hereafter use the term "group leader." What aims guide him if as a leader he is using a group-work approach? These will become clearer, we hope, in succeeding chapters. It is necessary here perhaps to define the over-all objectives that guide a leader's handling of specific problems. Throughout this book we use the terms "enjoyment" and "growth" to indicate what the group worker hopes may arise for the participants out of their experience in groups. Both are perhaps inevitably undefinable. Each of us must in the end define in his own terms what is the good. In this context, however, it is hoped that the reader will conceive of enjoyment as involving more than pleasure. True enjoyment in its fullest and most vital sense comes when the self is integrated and internally at peace, free of serious anxiety, envy and hostility, but more than that actively and vitally engaged, its powers expanding in fulfillment. For each person the objects and experiences which bring such consummations of life will differ. The search for the experience, however attained, underlies most of the enterprises upon which people embark in their so-called "free" time. The use of freedom, the search for enjoyment, the hunger for fulfillment, these are the common elements that bring people into the groups we shall be considering. To what ends can that freedom be put? In what ways can that fulfillment be found? These are the major questions with which we all are confronted. It is no mean achievement to find enjoyment in this sense or to help others to find it.

It is not enough, however, for man to seek enjoyment in isolation from others. Because of his essentially social nature his fullest growth comes only as he uses his expanding powers in conjunction with and for the benefit of others. For his own deepest growth he must become socialized. In these pages we shall mean by this his ability to establish mutual relations with others and the capacity to identify himself with the good of the social whole however he conceives it, to use his capacities in part at least for social ends beyond himself. Each must find for himself his social objects of devotion, but to discover them is as essential to fulfillment as to find the objects of his more personal loves. To hope for such attainment in however small a measure is no doubt the common goal of all who sincerely wish to work in some capacity with people.

We shall now turn from this excursion into philosophy. Having promised concrete goals at this point we may seem to the reader to have floated off into the abstract. Like Antaeus, whose vigor drained from him whenever he was lifted off the earth, we shall return to gain renewed strength from the concrete and immediate problems that confront the leader as he opens the door of the community center or hurries down from his office into the canteen.

By Way of Illustration

THE FOLLOWING CHAPTERS WILL deal with the major aspects of the process of group leadership in recreation or education groups within the leisure-time agencies. The author has selected nine sample groups from which illustrative material will be drawn at various points. These nine groups, while not containing examples of all the situations faced by group leaders, are, we believe, sufficiently representative to provide concrete instances of the problems and the approach of the group worker. The groups selected fall in age range between ten and twenty-five with scattered individuals below and above that line. This selection was made not because group work is particularly applicable to that age range but because the bulk of the clientele of the recreation-education programs falls within those limits. Furthermore, these were selected not as perfect illustrations of group work in practice but rather as indicating the type of problem with which group leaders deal.

An attempt was also made to select the sample in such a way as to illustrate different types of groups, a variety of agencies, public and private, with differing objectives and clientele drawn from the different social strata and various ethnic groups of a typical American community. Such a limited sample inevitably omits many types which may seem to have equally valid claims to consideration.

This illustrative material is drawn from masters' theses, term papers and narrative records kept by students who were working under the supervision of a trained and experienced worker. There is no claim made here that such records would meet the requirements of a research project. Careful and intensive research into group behavior is much needed and is so far limited. The limitations inherent in such record material as used here have only one compensating advantage, namely, that the approach used by these leaders is feasible for other group workers. The illustrative material has been disguised. Not only have names of individuals or groups been changed but minor alterations in the descriptions of the groups and their settings have been made to avoid identification.

The reader, like the group leader, if he is to understand the opportunities and problems that such leadership provides, has to develop a kind of three-dimensional insight. He must see the individuals as they seek through the group the basic satisfactions their personalities require. He must be able to observe and to feel the tides and currents of the group's behavior as a collective entity. He must be aware of the surrounding community in which both the agency and the group are set—including its class structure, its ethnic composition, its physical and social mobility, its aspirations, fears, values and traditions. In order to familiarize the reader with the groups that will serve as illustrative characters throughout the following pages, it seems advisable here to introduce each of them briefly and let them walk across the stage of this chapter as they might run, rush or stroll across the lobby of their clubhouse on the way to a meeting, a ball game, a class period, or a weekly dance in the canteen.

THE ROWDY ROBBERS CLUB

The first is the youngest group, the Rowdy Robbers Club, whose name remains a closely guarded secret revealed to initiates only at the moment of acceptance. This is a closely knit friendship group of twelve boys, although only eight can be counted on at an average meeting. They are eleven to thirteen years old. These boys live in a stable middle-class[1] neighborhood of a small suburban city. All their parents were born in this country of so-called "old American stock." None of the mothers work outside the home except one widow who is a telephone operator. The fathers are professional men and the owners of small businesses. They live in an area situated geographically and sociologically between a lower-class district where an immigrant population is giving way to Negro residents and the upper-class suburbs which represent the social aspirations of the financially successful of this neighborhood. Most of the boys attend Sunday school in the Protestant churches of the community in which many of their parents are active participants.

The clubroom in which this club functions is located in a public school building in which a community center program is carried on by the Board of Education. These boys live within a few blocks of the school and of each other and find in the atmosphere of the club the same standards and values with which they are familiar in their homes, and with which they are in basic conformity.

Predominant among the influences playing upon the Rowdy Robbers is the society of its peers and of the adolescents just ahead of them in junior and senior high school. This subculture of the younger generation provides for each rising group of this age the models it admires, the status scales it adopts, the forms of organization it initiates. This particular neighborhood is highly organized, especially with fraternities and sororities which reflect the social stratification of the parental society. To acquire some members from the favored residential districts of the upper-class suburb is to raise the level of any group—to admit the less desirable from the lower-class district on their margin pulls all down. These pulls and pressures are just beginning to affect the Rowdy Robbers.

This is no rebel group. It is a typical early adolescent clique to whom the warm accepting protection of their club provides a part of the social nourishment they seek in the process of growing up.

The leader is a young man of middle class background with several years of army experience and many recreational skills of interest to such a group.

THE SUB DEBS

The stage shifts at this point to an institution for dependent and neglected children. Here about eighty boys and girls from six to sixteen eat, sleep and play together, going to neighborhood schools and to some extent joining the nearby Y.M.C.A. and Y.W.C.A. and the Boy Scouts. Commercial recreation in limited amount also serves to bring them into the channels of community activities normal to their age group.

All the children are sent here because of family breakdown, tragedy or irresponsibility. They live for the most part in a dormitory setup, although the Sub Debs (being the oldest group) have the privilege of several smaller rooms containing only three or four beds apiece.

This group, although it had a cumulative enrollment of twelve during the program year, averaged nine in attendance. The club is a formed group planned by the staff and suggested to the girls by the group leader, who was a student member of the agency staff. The opportunity was eagerly seized upon by the girls whom the case workers and the superintendent selected for the club. All the children in the institution covet such opportunities but leadership is not available for all. This group was set up to include all the thirteen- and fourteen-year-old girls. Later two more mature twelve-year-olds were admitted.

The dominant factors in the backgrounds of these girls lie in the inadequacies of their parents and the family difficulties that resulted in their institutional placements. In six cases the parents are separated or divorced, in four they were never married, and another is the unwanted and neglected child of an immature, irresponsible couple. Several of the parents have prison records, one is prepsychotic according to the records of the Family Society, several are alcoholic, a few are reported as dull, one mother is deteriorating with syphilis.

So much human misery lies like a shadow over the Sub Debs that there is little wonder that the leader finds them starved for affection and security, for the privilege of understanding adult companionship, and for the chance at the normal pleasures of adolescence which the club can provide.

In some ways their backgrounds are diverse. German, Irish, Polish, Russian, Czechoslovakian strains, and even a Turkish father in two instances, have contributed to the ethnic make-up of these children. But with the disruption of family ties and the assumption of institutional residence little evidence remains of the significance of their cultural roots. In terms of social class the occupations of the fathers —largely in unskilled or casual labor—would indicate that they came from the lower-class levels of American society. The I.Q.

ratings on these children show two in the sixties, seventies and eighties respectively, four in the nineties, and two over one hundred.

The institution is a pleasant building set in wooded grounds in a middle-class American neighborhood. There is some tendency for these institutional children to find themselves segregated and stigmatized at school and on the streets. In certain ways the institution perhaps inevitably becomes a somewhat enclosed society within which the usual distinctions of class and caste are obliterated. Status levels do exist but they are founded on characteristics of the institutional society itself.

The Home has as staff a superintendent and house parents, who preside at tables and look after the needs of children within the dormitory units. The institution employs several case workers and regular case-work service is provided including work with the children and their families and the securing of foster home placement when that is desirable. The group worker who is the leader of this group is the only person available for planning a recreation program and has assistance in this from a few volunteers and from the other members of the staff as they can find time and opportunity. The leader of this group is a young woman in her thirties with considerable experience as a teacher and recreation worker and much to offer the children in warmth and understanding.

ROOSEVELT HIGH Y-TEEN CLUB

This club of twenty-one girls was organized as a part of the program of the Y.W.C.A. in a large technical high school. In age the girls run from fifteen to seventeen. About half are Negro and the other half are white of Polish, Jugoslav, Czechoslovak and Austrian background. Most of the white girls and one of the Negroes are Catholic. The other Negroes are divided between the upper middle-class Baptist and Methodist churches and a smaller number of store-front churches with lower-class memberships.

The parents' occupations are largely in the unskilled groups in the case of the Negroes and in the case of the whites such skilled jobs as mechanics, tool and die makers, pressers, or boilermakers. The only parent on the professional level is a Negro minister. The group is drawn from a wide area because of the nature of the school but the school is located between a Negro section and an area now shifting from Jewish to Negro in composition.

The group is a formed social club based on the customary program of the Y.W.C.A. for high school girls. Its inclusion of Negro and white is a direct result of agency policy and the learning of mutual appreciation is a recognized part of the group's program. It carries on various recreational activities. Although the club started as a school club it retains members after they graduate and is broadening its base by admitting friends from other schools. It meets in a Baptist church (white) not far from the school.

The leader in this case is a girl born in the Hawaiian Islands of Chinese background.

THE JOKERETTES

Contact was established with the Jokerettes after an article in a local paper had featured street fights among high school girls and had mentioned this group by name as one of those involved. This attack drove the group to seek respectability and protection by a loose affiliation with a community house. This connection provided them with a meeting place when desired and with a leader who acted in the role of "sponsor," a title often given in that neighborhood to adults who take under their wing one of the numerous autonomous social clubs of youth.

The Jokerettes is a group of sixteen Negro girls aged fifteen to seventeen who have been meeting for some months in each other's homes. They are all still in junior or senior high school but a few are also employed part time in the local market after school. They exist primarily in a so-called "booster" or "brother-sister" relation to a gang of sixteen boys, the Jokers. These boys, who have a formidable reputation in the neighborhood both in athletics and in gang fights, have recently been contacted by the Y.M.C.A. and have accepted leadership from a staff member. The relation of the Jokerettes to them is a usual one in the area as witnessed by several rival gangs and their girl "boosters" with whom these girls are in occasional conflicts. This relation seems to be based partly on individual attachments in which boys and girls date each other but also in mutual support of each other as groups through assistance at games, anniversary occasions, or if required in gang warfare.

These girls live in one of the worst districts in the community as characterized by the state of housing, income levels, and crime and delinquency rates. In this group three are in more comfortable circumstances and live "farther out," that is, on the edge nearest the higher-income areas to the south. Three families receive financial assistance in the form of Aid to Dependent Children and the remainder live precariously on the income of unskilled laborers. In only two cases are the parents of these girls living together. In all the others the mothers are either widows or in most instances deserted wives. All the parents are southern born but most of them moved north about fifteen years ago so that the young people have all been educated in the northern city schools. Among these girls one has had a court record for stealing, one has married because of pregnancy, and one admitted to the leader that she always carried a knife given to her by her mother for protection. The leader's impression is that some of the girls have had sex experience.

In spite of these indications, the Jokerettes regard themselves as a "good club." They consider the newspaper article an unwarranted attack on their fair name. Several of the members have aspirations toward middle-class status as indicated by residence in the nearby housing estate and ambitions to complete high school. This desire for the group was voiced by its president in her attempt to get the girls to be "ladies and cultivated"—or, as frequently stated by them, to be more "seditty" (sedate), a colloquialism referring to the respectable and controlled behavior associated with middle-class standards.

This group exists on the edge of the community house program. Its former history as an autonomous group and its tie to the Jokers (associated with another agency) have kept it from joining wholeheartedly. It also rejects the agency clientele as "tough"—a reaction to their own lack of acceptance. However, the advantage offered by the facilities for meetings and dances and most of all the protection and assistance toward a respectable status provided by a sponsor have strengthened the tie to the House.

The sponsor—or leader—in this instance is a young woman (white) who has had several years' experience in other agencies but is new to this type of neighborhood and to the role of sponsor to a semiautonomous group.

THE BUCKEYE BULLDOGS

The Buckeye Bulldogs is a boys' gang of ten members of fifteen and sixteen years of age. A few have already gone to work and the others are likely to drop out of school at sixteen as soon as the law releases them from its unwanted privileges. These boys have grown up together in a neighborhood where gang behavior is the accepted mode. The gang has at an earlier period been a part of the nearby Catholic parish but they were ousted from their church clubroom for bad behavior and vandalism. For a while they maintained a clubroom of their own in a ramshackle deserted building by the waterfront. This proved unsatisfactory and they were driven to accept the hospitality of a public recreation center. This involved the acceptance of leadership, which they grudgingly agreed to, weighing its undesired controls against the pleasure of a good basketball floor.

The neighborhood, known locally as Whisky Corners, is an industrial area on the flats near the river. It has a long and proud tradition of producing the toughest politicians, the toughest prize fighters, and the toughest gangs in the city's history. The population was originally Irish but has now an infiltration of Slavic peoples from a nearby district. Because of its bad housing and other social handicaps it was selected as the site of one of the housing estates built during the past ten years. While this has eliminated much of the slum housing, it has not as yet transformed the social structure of the neighborhood especially in the fringe of old houses bordering on the estate. The gang tradition still lives and produces in every generation of its youth a hierarchy of gangs of various ages. In this structure the Bulldogs must win their place by physical prowess, athletic attainments, and antisocial behavior. Their outstanding member and central figure is a graduate of the local reform school still on probation. He holds his position among them by virtue of that attainment and the fact that he already has a job on the boats along the waterfront and is the oldest and the most aggressive. No member of the Bulldogs can be a sissy. They must be able to stand up and fight both literally and figuratively for their status as a gang group in the area.

Their leader is a young man in his early thirties with considerable experience in dealing with this type of boy.

THE CANTEEN COMMITTEE

The next group to present itself briefly here is the executive committee of the Gay Teens canteen established, like so many others, in recent years to provide recreation for youth with the sanction of an adult group of sponsors. This canteen occupies a former store just off a busy thoroughfare. The neighborhood is made up of small two-story houses largely owned by the families who live in them. The parents are the second or third generation of a variety of nationalities and the parish Catholic church occupies a central place in neighborhood organization. The fathers are skilled workers or proprietors of small stores or businesses. It is a responsible, steady population which for the most part sends its children through the senior high school and into the skilled or white-collar occupations.

The canteen was organized at the suggestion of a nearby settlement house but is itself an independent enterprise with an adult sponsoring committee of parents to give community support and an elected representative committee of young people who assume the responsibility for running the canteen program with assistance from an adult adviser. In the limited space its store front provides the canteen offers the usual canteen activities—dancing and table games, ping-pong, a soft drink bar, a place to hang out with one's friends for the five nights a week it is open.

The Canteen Committee consists of fourteen senior high school students, eight boys and six girls between the ages of fifteen and eighteen. The ethnic composition of this neighborhood has now become so mixed that in this committee youths of many strains accept each other without apparent awareness of any difference. German, Irish, Polish, Scotch and Spanish as well as older American names appear in the roster but beyond that relic of their inheritance little evidence remains. They are united, however, in opposition to the Negro group that is moving into the edge of this neighborhood.

The leader in this case is a young woman in her late twenties with some previous experience in business, teaching, and recreation overseas during the war.

THE MIKE CLUB

The "Mikes" is a small club of nine young people, six boys and three girls between the ages of eighteen and twenty. They are all of Italian descent and live in a close-knit Italian community. Five are in the last year of high school and are taking commercial or technical courses which will see them in skilled occupations within a few months. The others are already at work as salesladies or skilled workers with the exception of one who has entered a nearby Catholic college. All the members are Catholic except one of the girls, whose family was converted to Protestantism in a nearby mission church. With these exceptions the group is homogeneous in economic status and cultural background.

This group was organized in a Neighborhood House by the leader, who invited certain individuals whom he had known through the house canteen and other contacts and who he had reason to believe might be interested in a radio dramatics group.

The nine who responded to his invitation came for a variety of reasons. One or two had been on the air in some singing contests in local radio stations. One had a vague vocational interest in radio acting. Several were interested in visiting local radio stations and others thought they might write radio scripts for their own acting. Through it all played the customary social relations of these young people who had grown up together mingled with the rather vague and dispersed educational objectives. Although called a club, this group was in fact an educational group with a sociability frame.

The leader was a person with considerable experience and skill in radio script writing and production. In this case the agency had in mind that such a group might give an opportunity for introducing some education on broader community issues. Racial tensions with a nearby Negro population were running high and the tightly closed character of the neighborhood made it desirable from the agency viewpoint to introduce more contact with other groups and new points of view. This, it was felt, the leader could do through his selection of scripts and his discussion of attitudes as they were expressed. The group accepted him in the role of teacher and coach.

THE TEEN TATTLER STAFF

This group is the staff of a newspaper issued in a branch of a Jewish center. The group consists of seventeen young people who have attended at various times during the year. All of these seventeen attended at least three meetings but a nucleus of five have been present at more than half the twenty meetings of the program year. In the group are five boys and twelve girls ranging in age from fifteen to seventeen. Several of them graduated from high school in the middle of the year. The majority of the remainder are seniors with a sprinkling of juniors who will be the continuing nucleus for next year's staff.

This group lives in a middle-class neighborhood of a suburban community, Oakdale, in which they are in contact in school and elsewhere with non-Jewish youth. Several of this group will enter college in the fall. They have reached an age in which they are aware of their position as Jews and the impact of this realization in their social setting has differing effects upon the members of this group.

The group was organized through the efforts of its editor in chief, Melvyn. It takes the responsibility for collecting, editing and producing (by mimeograph) the *Teen Tattler*, a typical five- or six-page sheet featuring the news of the center and of the school and the opinion of the editors on significant public issues as they see them.

Its leader is a Jewish young man with some newspaper experience, also of middle-class background and with considerable interest in broader social questions.

THE SOCIAL ACTION COMMITTEE

The Social Action Committee is a group of twenty-four people who were sent as representatives to a state-wide conference on social legislation. The conference was called under a sponsoring committee which included representation from the settlements, the Y.W.C.A., certain unions of both A.F.L. and C.I.O., and the Consumers League. Its purpose was to consider four bills about to come up in the legislature—a bill to establish fair employment practices, a bill to improve the child labor law, a bill opposed by these organizations to lengthen hours of work for women, and a bill also opposed by this group to weaken the state unemployment compensation law.

The call sent out for a state conference went to the local units of groups represented in the committee. Twenty-four people responded from this particular community. Of these four were from unions, two from the Consumers League, three from social workers' groups, five from clubs of the Y.W.C.A. including business, industrial and young married women's groups, and ten from three settlements representing one youth canteen, two locals of a political Youth Group meeting in the agency, and the Federation of Mothers' Clubs. In age the delegation ranged from seventeen to fifty, with the large majority between twenty and thirty. It contained four Negro, one Oriental and nineteen white persons. In occupation three were students, eight were homemakers, two were social workers, six were clerical workers, six were factory workers. Although a few were college graduates, the majority had less than a high school education.

The delegation was organized by one of the settlement workers before the conference in order to prepare them for the speeches at the conference and for their consultations with the legislators from their community which were planned during the conference. After the conference the delegation organized to continue its pressure on the legislators and met to discuss how to inform and interest the constituent groups of which they were representatives. In this case no detailed records of meetings were available but a study of the results accruing from the conference to the organizations contained information on individuals from which material here is drawn.

These nine groups will appear within the following chapters as their experience can serve to make more concrete and vivid the aspects of group leadership discussed in each chapter. Some groups will appear only once or twice, some more frequently, but as they get their cues and play their parts it is hoped that the reader can get through these pictures of American youth in action a deeper and more perceptive understanding of the problems and opportunities that group leaders face.

CHAPTER IV

The Formation of Groups

EVERY GROUP LEADER MUST DEAL
with questions of how to organize his groups in order to provide
the greatest satisfaction to the participants. If he is to go at this in
more than a haphazard fashion he will need to consider first what
people are really seeking out of this experience and then how he
can help them to find within the groups and activities available the
greatest opportunities for the enjoyment and growth they seek.

It is not easy always to discover what it is that people actually
want. A new member may register with an apparent interest in basketball, international affairs or interpretative dancing but it soon becomes
evident that mixed into this stated interest, and in fact often of more
importance to him, is the search for intimate companionship, the
need to exercise dominance over others, or the hope of escaping the
surveillance of an oversolicitous parent.

Among the groups available for such a person may be a club or
an interest group whose major purpose seems to fit the stated desire
of the participant. If one understands, however, that there is really
more involved here than meets the eye, one will see that the less
obvious but equally important needs must also be met if the experience
is to yield its full satisfaction. Each individual is unique in his
capacities and needs, his interests and emotional drives. By the time
he is old enough to come to a recreation or education group his
personality has already taken shape in patterns of aggressive or sub-
missive behavior, in capacity for love and hate, in intellectual
interests, and in many unconscious needs which will determine how
he makes use of any group experience.

THE PROCESS OF FORMATION

Collective behavior is something more than and different from
the sum of the individuals who produce it. As the members gather,

organize, decide on program, they interact to create a new entity, the Buckeye Bulldogs, the Mike Club, the Jokerettes, as the case may be. What is the process by which these new social units are born and what is the anatomy of their being?

Every group of this type as it defines itself from its surrounding community takes three steps. It develops a bond which unites the members into one. It selects and accepts those whom it will include. It adopts a pattern of structural relationships in terms of club, class, team, council or committee in line with the function contained in the bond it has formed. Every group leader who assists at the birth of a group will need to help it to define itself in these three terms before it will be able to step forth into the agency and the community.

The psychosociological process by which a group comes into being is still largely a mystery beyond the present confines of research. However, the group leader may be helped to understand such collective behavior if he will look at the bond that ties them in terms of three levels of visibility. Most groups will have in some articulate form a conscious purpose which they consider to be the raison d'être they present to the world. Such purposes, for the type of recreation or voluntary education group we are considering here, are usually expressed in terms of either sociability or friendship, as in the social clubs, a recreational or educational focus, as in interest groups, teams or classes, or in the case of committees or councils, administrative responsibilities or social action programs.

The second level of such group bonds can be found in assumed, often unavowed objectives which float in the shadowy area between articulation and the unconscious motivations that may give rise to them. Among such unavowed but potent objectives may lie, for example, the achievement of status through group accomplishment in a hierarchy of similar groups. The ego expansion and assurance arising from the status value of group membership provides for many individuals their strongest tie to the groups, especially in those situations in which competition between groups is keen and social distinctions of major significance.

A second type of unavowed interest evident during the adolescent period is the courtship basis for much group activity. As children emerge from puberty and the first interest in the opposite sex begins to stir them to unaccustomed emotions, the first approach is often through their groups. Long before this can become the open and avowed objective, as it has by the late teens, it appears fleetingly and unavowedly behind the absorption in athletic prowess or the interest in dancing and dramatics. Its emergence into a conscious and avowed objective marks the maturing of the group into full-blown adolescence and the beginning of the courtship period.

As obscurely at work in the creation of these collective bonds lie the opportunities to express through interrelation and activity the other unconscious drives that so largely determine behavior.[1] Among the chief underlying and unconscious bases of groups such as these is the opportunity they afford for the sanctioned release of aggressive behavior, the recognized and controlled escape into a world of re-laxation from the excessive demands of reality and the sublimated outlets for unused erotic impulses in creative activity. One of the major functions of play, as Robert Wälder puts it, is to afford "a leave of absence from reality as well as from the superego."[2]

With these approaches in mind let us turn to the responses of our sample groups. Within the leisure-time agencies many types of groups are commonly used. In this book we shall consider only four of the most common types: the friendship and acquaintance groups; avocational interest groups; units organized by national program agencies; and administrative groups, including committees and repre-sentative councils. Several other types are commonly used. There are, for example, teams of all kinds, short-term projects, loosely organized play groups, large canteen groups without organization and federa-tions of clubs.

FRIENDSHIP AND ACQUAINTANCE GROUPS

We shall look first into the Rowdy Robbers as its leader sizes up the underlying process of formation.

"The R.R.C.'s have no formally stated purpose for the club, no constitution. They will say that they are in the club 'to get together to have fun,' to play games, take trips, have parties.

"They made an early and emphatic distinction between the voluntary, pleasure atmosphere of the club and the compulsory nature of school when they said they would go to the Health Museum but not the Art Museum because they have had to go to the latter with their school teachers. On a conscious level they want a club because they see clubs and organizations all around them in their highly organized community.

"But there are deeper satisfactions and needs of which the group is not aware. Fundamentally, and this is obvious to the adult observer, they are using the club in their almost desperate strivings to grow up. They are experimenting with relationships among peers of their own sex and they are beginning to stumble awkwardly into relationships with girls. The shifting of friendships within the group attests to the former; the boisterous chasing and teasing of the girls in the agency point to the latter. Above all, they are learning to work together, to develop loyalty to a group, and to subordinate individual needs and drives in order to obtain the benefits of group activity.

"It is this training for democratic, adult living that coincides with the agency's primary objective. But the boys in this case are part of a community studded with fraternities, sororities, young adult groups and adult organizations and their drive to imitate some of these occasionally runs at cross-purposes with the agency's goals. This is especially true of the agency's attitude toward fraternities, which is to discourage the snobbish, exclusive and often cruel practices which are part of the Greek letter societies. The leader once expressed the agency's view on this when Greek letters were proposed for the name of the club. He said he hoped the club would remain free of the objectionable features of fraternities. Bob, reinforcing the leader's statement, said, 'Our club is open to anyone we think is a nice guy.'

"These purposes have determined their membership policies. At first, in their rush to get members, anyone could bring a friend down to a meeting and the prospective member would be voted in, without much thought being given to how he would fit into the club.

After two months of this almost open membership policy, the group began to show signs of measuring prospective members by a set of standards that reflected their middle-class backgrounds and their growing cohesiveness. For example, there was strong opposition to one Nathan P. on the grounds that he was disruptive, disorderly and disobedient, observations members of the group had made in his home and at the Cub Scouts. A few weeks later another boy, Ted N., also was rejected because he was 'silly, dirty (in the use of obscene language) and too wild in school.' He came in fact from the nearby lower-class area generally looked down upon by this group. It was at this point that Seth insisted that if the group did not begin to select its members carefully, they would have all the 'trash' in the club. Some weeks earlier the group leader had asked how many members would eventually be in the club, suggesting that some limit be fixed. A limit of fifteen was decided upon and this probably had some effect on the increasing selectivity.

"Gradually the group became more critical of prospective members. A process somewhat evident from the beginning became more obvious. In general only boys who measured up to the group's unwritten, unspoken and largely unconscious standards were ever considered. These standards, characteristic of their middle-class homes, required the suppression of impulsive disorderly behavior and put a high value on controlled cooperative attitudes. Hence even these normally healthy and boisterous boys were capable of rejecting schoolmates they considered too wild and boisterous. Coincident with this was an emphasis on intellectual capacity and achievement. They preferred 'smart' as contrasted with 'dumb' prospects. The boys seemed to use their club unconsciously to express and reinforce the standards learned in their homes and in the community."

It is evident that the Rowdy Robbers Club is providing for its members the essential social nourishment found only in the intimate friendship group. This type of group relation has been discovered and described recently in many quarters. In industrial relations,[3] in labor organization,[4] in institutional management,[5] in community structure and organization,[6] the significance, psychological and sociological, of such close-knit mutually accepting person-to-person groups is being

realized. Since they function largely in leisure time, their presence
has been familiar to group workers in what have been termed by
them rather ambiguously "natural" groups. Although titles differ,
the phenomenon is obviously the same. We shall here call them
friendship groups, since that is the most familiar name in the
recreation-education agencies.

The common characteristic of this familiar type of group is that
they depend upon the mutual acceptance of the members in terms
of their total personalities, rather than on the basis of single
interests.[7] They involve positive emotional response to the members
of the group which, while it may not prevent mutual criticism, does
not carry hostility to the point of rejection of the person as a whole.
Within the confines of such intimate groups the person feels as free
as he normally does within the family to be himself with the assurance that he will not thereby lose his relationship with the group.

This type of group is found apparently in all social levels and to
some extent among all ages. It penetrates and partially organizes
neighborhoods, places of work, schools and colleges. As "clique,"
"crowd," or "gang" it draws people together in powerful and
intimate relationships which have in many cases a major significance
in satisfying individual emotional need.

In the recreation-education agency the domesticating of the friendship group by organizing them into social clubs has been common
practice. The process of domesticating consists of establishing
organized government by elected officers as distinguished from the
domination by so-called "natural leaders," of suggesting program
activities and of adding to the group a leader representative of the
agency.

The full value of such intimate group experience to the Rowdy
Robbers is obviously far beyond their present ability to comprehend
or to articulate. The inadequacy of their language "to get together
to have fun" will not conceal from the perceptive leader the deep
satisfactions available in the secure accepting congeniality which
group experience provides at the threshold of adolescence.

If we exchange the well-ordered respectability of this community
surrounding the Rowdy Robbers for the disorganized, violent and

deprived arena of the Jokerettes, we find the same phenomenon with a difference. Here too is the same reliance on close-knit acceptance and mutual loyalty in a person-to-person relation. Two factors, however, are added here. The Jokerettes have matured into an interest in the boys but this interest is not yet strong enough to break the bond between them as a girls' group and replace it by the serious dating that will lead to marriage. This commonly comes at a somewhat later period. The process has begun, however. The curious assumption that the two groups hold, as they say, a "brother-sister relation" along with the fact of some individual dating and probably some sexual promiscuity is an unconscious indication of the transitional phase through which the group is passing.

A second major difference arises for this group from the threatening environment in which they function. They live constantly in fear of attack from rival girls' groups attached to gang rivals of the Jokers. They and their parents in several instances have run afoul of the law. Their dearest desire, to have an all-night house party in one of their homes, is regarded by the police as an illegal form of recreation. It is not surprising, therefore, to have their leader define their function in terms which show some marked differences from those of the R.R.C.'s:

"The leader's connection with the Jokerettes began on October 2. At the Tuesday night Canteen she was introduced by a member to Queenie who had been jitterbugging with extreme grace and smoothness. Later a staff worker called her over to where Queenie and Betty were sitting, saying that these girls were interested in a club which would not meet necessarily at the settlement but might want to continue meeting in the girls' homes as it had been doing. Queenie and Betty asked the leader to come to their next meeting to talk about being their 'sponsor.' When queried on how they felt about meeting at the settlement, the girls after some hesitation said some of their mothers preferred not to have them come because 'the settlement had a bad name a while back.'

"On several occasions following this first contact, the Jokerettes discussed their purpose. At one meeting the girls talked about a club motto, and when the leader suggested that thinking about the club purpose might be helpful first, Nora said, 'To boost the Jokers.' The others nodded, and Queenie summed up their feeling by saying, 'Yes, that's all we're for.' Betty expressed another purpose vaguely at one point by saying that the club was a 'sort of social club, for parties, also a sort of athletic club.'

"It is undoubtedly true that association with the boys' club is a major factor for the existence of the group, although the importance of the relationship has varied during the year. In November the two groups mutually questioned their relationship in a joint meeting instigated by the girls; the girls were insistent that the boys did not invite them to parties, called them 'bad luck' at their games, and had made disloyal remarks; the boys felt the girls were not cooperating with them in their pending anniversary, and had not shown interest in supporting them at athletic events or in casual contacts with others. The two leaders suggested the importance of frankness between the groups and realization of mutual responsibilities if the relationship was to continue. The girls voted to remain boosters if the boys wanted them, and at the next meeting of the Jokers the boys voted their acceptance. Several Jokerettes attended the Jokers' anniversary party.

"With this clarification the relationship between the clubs improved, and the Jokers became increasingly a pattern for the girls, who wanted to have the same number of members in their club as in the boys' group and to hold their own anniversary in the same YMCA room used by the boys with many similar features. In late February the YMCA refused this room to the girls following a destructive evening attended by both groups during which an outside group attacked the Jokers, and the girls decided to call off their anniversary. At this time the girls turned with some relief to securing sweaters. This seemed to be evidence of the girls' increasing sense that their club was a separate entity, and despite frequent association this tendency seems to have continued.

"The other stated purpose, a 'social and athletic club,' is reflected in collective activities which they have chosen and which have tended to conform with patterns of club recreation in many lower-class agencies—parties in homes, including a Christmas party and one to celebrate the release of a Joker from a brief stay in jail, two agency dances to raise money, plans for an Anniversary party, a baseball team last summer and a joint team with another club this summer, a popularity contest to raise money, and the often considered plan for a 'house party dance' to be held in someone's home.

"Behind these stated purposes the leader sees several unavowed purposes of which she feels the girls are nevertheless conscious. Most important of all is a desire for security. These girls from broken families, extremely deprived homes, and in most cases unfavorable early childhood parental training, feel that together in a club unit they can face the pressures of low income, unwise family handling, school demands, and the drabness, conflicts, and lack of privacy of a sick community. The club grouping helps them also accept the stresses of adolescent growth. Here they can talk out individual pressures and relieve to some extent inner and outer insecurities and tensions. The girls have not been vocal about a desire for security, but they have given various indications of it by their aggressive or shy behavior when attending a few of the agency functions. Clarice, the president, said, for example, 'Lots of people didn't like our club, but if I can have my sweater in June I don't care a gosh darn.'

"The leader feels a second unavowed purpose, less important than the desire for security, is a desire to rise to a more middle-class status, as a group and in most cases, individually. They are ambivalent at this point for they also give evidence of not wishing to conform to more rigid standards of behavior represented by the agency.

"The first night when Queenie and Betty discussed the possibility of a 'sponsor' the other staff worker present questioned the wisdom of the name Jokerettes, in view of the poor reputation of the brother club. Queenie said earnestly, 'But we want to do things that make people raise their ideas about the club, and keep the same name.' "

Both the R.R.C.'s and the Jokerettes indicate as the fundamental bond that unites them the need of these adolescents for the close intimacy and full acceptance of the typical friendship group. The additional elements in their purpose, some of them below the level of avowal or even of consciousness, show the impact of different social settings molding psychological needs by the social pressures within which they must seek their satisfactions.

It is valuable to turn from these "natural" groups spontaneously formed to meet urgent needs to the artificial situation of the Sub Debs. In this case, at the instigation of the staff, a formed social club was created within a children's institution to provide an experience similar to that of a friendship group to girls who seemed unable or unwilling to create one for themselves. Observation in this institution seems to indicate few spontaneous friendship groups. It is not yet clear to the social workers studying this whether this lack is due to the rejection or neglect by the families which may have made these girls less able emotionally to establish meaningful relationships or whether it is because they hope and expect their stay to be brief and so do not want to commit themselves to a mutual undertaking. At any rate the usual friendship groups are largely absent. Obviously no artificial formation can quite take its place. However, the staff has felt that perhaps the largest element lacking for these girls was the experience of warmth and acceptance from their peers and from an understanding adult in a group small enough so that the relationship would not have to be too diluted. It is in the light of this purpose on the part of the staff that one must interpret the following account of the group's formation:

"The Sub Debs was formed in October. After a few days of becoming acquainted in an informal way—at the table, in the playrooms and in the yard—the leader invited the thirteen and fourteen year old girls to meet with her in the recreation room. Because of their familiarity with the program at the Home, they knew that this meant the possibility of a club even though it was not mentioned. Eight girls came and all said they were thirteen or fourteen. As they gathered she wrote down each girl's name and then explained to them that they could form a club this year if they so desired. They were enthusiastic at once, for belonging to a small group at the Home has come to have status value in itself and to carry special privileges as well as meeting the desire for a small group. Hence the suggestion at once formed the club.

"They felt no need for a purpose; the formation of the club seemed to them like the granting of a privilege and they were inclined to see no further than that. Hence the leader took the initiative in asking the group to think about what they wanted to get out of belonging to a club. This question was too theoretical to get much response; so the leader shifted her question to the possible activity and asked what the group wanted to do during the club periods. The response was noisy and confused. Some did not know what to say and others began all talking at once each trying to be louder than the rest. There seemed to come out of this discussion a fairly unanimous agreement that they wanted to go roller skating and swimming, that they might sew and knit and cook (the latter suggestion met with not much enthusiasm), and that they wanted to have a party without the rest of the Home. As far as the worker could see, their purpose was to have privileges which non-organized groups within the institution could not have.

"This group never developed a written stated purpose. Its verbal purpose is 'To go places, have parties, and have fun.'

"Judging from its behavior the dominant purposes of the group included many unavowed and some unconscious motives. It is very well understood that belonging to a group brings privileges like being allowed to go on trips, to get special materials with which to work or play, to get away from the noisy and crowded playroom at least one evening a week, to have parties, to have special food occasionally, and to have the leader in a closer relationship. Children in organized groups seldom voice this privilege motive but those left out voice it very loudly. It is a strong motivation even though un-avowed by the group. The group's choice of activities following this purpose is proof. The agency plays into this motive quite overtly because special privileges cannot be granted to children without an adult sponsor. A less conscious motive is the desire on the part of these children to seek a relationship with an adult. They want love, approval, understanding, and individual attention. At the same time their experience has taught them to be suspicious of adults and they feel required to test the adult's acceptance of them often through overt misbehavior. Their own feelings in this respect are frequently in conflict. They will fight for attention and affection and thus put their wrong foot forward. Realizing their own lack of cooperation then, they are unhappy with themselves. They want the leader to make them want to do what will make them happy. The leader believes the children in this group have some awareness that part of their purpose is to be close to her but she thinks the reasons for this desire are largely unconscious.

"The leader has had two big purposes for the group: To try to meet the individual needs for an adult relationship by being accepting, non-punitive in attitude, impartial, steady, consistent, responsive, and understanding insofar as she is able, and to try to create some group feeling—an appreciation of the needs and wishes of other members, a willingness to negotiate and cooperate with the desires of others, an ability to see beyond one's own self and find pleasure in group as well as self-centered feelings.

"The leader sees these as basic needs and feels that in a relative way this group experience has helped the girls to move in a constructive direction but she realizes that there is still a long way to go. An appreciation of the deprived background and present emotional disturbance of these children makes relative progress satisfying and patience enduring. The members of the group have received some satisfaction too in that their overt purposes have been pretty well met and some of their basic needs have been constructively modified."

As we shall see in a following chapter this group, which started on a basis of relationship to an accepting adult and the pleasures of exceptional activities available to them, developed in time much of the mutual acceptance and group identifications characteristic of the spontaneous friendship group.

The friendship group, usually of five to fifteen members, is not the only variety of relationship that is rooted in person-to-person interaction. In the larger social clubs, such as Hi-Y or Y-Teen clubs, youth canteens or young adult clubs of from fifteen to a hundred members or more a more superficial but still personal interaction is established. They are acquaintance rather than friendship groups. Closer observation will often discover that one of the main functions of these acquaintance groups is to provide a hospitable opportunity for locating the congenial spirits out of which close friendship groups can form for those capable of establishing them. A large canteen group of eighty to a hundred boys and girls recently studied showed within it nine friendship groups already organized into clubs, several others clearly discernible but not crystallized into organization, and a considerable number of drifting, or isolated individuals. Some of these latter are in process of locating their intimates; some are unable because of either mental inadequacy or emotional incapacity to win their way into the mutual acceptance required for the friendship group membership.[8]

The objections sometimes raised by leaders to so-called cliques within large groups arises from a mistaken conception of basic needs. It is these cliques which often provide the deeper and more meaningful relationships. The problem is to relate them in valuable interaction with the inclusive purposes of the over-all group that they also share. Among our illustrative groups the Gay Canteen illustrates this type of group formation. Within the friendly atmosphere of a large group organized for various recreational activities, friendship groups and courtship pairs can find opportunities to function.

Avocational Interest Groups

A second major variety of group relationship used in recreation-education agencies is that which we shall here call avocational interest groups. The common characteristic of these groups as distinguished from the person-to-person friendship or acquaintance type is that they rest on a similar interest among individuals which requires collective expression. Persons touch each other, as it were, with one facet of themselves, their interest in ceramics, in international affairs, in Polish cultural values, for example, but do not commit themselves to each other in the full mutuality of friendship. Such relationships are not necessarily superficial. They may reach deep needs and provide essential satisfactions at the points at which individual interests coalesce. The emotional root of such interest often lies far below the conscious level. The ability of these pursuits to call forth effort, to enlist capacities, to establish absorbing and enriching outlets for unused energy is only beginning to be recognized.

Recent studies of the incidence of such interests in persons treated in a psychiatric clinic show not only that they have fewer hobbies than those common among a group of normal persons but that such hobbies are of shorter duration and are pursued in a more desultory fashion.[9] This conclusion would seem to indicate that the ability to find satisfactory sublimation through such pursuits is itself an indication of and an assistance to mental health.

While the unconscious bases of individual avocations are only beginning to be understood, enough is now clear to indicate their importance for a well-balanced life. As the Menninger Clinic experience shows, the real difference between work and play lies in the use made of the activity and not in the actual occupation itself. As stated in the study of such avocations, "the psychiatrist plays at being a photographer, the professional photographer plays at being a horticulturist, the florist plays at being a carpenter, the carpenter plays at being an artist, the artist plays at being a cook and the cook may along with several million other blithe spirits be playing at being a psychiatrist."[10]

Such avocations give an opportunity within sanctioned limits for the creativeness and unpunished expression of aggression which the rest of life often does not permit. They can give scope for adventure and pioneering and for the satisfaction of achievement in the avocational worlds created by those who share intensely in such pursuits. Recent research would suggest that mental health will be improved as society acting in the role of the approving parent gives scope and opportunity for such indulgence.[11]

For the group worker the realization of the psychological significance of avocations has many implications. It should make him more alert in providing assistance to individuals in finding what will for each of them fulfill this need. Because many people will have to have groups in which to pursue such avocations, it will require him to provide the group in which such avocations can be found. In the drama club, the dance group, the discussion class, the social action committee, he will catch the sense of absorption and delight in accomplishment that gives him the clue to the fact that through these interests underlying drives are finding fruitful outlets. It is a part of his function to provide rich opportunities for experimentation with such interests and the facilities necessary for their expression.

There is often apparent a mistaken conception that what ties people to such avocational groups is simply and predominantly the obvious interest basis of the group. Closer examination reveals that the program interest is only a part—perhaps a minor part—of the true bond. Of the two interest groups among our samples, the Mike Club and the Teen Tattler Group, we shall select at this point the latter. The leader's report on its formation shows clearly the interplay of needs and motives of which an interest in journalism was only one.

"This record of a teen-age newspaper group must begin with Melvyn Jacobs, for he was the dynamo who set the activity in motion and charged it with his restless energy for the eight months of its rich development.

"Even before the House officially opened its doors in the Fall, Melvyn had spoken with the supervisor about his one absorbing interest—journalism. They had discussed the publication of a teen-agers' newspaper and when the leader assigned to this activity met Melvyn at a Sunday afternoon open house, he had with him detailed, written plans for the format and organization of the paper.

"In this first meeting with the leader, Melvyn explained that he was writing a weekly column for a local newspaper and that he wanted all the experience he could get in journalism. He clearly saw himself as editor and finally led up to the suggestion that he be designated as the representative and spokesman for the teen-age group through the newspaper. He said he would invite a group to a meeting that week.

"At the time Melvyn was eighteen and a senior in the high school of a suburb adjoining the one in which the agency was located. He was an only child and his family had moved to the community three years before. His father was a salesman and their socio-economic status can be considered middle middle-class.

"In appearance Melvyn is of slight build, his face is freckled and his skin is usually in poor condition. He wears glasses and dresses neatly. Through his membership in a fraternity of Jewish boys with fairly high status and his participation in the agency, he is identified with the Jewish community, but his consistent efforts to separate himself from Jewish religion and culture betray a deep feeling of uneasiness about his Jewishness. His manner, behind the facade of the ace newspaperman, is compounded of the twin elements of aggressiveness and insecurity.

"Melvyn was running from one activity to another—his weekly column, his fraternity which placed a high value on athletic achievement and from which he withdrew after a few months, his position as publicity man and manager for several high school dance orchestras. For him recognition, fame and the opportunity to appear with his 'steady' girl were important though hardly conscious motivations for his active participation in the group. Perhaps he was too insecure to seek openly the friendship of other boys and girls, but his grasping for recognition seemed always to be related to adults and to the teen-age community en masse rather than to the individuals in the newspaper group.

"Melvyn was 'going steady' with Shirley Robb, an attractive but extremely tense and insecure girl, whom he brought to the paper as the art editor. Melvyn wanted this to be considered a stable, adult relationship, but built as it was on two insecure personalities, it proved to be fraught with more than the usual adolescent instability. Shirley had some skill in drawing and was taking lessons at the Art Museum. Melvyn and Shirley were deeply dependent on each other, but had few other close and friendly relationships. Out of Shirley's insecurity grew a strong need to dominate everyone, particularly Melvyn, as well as a need to prove that she could attract other boys. She used the group to serve both these needs.

"For the first meeting, in addition to his girl, Melvyn had rounded up three of his fraternity brothers, who dropped out of the group after a few meetings. The sixth member at the first meeting, Ruth, had been invited by the supervisor of the branch.

"Ruth was seventeen, quite attractive and in her last semester of high school. She had, despite an outward reserve, a great deal of poise based on real inner security. She had many friends and though she attracted high school boys, she had begun to go out on dates with college students. In addition to many activities in the Jewish and general community, she was interested in becoming a volunteer leader in the agency. Above all, as the daughter of warm and understanding parents, who had been born in Europe and whose family life embodied a rich heritage of Jewish culture, Ruth was comfortable and at home in her Jewishness. For Ruth the newspaper group meant stimulating activity and a relationship with an adult male leader.

"These three—Melvyn, Shirley and Ruth—provided the stable core of the group throughout its existence. Each of them attended at least twenty of the twenty-five meetings of the group from October through June.

"Within the first few weeks a girl and three boys, all of whom were very active in the highly organized Jewish community, joined the group. The three boys came to the group from another Jewish organization, a local unit of a national fraternal order.

"For four months these seven made up the staff of the paper. They came, ostensibly, because of their interest in working on a newspaper and learning some of the techniques of writing, editing and make-up. Certainly that is what they would and did say was their avowed purpose. But they were all well into their adolescence and the need for boy-girl associations was a strong and determining factor in their participation in the group.

"The end of the first semester at the High School, where every member of the group except Melvyn was a student, produced some sharp and interesting changes in the membership of the newspaper staff. . . . A number of the group were completing their high school education and were already oriented toward college. Their interests were expanding, their curiosity was reaching out to areas and problems in the adult community and unconsciously some of them were using the group and its leader to help them cross that bridge. But the crystallization of this need into clear-cut form was expressed soon after the mid-year graduation in the formation of a definite subgroup of four who were waiting to get into college.

"Of these Ruth had been coming regularly. Immediately after leaving school, Elsie Ryder, Doris Wolf and Bernard Wise became active members of the newspaper group. Doris and Elsie had neither too much security nor breadth of interest. To them coming to the group and the house was largely a means of keeping up social contacts. They spoke continually of college but it meant to them preparation for marriage and not a career.

"Bernard, the fourth member of this sub-group, was an extremely sensitive and intellectually mature boy with a deep interest in the theater and in music. He was ill at ease with girls and though he was strongly drawn to Ruth, one wondered whether his highly developed intellectual and esthetic interests were not defenses for his social discomfort. The group, however, served both his conscious interests and his less conscious needs for socialization.

"All of these four graduates were working, marking time for a semester until they could enter college in the fall. They were cut off almost traumatically from their high school activities and associations. Doris and Elsie had to adjust to a sudden change, to the status of 'passives' in their sororities. These four felt severed from their normal group affiliations and they grabbed on to the newspaper staff to help them through this period. As Elsie put it when the other members of the group saw her there for the first time and expressed some surprise, 'Just because I've graduated doesn't mean I'm dead.' Often this sub-group stayed long after the meeting was over to discuss with the leader books, music, the theater and broad social and political problems.

"In general the boys and girls in this group were meeting their needs for heterosexual associations, for a stimulating experience that helped to raise their intellectual and social horizons and a relationship with a young adult leader. The latter was particularly important to the late-adolescent girls in the group.

"What was the background of these boys and girls, the socio-economic and cultural patterns of the community of which they and the agency were parts? Without exception they came from middle-class Jewish homes.

"For the most part Jewish people in Oakdale literally looked down on the dress, speech and mores of their erstwhile neighbors, who still had some of the characteristics associated with the immigrant and his European-Jewish culture. The Oakdale people had modernized their religious activities, softened their speech and taken on middle-class standards of behavior.

"To the extent that an individual, a family or a group reflected the 'city' mores, they were socially rejected. On the other hand, the 'city' Jews were straining to move to Oakdale or if that were not possible because of their income or the housing shortage, at least to move their social life to that community. Consequently within the national organizations, the status of a chapter depended on the number of 'city' boys or recent newcomers to Oakdale. One evening some of the 'Teen Tattler' girls met the members of one of these groups and asked, 'Who are those Dead End kids?' Floyd Merriam, with his more aggressive manners and less controlled behavior, represented this conflict within the newspaper group. He was never given full acceptance and his attendance thinned out.

"But the population of Oakdale was only half Jewish and relations with the Gentile half were what they are in most American communities—not unfriendly but not without definite distinctions. Melvyn, so quick to disparage the use of Jewish words or an 'over-emphasis' on things Jewish, once insisted that an article on vocational opportunities be realistic and discuss job discrimination against Jews and the fields that are open or closed to Jewish youth.

"There can be no single generalization, however, about the attitudes and feelings of Oakdale Jews toward Gentiles and toward their own Jewishness. Some, like Ruth, were secure in being Jewish and secure in all their social relationships. Others, like Melvyn, were caught in the conflict between the realistic position they had as Jews and their unconscious desire to run away from being Jewish. In any case, the multiplicity of organizations in the Jewish community may well be a compensation and a defense for the discrimination and prejudice that still exists.

"The group began discussing the role of the paper in relation to the agency and to youth groups in Oakdale. Shirley immediately raised the question of relations with non-Jewish groups. The group wanted to know the agency policy in that area. The leader explained that agency membership was open to anyone who wished to join provided they understood the Jewish orientation of the agency. The fact is that despite strenuous efforts on the part of Melvyn and Shirley, no non-Jewish boy or girl ever joined the 'Teen Tattler' staff, though some cooperation with individuals in a church group was achieved.

"The group went on at the meeting to ask about the agency itself. When the leader had explained the structure and function of the agency, the group returned to the discussion of relations with non-Jewish clubs and individuals, particularly in school. There was general agreement that these relations could and should be improved. Shirley felt the newspaper should make active efforts to break down barriers. Ruth said this was not the function of the paper. Discussion finally brought agreement that the paper would serve primarily to report and reflect events and developments among Oakdale Jewish youth and that this necessarily involved their relations with non-Jewish groups.

"The group ended its first meeting by setting as its three immediate tasks establishing relationships with all Jewish youth groups in the community as news sources and as channels for distribution, expansion of the staff and preparation of the first issue. The group was quick to see the positive implications of their plans for increasing participation in the agency's program."

The group leader has here to deal with a complexity of interests. The interest in journalism, while active, is blended with courtship concerns, the transition between high school and college, and most of all the search for a satisfying adjustment to their position as Jews in a mixed community of Jews and Gentiles.

NATIONAL AGENCY GROUPS

As already indicated many agencies have been organized not for recreation or education alone but to promote a viewpoint through the recreational and educational activities they offer. At the point of formation this may appear in two ways—agencies may establish the purpose first and recruit members interested in it; they may select individuals for organization in order through certain social configurations so produced to affect social attitudes.

The turning of agency purpose of this type into group program is clearly seen in the familiar youth-serving agencies—the Scouts, the Camp Fire Girls, the 4-H Clubs, the Junior Achievement Groups, the Hi-Y and Y-Teen programs.

A complex set of recreational activities is designed to embody the values which the agency aims to promote. A kind of avocational curriculum is developed which appeals to many interests and meets many unconscious as well as conscious needs. The sense of belonging to a large and powerful national organization, the prestige accorded by adults to the uniform and ritual, the well-ordered and controlled movement of the program giving to some uncertain adolescents a stability and conformity they require—all these are offered through these programs in addition to the joys of intimacy often present, and the pursuit of absorbing recreational interests.

The case of the Y-Teen group illustrates this combination of group purposes. It is interesting to note the modification of the agency's prepared program by the bond formed after the group was organized. The leader reports the process as follows:

"The Y-Teen Club was organized after extensive publicity in the school. It was not a natural group formation, but a group who came together to take advantage of an agency program. All had differing needs and interests, but each hoped to find in the agency program some satisfaction for herself. At the opening membership meeting, girls were asked to indicate their choice of committees or interest groups they wished to belong to. These committees included: membership and publicity, program, social, public affairs, and worship and community service. On the basis of these individual choices, the group was divided and chairmen were appointed for each of the committees. At this first meeting there were six white girls and eleven Negro girls.

"At the opening membership meeting girls were given a checklist of desired club activities, giving in more detail the general activities listed in the publicity folder. On the basis of the findings of this survey list, the officers made out a tentative plan of club activities, to help realize more meaningfully the purposes for which the club members formed the club.

"Stated in Y-Teen goals, the purpose of the Y.W.C.A. helps a girl: (1) to grow as a person; and (2) to grow in friendship with people of all races, religions, and nationalities. In terms of the above-stated Y-Teen goals, a Y-Teen club builds its program around six program emphases: the arts; health; personal and family relations; problems of social concern; religion; and work. Some of these program emphases are included in the club program only incidentally; and others have a major part in the program. Interpretation of these goals is consciously made in ceremonials and in other program areas of work; but the readiness to accept these goals differs with each individual girl. She may have what she thinks are very different goals, such as, having fun with boys; but the leader sees her immediate goal not in conflict with the stated Y-Teen goals, but only as the individual's way of expressing what she thinks and feels is her personal growth area. Because of its interracial aspect, these goals hold much meaning and significance for the members of this group. Some of the members are matured enough in their thinking to grasp the meaning of these goals broadly and have helped the others along.

"As the leader gained a better understanding of individual and group behavior, the following seem to be the dominant purposes of the group: to make new friends with girls of their own age and racial groups; to participate in more recreational activities; to meet 'nice' boys and have fun with them; to learn certain recreational and other program skills. Underlying these dominant purposes are certain evident needs, some of which were lacking in the homes. They seemed to have a need for security and affection which they sought from belonging to a group."

At one point, however, in the determination of membership the agency's policy had a major effect on the group process. The agency policy is, in this case, to include in a club organized within a school anyone attending the school. In a school like this one this meant that the club was open to both Negro and white girls. Moreover, it was a part of the agency's program to encourage mutual understanding and activities without discrimination. This policy required interpretation although it was understood by all who joined the club in the first place. The leader indicates the concrete way this agency aim affected membership practices:

"In their desire to increase the club membership, and to have full responsible participation by dividing club responsibilities, the Negro president and the colored members in the group who comprised the club majority were emphasizing the role of the Negro girls in the club and in turn giving less place to the white girls. More of their colored friends were invited to join the club and important club responsibilities were delegated to them. The white girls gradually lost interest in the club. It became necessary for the leader and the cabinet to think through this situation in order to bring a wider club participation. The result of joint thinking was a recommendation to change the meeting time for the club to a time desired by the white girls. Through this change the white members were able to invite more of their neighborhood friends to join the group, and so the club was able to maintain its interracial balance and realize more purposefully this objective."

The effect of this interracial membership in determining relations within the group will be discussed in a later chapter.

The Y-Teen Club shows in its process of formation many of the characteristics of agency-determined groups of this kind. A program of activities is offered by an agency through the usual publicity media—folders, school radio, and other means. The response is in part to the activities offered, in part to the reputation the organization has acquired among potential members, and in part to the opportunity such groups offer to satisfy basic needs through or sometimes in spite of the agency's program.

As one compares the dominant purposes of this group, unavowed but evident to the leader with the neatly formulated program emphases presented to them on admission and tacitly accepted in order to become members, one is tempted to wonder how in reality the twain can be made to meet. This is not an unusual situation in adult-planned youth programs. The saving element often lies in the capacity of youth to secure their essential satisfactions through many channels unbeknownst to their sponsoring agency. However, the approach of the group worker to such groups rests rather on a realistic understanding of what are the true motivations forming the group, unavowed and unconscious but still clearly indicated in acts if not in words. As this leader comes to see the individuals and their needs, the agency's objectives formulated in its program remain as a guiding direction and, when the group's interest is ready for it, a set of activities available for them to use. Only where there is emotional readiness can real education ensue.

Where the ideological purpose of the agency is related to the promotion of social viewpoints his purpose is likely to appear in direct teaching through promoted programs, as in the case of the Mike Club. In many cases it also affects the selection of group members for organization. Agencies, for example, with aims related to ethnic cultures, Jewish, Polish or Italian, are likely to organize their groups to secure homogeneity of this type. If their purpose is to promote intergroup understanding, this obviously will produce membership requirements opening the groups to people of all racial or nationality backgrounds. When they aim to produce interest in economic problems of particular groups, such as young business girls, household employees or industrial workers, this objective will affect grouping in order again to strengthen this interest by securing a group homogeneous in this respect in which loyalty and concern for common economic problems can be built. On the other hand, where an organization such as a settlement house aims to produce interest in and loyalty to a neighborhood, it will organize its groups not only within the neighborhood geographically but of such a composition as to unite in co-operative effort elements in the area which are isolated or hostile to each other. In areas of differing ethnic composition this may mean the conscious use of both program and organization policies to produce acquaintance, reduce fear and prejudice, and eventually unite for common recreation activities and common projects of neighborhood improvement.

In all groups of this kind, whether clubs, classes, teams, canteens or committees, the basis of formation contains an element of purpose injected by the sponsoring agency. Person-to-person responses and avocational interests provide a considerable part of the bond that unites these groups as they do others. The objective of the agency, whether it involves transmission of religious teaching, "character" values or social viewpoints, will in fact be fulfilled only as the group members respond to and sincerely accept the agency's aims. The validity of providing within the community opportunities for such education seems beyond question. In a society such as ours, one of the essential freedoms is the opportunity to attempt to convert others and especially to bring up the young in the values cherished by groups of adults. In terms of the method here used by the agencies it is essential that group leaders look realistically and penetratingly at the social process with which they are dealing. If agency objectives appear only on the level of the avowed and articulated purpose of the group, but there is evidence that the more potent ties are actually other than or even contradictory to the agencies' values, it is well to reconsider the methods being used. One is tempted to wonder how many small boys learned effective lessons in deceit and hypocrisy when their only way of securing a coveted trip to camp required them first to join the church and then the church choir. Moral values sugar-coated with recreation are liable to produce spiritual indigestion.

However, the introduction to new and different viewpoints and values initiated through or combined with recreation activities is often a highly successful entrance into deeper and richer satisfactions. This growth in social understanding through experience is in practice the sound basic educational principle of beginning where people are and leading from existing interests into more mature and more socially desirable experiences. The leader must keep a realistic eye on group motivation in order to be sure what the bond actually is that holds its members together. As he understands this he has the solid foundation on which to build. He will then begin with the actual motives as he can discern them and by exposure to new experiences rooted firmly in the existing needs and interests of the individuals he may start the sprouts of growth in the desired directions. As a group worker he will cultivate such growth with an understanding of the unique need of each person to fulfill himself. He will avoid a mass plowing and planting of acres of youth with a prepared seed mechanically distributed in neat program rows.

ADMINISTRATIVE GROUPS

The third type of group familiar in all such recreation-education organizations includes the committee and the representative council. Such groups exist not primarily for the recreation or education of their members but to accomplish certain collective purposes which the groups have established. Administrative groups are of many kinds. They may be elected by an organized group. They may be appointed by officials to carry out specific assignments. They may consist of representatives of a number of groups working together on an intergroup project. Although it might appear that the bond uniting such groups would be clearly and simply the execution of its assigned function, it is, of course, true that here too unavowed objectives flourish alongside and at points overshadow the overt purpose. Here too unconscious drives for domination over others, the craving for prestige, or the pleasures of creativity play into the committee's life.

Among our samples we have two groups of this variety. Let us look at the Gay Teens Committee as described by the leader:

"The purpose of the Gay Canteen as stated in their constitution is to furnish enjoyable recreation for youth. It is a little difficult to separate the purpose of the so-called Youth Committee from that of the Canteen. In a sense they are one and the same, with this difference—the Committee has the administrative function of seeing that this purpose is carried out for the Canteen.

"Although this administrative purpose is the recognized and avowed purpose of Committee members, actually the members come to the meetings with much the same ideas that they have in coming to the Canteen. It is a place where they can meet with the other young people—boys and girls—only, in a more intimate situation than obtained on Canteen nights. They not only hold their business meetings, but they have fun while doing so. Before the meeting is called, ping pong games, improvised basketball and baseball are played in the dance room. Groups gather in lounge and coke bar rooms talking about school and other affairs, while one or two of them will play the juke box. After the meeting is adjourned members will remain to talk awhile, and then will begin to leave in groups and in couples—for one of the main unavowed purposes is the desire for boys to be with girls and girls to be with boys.

"An additional unavowed purpose, only partly conscious, is that belonging to the Committee definitely gives status in the Canteen. Members feel that there is a certain importance attached to belonging. They are the Canteen representative body. Unconsciously they all have this need for status in the large Canteen group, for recognition and acceptance, and for the security of having been elected and of belonging to this group. All of these unconscious motivations and unavowed purposes keep them coming to the Youth Committee meetings.

"The need for boy-girl relationships . . . can be seen in Fannie's and Josie's giggling behavior with Jack and Tom, their entering into basketball games with them, their side conversations and 'horseplay' with them during meetings; in Chick's waiting for Herb and attempts at indifference while acting in such manner as to call attention to her when Herb is present, her evident appreciation of attention from Pat, Ted, Nat and others, who also show their evident interest in her; Helen's patiently waiting around until Pat, her boy friend, chooses to recognize her, and her choice of boys' groups, often, to talk with in preference to girls; Pat's and Ted's teasing of all girls and their enjoyment of it; Nat's rather shy overtures to Chick and others of the girls; and conversations in general between the members and on the subject of boys or girls.

"That they see status and recognition in belonging is shown in their attitude in the Canteen and their mentioning of meetings to other members; their discussions and the seriousness with which they approach Canteen business. This status and recognition motivation tends to get them down to seriousness in business meetings, while the need for boy-girl relationships can frequently be disrupting in meetings when giggling and silliness distract from the business."

In any group of this age and composition the heterosexual interests could normally be expected to predominate no matter what other functions it assumes. It is essential for the group worker to recognize and make place for these in any assistance to the group. The status element in leadership groups of this type provides the return that the larger group makes for the services of its elected leaders. So long as it is earned by effective service to the group and not perverted into special privilege, this expectation of recognition is valuable for both individuals and the group itself. One of the symptoms of a sick group is often either the refusal of the group to accord status to its indigenous leaders or their abuse of their leadership position through irresponsible or ineffective administration, misuse of funds, or claims to special privileges in the agency.

The second type of administrative group illustrated by the Social Action Committee represents a more complex situation. Individuals were sent to the committee and so to the state capital as representatives. Although the exact functions involved were not clearly defined by the sending groups, it was clear that some responsibility was assumed for expressing the opinion of constituents and for channeling back the results to the senders. The job of the committee was defined as follows:

"The delegation met as a Social Action Committee before going to the conference. Its purpose was to prepare itself by learning about the legislation to be presented later and to have presented to it the purpose and program of the Conference. Following the Conference the Committee met to consider how they could present what they had learned to the groups that sent them and how they might arouse public opinion on this legislation.

"In terms of the functions assumed by the members there were evident several unavowed purposes at certain points inconsistent with the major purpose of the Committee. The two youthful representatives from the settlement Canteen were to some extent 'going for the ride' and were somewhat immature to make the most of the occasion. To a less extent several of the young married women went for similar reasons. Such distortions of purpose became evident in the fulfillment of the Committee's responsibility to its constituent groups.

"The absence of sociability as an element in this group and the nature of a representative body made easy the inclusion here of individuals of differing ethnic backgrounds, educational and economic levels. Such inclusiveness was in this case related also to the social objectives of the Committee.

In these four major types of groups used in the leisure-time agencies it is evident that there are opportunities for many individual satisfactions related to the groups' objectives. The group worker, while he helps the group to formulate its avowed purpose, to determine its membership policies and to get itself organized, must also be aware of the deeper and less obvious psychological elements that enter into formation. What is his part in this process?

The Group Leader's Part in Formation

WHAT IS THE GROUP LEADER'S relation to this process by which a group comes into being? It will differ according to the type of group and his recognized function within it. If he is dealing with a friendship group like the R.R.C.'s, the Bulldogs, or the Jokerettes already organized and often provided with its own indigenous leadership, his role is likely to be one of assistance in organizing it into a club in which democratic process can replace indigenous dictatorship and the group values can be brought into closer conformity with acceptable social behavior. If it is an interest group like the newspaper group or a collection of individuals recruited by advertisement and unknown to each other, it may be to meet first their demands for increased skill and then to give scope to their unavowed need for personal relations by the way the group is conducted. If it is a committee, his role may be that of an executive secretary[1] enabling the group to fulfill its function but at the same time aware of the less obvious but potent demands for personal relations or a well-earned recognition among their peers.

The group leader who represents an agency in such groups is at times a club adviser, at times a teacher or coach, at times an administrative assistant. In all these roles, if he is a group worker he is aware of individuals and the opportunities for their enjoyment and growth. He should also be equipped with insight into the complex process by which the collective entity is created out of articulated aims, unavowed objectives and unconscious drives. His function as a group worker consists at this point in his making available to them his knowledge of the varieties of group experience in his agency, his skill in the program activities, recreational or educational, and his understanding of the psychological and sociological factors significant in their situation.

The group leader, if he is using a group-work approach to his groups, will bring to bear upon this process of formation and the grouping of people both his specific knowledge about types of groups, methods of organization, and the individual needs of particular persons and also a generalized knowledge of what he may expect from people in certain age ranges and affected by certain social factors of significance in their environment. We will first consider here those general aspects of concern to group workers dealing with youth.

PSYCHOLOGICAL FACTORS SIGNIFICANT IN GROUP FORMATION

It is well for the group worker to keep in mind first the place of leisure-time experience in the total life situation of young people. In most cases people are seeking in these activities enjoyment, relaxation, new forms of intimacy outside the family, the release of drives inhibited in the hard reality of school or work, the use of capacities in mutually satisfying relations and in learning for its own sake, or at times, in the more mature groups, a way of participating in the larger community.

In dealing with youth who are emerging from childhood into adulthood, it is important for leaders to realize the need to readjust the place of work and play within the individual's scheme of life. School activities in the early part of this age period represent the work element of life and should do so in providing education not only in subject matter but also in the discipline, work habits, and acceptance of responsibility that mature employment will require. At the same time, the shift from school to job that occurs during these years requires a major life adjustment. Youth are in process of determining their vocational choice, of finding their first jobs, of meeting the requirements of foremen and employers, of receiving their first pay, of learning how to adjust to their fellow workers, often of joining a labor union. Both the amount of time available for leisure and the use to which it will be put shift as young workers enter employment. Because of this new experience they may need to spend time in talking out and working through the meaning of the job or in learning what vocational opportunities there are, what legal protections they have as workers, and what organizations they may wish to join.[2] As they learn their jobs they begin to find their place in the social life of the factory, store or office. This will begin to determine their choice of friends. Their leisure must supplement or at times compensate for their work experience. It is extremely important, therefore, that leaders be informed of the job experience their group members are having and its significance for their leisure.

Beyond such realization of the place of leisure activities in the total life situation, when dealing with youth the leader needs to be aware of the special function of group experience in the maturing process.

As the adolescent grows his emotional needs will lead him to seek a variety of social experiences and avocational interests. There is increasing understanding of the psychological significance that group membership has in the adolescent period. The first group experiences that seem to come in the nursery years serve mainly as a first support in the break away from the maternal tie so close in infancy. The child is by that time capable of enlarging his affection to include not only the parent but also a group of children. This provides him with the first form of social identification. It is not, however, until adolescence that the desire for a group becomes imperative. The emotional upheavals of adolescence give rise to the needs that produce the many close-knit friendship groups of which the R.R.C.'s and the Jokerettes are types.

As the adolescent seeks to establish his independence he necessarily turns to some extent away from the family. This breaking away from the parental family must be accomplished before he can establish the mature sex relations toward which he is now reaching. In this period of conflict and confusion the close-knit friendship group acts as a kind of substitute or vestibule family in the affectional support it provides. In the group and its members the adolescent finds new love objects which help to carry him through the break with the parental home. Within such groups of his own making, however, he can develop the capacity for mutual affection, he can experiment with rebellion, he can assume at times the role of leader (forbidden at home where the parent exercises authority). He can revolt against the group leader without the guilt associated with parental revolt. He can also identify with him and so move on by this means toward adulthood. The alternation of dependence and independence, of submission and revolt, which the group permits, provides in early adolescence an essential opportunity for experimenting with approaching maturity.[3]

The capacity for developing strong group loyalties seems to vary somewhat between boys and girls. There is some evidence that boys belong to such groups more frequently than girls.[4] Moreover, recent studies would indicate that boys tend to use such groups more frequently to express their need for attack on adult authority, represented by the teacher, the group leader, or the local police. Girls, unless they have a tendency to compete with boys, are more likely to use their groups as an opportunity for intimate friendship pairs and triangles.[5] When one considers the differing role that the sexes are destined to play in the adult family and in vocational life, it does not seem extraordinary that we should notice this difference.

An interesting evidence of their difference in focus is familiar to most group leaders who have ever been in charge of a game room or canteen. The boys use such facilities chiefly as a place to play competitive games, especially ping-pong or pool, or to flock about in gangs with a hostile eye out for a rival gang. The girls use the same facilities in most cases as an occasion to attract the boys through horseplay, exhibitionism of various kinds, and dancing. They seldom seek to play competitive games and almost never succeed in getting a chance to do so.

There is a danger in the one-sex group after early adolescence if it does not serve as an escalator to move the group along toward the more mature relations. For some children it provides a secure haven from this often-fearful prospect. For some it makes too attractive a social life with their own sex. There is sometimes a tendency on the part of leaders to prefer to keep children on an immature level— perhaps because of some unconscious need of their own to infantilize them and to keep them dependent upon the leader or perhaps because the complexities and dangers of helping them into the courtship era are frightening to the leader. However, as we realize the opportunity that such groups afford for serving as the bridge into normal and satisfying heterosexual relations we recognize them as one of the effective means to move into relations with the opposite sex.

By the mid-teens the rising heterosexual interests are likely to be obvious and should provide the focal point for programming for one-sex groups. This involves the provision of the appropriate and age-old activities of courtship—dancing, dramatics, music, for example —and also the opportunities for acquaintance and knowledge of each other that come by way of common projects in clubs, committees, councils or canteens.

The responsibility of the community to provide socially sanctioned and desirable facilities to meet this need is still not fully recognized. Our attitudes in the past have been too largely fearful or negative. We have forbidden and controlled. While certain controls are obviously necessary, a positive acceptance of this concern and socially acceptable provision for it will go far to make such controls more easily established. The vital contribution made by the approval of the community as a kind of sanctioning parent does much to remove the essential courtship functions from an "alley" activity into the broad light of well-established and controlled environments.

It is important also to recognize the contribution that program activities in these years provide for teaching the masculine and feminine roles. The association of masculinity with athletics is no accident. In the need to develop strength, controlled aggressiveness, courage and persistence sports and games create the stage on which the accepted masculine attributes can be acquired. The function of the girls in providing an admiring audience, as evidenced in the Jokerettes, is an unconscious recognition of this process. Acquaintance with girls' groups of the same age shows an equivalent process of femininity in the making. This is shown in the absorption in clothes, cosmetics and glamour, the spontaneous attraction of dancing, the identification with actresses as symbols of the successfully feminine, the constant discussion of boys, petting and dates, and at times the need to use the attractive young leader as a model of femininity. Here too the leader needs a sympathetic understanding of the urgency behind these concerns if the new emotional capacities are to come to fruition within the accepted mores of our society.

A third element in the maturing process is related to the use youth can make of group experience. A part of successful adulthood in a democratic society requires the capacity to identify with the community. The growth of the socialized personality from the narcissistic phase of infancy to such enlargement of the self comes about gradually. The true significance to society of this succession of group experience is the contribution it can make to increasingly wide identification.[6] In early adolescence socialization has usually not proceeded beyond the capacity to identify with the friendship group. It often expands to include the school, sometimes the neighborhood. Identification with religious bodies, cultural traditions, or racial units often begins with the early teens. Vocational identification with occupations or economic classes more easily occurs apparently after people have taken jobs. Citizenship at twenty-one indicates the expectation of the community that by then individuals should be capable of concern for the larger whole.

The early stages of such stretching of the self require personal contacts and immediate returns in the affection and security of intimate group life to justify the demands made by growing mutuality. The emotional maturity of the well-balanced adult includes the capacity to respond to less personal but still vitally important group demands and to assume responsibility to give without the assurance of immediate reward. This is the capacity upon which a democratic society rests. It is, moreover, the ability that makes possible the extensive growth of voluntary Associations with various public purposes—economic, ethnic, political, philanthropic or civic. As Grinker and Spiegel point out, the wartime experience proves that "not all Americans have been able to develop a range of identification large enough to include the nation and thus to develop strong feelings of loyalty and obligation. To some extent this ability seems to be a measure of social maturity."[7]

Many people, even when identification with less personal objects becomes possible, become fixated at some halfway point along the line of full social maturity. They can identify only with their home town, their social class, their neighborhood, their ethnic group, or their section of the country. The inclusion of the good of the nation —and of the world—is beyond the elasticity of their particular skins. These partially socialized personalities present one of our most serious problems today. Moreover, the group organizations that arise to meet the needs of such partially socialized persons often become symptoms of social disorganization. The danger that our society will be torn apart by highly organized hostile pressure groups and power blocs is a real one. The only cure for this disease of the social body is a satisfying outlet for the social needs of men which produce the mature response to social responsibility for the total community.[8]

The dependence of a successful democratic society upon this type of identification is clear enough. Unless the citizen does feel his oneness with the whole, assumes his responsibility readily and carries it effectively, the democratic system will rot away at the roots. Any democratic society requires a delicate balance between independence and dependence, between individualism and conformity. It must provide opportunities to act independently and with initiative but with the recognition of the interdependence with others and their rights. It must leave freedom for the uniqueness of each within the voluntarily accepted control of each by the good of the collective whole. Within the smaller compass of the voluntary group this delicate balance can be learned and practiced if its true significance is understood. In serving the collective interests of the groups he joins youth can find those extensions of the self which will lead to his identification with the larger good.

For the group worker an understanding of these psychological factors lends meaning to the experiences that represent the various stages in social growth.

SOCIAL FACTORS IMPORTANT TO GROUP FORMATION

As he starts to organize groups for various purposes the group worker needs to be aware also of certain social factors which will act in many subtle ways to determine whether a group can be organized at all, and how it will function. In an already highly complex, interacting social situation, a new equilibrium is required each time a new social entity appears.

Of major importance is an understanding of the social differentiation already established in the community into which a particular group is born. The agency and any group within it are affected by the structural lines that divide people into large subgroupings. The class formation establishes a well-recognized hierarchy indicated by differences in custom, mores, education, language, and many other symbolic manifestations.[9] While economic status and occupation may act as major determinants of class, many secondary characteristics arise around them to produce the differentiations with which we all are familiar. Caste marks in addition to class lines are present in certain communities.[10] The established hierarchical patterns based on ethnic origin interact with class distinctions in most of our American communities. Intertwining with class and ethnic differences age and sex lines create further complications.[11]

For those who work with youth, it is important to realize the existence also of the youth subcultural groupings, whose values and standards may be a potent influence on a particular group. The evidence of such a youth culture is familiar to group workers in the costumes and lingo of the modern adolescent, the heroic figures of the national athletic hero which guide his aspiration, the "swell guy," and the "glamour girl," the current literature aimed at this age group, the moods and crazes that come and go regarding popular amusements.[12]

The significance of social differentiation to group organization appears at several points. In the first place, as has been revealed by recent research, habits of social participation differ within these social groupings.[13] The amount of social participation expressed in group affiliations, for example, varies with income and occupation. In kind as well as amount, members of different social groups vary in the types of organizations they form or will join. Recreational and educational interests reflect social position.[14] Ethnic groups also seek through organization to express their cultural values or to protest their depressed social position.[15] Unless he is aware of the customary and accepted group affiliations in the social group with which he is working, the leader is functioning in the dark. This does not mean that he will necessarily accept all such customs as desirable. Like the interests and needs of individuals, they provide the foundation on which he must build. In fact the way he organizes must take into account more than existing social relations. Whether he knows it or not, the bases of organization he encourages add to or subtract from the existing pattern in some way. It is essential, therefore, that he understand the social anatomy on which he operates so that his efforts will lead to social health—as far as that can be defined.

If he understands the participation habits of those he works with he will be prepared to meet at times a lack of response and perhaps even resistance at points where he and the community back of the agency are likely to feel there is the greatest need for his services. For example, the response of middle-class children to the program of the adolescent-serving organizations, such as the Boy and Girl Scouts and Camp Fire Girls, leaves little to be desired except the need for more money and more leaders to meet it. This is not the case, however, when one is dealing with certain low-income areas or with certain nationality groups in the lower status levels.[16]

For those who work with youth one of the most important aspects of the peer society of youth is that which consists of the participation in autonomous groups within it. Although a full exploration of the prevalence of autonomous groups among youth is still not available, evidences point to the fact that this phenomenon is not confined to any one economic or ethnic group. While the forms it assumes differ, the urge to organize seems to rise spontaneously and independent of adult control among youth of all kinds. The gang life in the interstitial areas of Chicago[17] or the cellar clubs of New York City[18] can be matched by a similar number of social clubs and fraternities and sororities in a lower middle-class area of Jewish and Negro people in Cleveland.[19] Sixty unaffiliated social clubs of Negro girls were discovered, for example, functioning in one senior high school.[20] The social clubs, fraternities and sororities of the college community are only another expression of the same ineradicable need of youth to organize its own groups under its own control. Such autonomous youth organization is so universal that we need to understand its implications for all who work with young people in the established youth programs. It seems to prove for one thing that self-selected intimate groups are so essential to the social nourishment of this age group that they will exist against all obstacles, including poor facilities, police interference, the disapproval of school authorities, even the outlawing of their existence by legislative action. This persistence and extensive prevalence should make clear that the need for intimate companionship they express must be provided for in some way and should be recognized by the community.

These groups in the latter adolescent years are in essence the means of approach to the other sex. The brother-sister motif, evident in the relation of Jokers and Jokerettes and the use of brother and sister terms in fraternities and sororities should give us the clue to their unconscious roots in the familiar family ties from which youth are gradually freeing themselves. These are in feeling groups of siblings and by that curious transference at which the subconscious is so adept these groups in the early stages of courtship also seem to appear as brother and sister groups. However, they soon emerge into becoming the means for courtship.

As courtship devices it is important to note how they reflect the communities' patterns of eligibility for marriage.[21] Current patterns of endogamy and exogamy appear in the dating procedures between these groups and therefore are reflected in the membership requirements of groups which are to serve these purposes. This accounts for the class and ethnic qualifications on membership often imposed. It is true also that, while some of these groups become the means to sexual freedom and promiscuity, many of them control sex behavior within the prescribed socially acceptable conventions. Occasionally the double standard is manifest in instances where sex freedom is allowed in boys' groups on club premises or for group members with certain girls, for example, but another set of girls are, as it were, reserved for marriage. Members are not expected to marry out of the girls' group which has served these casual purposes. When they mature to the point of marriage ethnic or class considerations come into play as is not always true in the casual contacts recognized tacitly at least by the group.[22] Again the need for a social instrument to make courtship possible, to bring together eligibles, and to provide for the acquaintance out of which courtship can arise should provide significant clues to the efforts of the group worker.

Where such groups have grown up in sick communities like those surrounding the Bulldogs or the Jokerettes, they will take on pathological features. They may become the means to promote delinquency of all kinds. And the answer must lie not in an attempt to eliminate them. If society tries to break them up it merely drives them underground in most instances. The answer must come rather in their transformation into socially acceptable opportunities for securing the intimacy needed with their own sex and the fulfilling of their function as a medium for courtship.

From the viewpoint of the group leader, therefore, a recognition of this phenomenon as prevalent in some degree among the youth with whom he works will have several results. In the first place, he needs to recognize the place these groups fill in the lives of youth. Many of the members of agency groups will also belong to autonomous groups.[23] This interlocking of membership means that the group leader needs to know what such affiliations mean to his members.

In the second place, experience seems to show that a considerable number of such groups would welcome help, in program planning and in leadership from the community if they can be assured that their autonomy will be respected.[24] This requires a special skill in leadership and an ability to work with their indigenous leaders which is only beginning to be developed. It is important to recognize in this relation that part of the suspicion encountered here is due to the fact that this group represents a revolt against the encroaching adult world. If skilled leadership especially equipped to deal with such groups can be found, a considerable number like the Bulldogs and the Jokerettes will welcome the chance to affiliate with organizations. Even where this cannot be accomplished, the group worker needs to be alert to the functioning of such autonomous groups if he is to understand the peer society of those with whom he works. He will find depicted here in glaring colors the values actually dominant among youth—learned, of course, from their elders. The emphasis on wealth and social position as related to marriage, the current racial and religious prejudices, the achievements, sometimes antisocial, that bring prestige—all these will be dramatized within the youth world by these autonomous groups.

Another by-product of social differentiation with which any group worker deals is the attitudes of social distance, of public esteem or stigma with which people regard those who differ from themselves. Through the tendency to react by stereotypes, these attitudes will determine responses to contact with others who are felt to be different, whether superior or inferior.

The major groupings within our society have already established patterns regarding intimacy of association. These control not only marriage but to a large extent friendship and social acceptability, and so inevitably the companions selected for leisure-time groups.[25] Such patterns will determine what kinds of people are likely to mix easily in which kinds of activity. These social hierarchies, whether based on class, race, sex or age or some other form of social distinction, determine the consciousness of kind we each have and the social distance we feel between ourselves and others. One problem for the group leader is to discover what is the basis of this consciousness of kind in any particular group. Do they think of themselves primarily as Italians or Jews, as women or men, as workers or professional people, or as residents of "the flats" or "the Heights"? The sense of at-homeness that arises out of the accepted consciousness of kind is essential if people are to enjoy themselves. It often is determined by patterns well defined in the minds of group members and obscure or invisible to the leader who may come from a different social setting. In certain communities, for example, economic class lines are so clearly drawn that office workers do not naturally spend their leisure with factory workers. Household employees are often cut off from others of their age and educational level not only by their hours of work but by the inferior status of domestic employment. In a Catholic community, for example, the few Protestants in the area—the members of a mission church—suffer from social isolation in all the adolescent activities of the neighborhood. In a Negro community in which place of residence is symptomatic of social status, those living above one of the main traffic arteries maintain their social homogeneity in recreation groups by excluding those outside a limited number of streets.

The social basis of homogeneity that makes people feel at home together must be recognized by the leader and used as a starting point for group organization. It will differ in each community. If the sense of comfortable at-homeness is possible only within a restricted social grouping, such as those in one occupation, one sex or one racial group, it is often necessary to begin by organizing only within those confines and developing through group activities greater security and pride. If the group suffers from a sense of social inferiority, as is often the case with those in stigmatized parts of the population, then, by building the program around the social factor itself it is sometimes possible to create a new pride in racial accomplishments or nationality traditions, the contribution of the industrial workers, or the position of women, as the case may be. The voluntary separation of such groups and the creation of group esteem must be handled in such a way as to prevent the reality or the appearance of segregation. The program must be geared so that satisfaction in their own group accomplishment does not heighten their isolation or create intolerance of other groups. As soon as sufficient self-esteem and self-confidence are created within the homogeneous group it is important for the group to broaden its contacts by intergroup activity or by individuals' moving on into more heterogeneous groups.

A further significant by-product of our highly differentiated society is its effect on our mores. While our society produces certain mores that function throughout with a fair degree of uniformity, these social pockets formed by class, race, residence, age and sex and their combinations show wide difference in accepted customs and standards of behavior.[26] Concepts of right and wrong in regard to honesty, sex behavior, civic responsibility, for example, vary as between the neighborhoods surrounding the R.R.C.'s and those in which the Jokerettes are growing up. The accomplishments that give status and recognition and those which mean disgrace and failure are widely different within these partially separated worlds of our complicated society. It is the functioning of such values—whatever their content —that provides in part the dynamic for individual ambition or group recognition. It is essential, therefore, for the group worker to understand what forces move below the surface of the community he deals with. It is these social pressures and pulls that will prohibit some behavior, stimulate in some directions, guide the more competent individual to success *as he sees it*, or depress with inadequacy the individual who cannot measure up to the standards he knows and accepts. These values must be related to those of the agency and of the larger community that the group worker inevitably represents. This integration will be illustrated in later chapters.

One additional aspect of the social setting must enter into the planning of the group leader. If he is concerned with the active social participation of people in improving the community in which they live he must be thoroughly acquainted with the social and economic conditions that affect them, their feeling about such conditions, and the points at which improvement might be effectively attacked *by them*. This involves an understanding of their attitudes toward what is most in need of change as well as a realistic facing of the resources with which such social programs can be effectively carried through. It includes the assistance to social action based on intelligent knowledge and related to the agency purpose as well as to group interest.

In all of this consideration of the social elements significant to group organization there are obviously certain common approaches. In the first place, the group leader needs to *enter into* the social experience of those he works with. He must cease to be socially naïve in regard to his own attitudes—also, of course, socially produced. When he has accomplished that he is prepared to see the world through the eyes of others who have entered life from a different place in the social scheme. He will see with them the barriers that shut them in or others out, the platforms by which they climb to social esteem, the levers they have in their hands to hoist up the level of life as they live it. With such understanding he will combine his own viewpoint, accepting his role as an agency representative and as a professional person expected by the group to assume a degree of leadership.

THE PROCESS OF GROUPING

We have been considering in the preceding sections the underlying psychological and sociological factors that will affect any group as it begins to form. We need also to consider how the group leader must in reality deal with the concrete questions presented by the R.R.C.'s, the Teen Tattler staff, the Y-Teen Club, or the Gay Canteen committee. How does he help them get organized, decide on their purpose if it is to be formulated, determine membership requirements, and establish their structure?

As indicated in the illustrative material, the most important element at this stage is the true basis of the bond that holds them together. These illustrations indicate how complex that may be. Avowed purposes, like the tip of the iceberg rising above the water, are only indicative. The process of clarifying group objectives, as the leader did with the Jokerettes, for example, can be a very useful one. Obviously the stated purpose will express only that which can be brought to light but the group leader in the process of such discussion is likely to see considerably more below the surface. With this understanding he is better able not only to help in organization but to get clues to what the program activities should be. Not all such motives can or should be satisfied because they would be harmful to individuals or socially undesirable. However, there are many outlets for such needs as the search for status, the hunger for security, or the obscure gropings toward mature emotional expression. To channel them in fruitful, socially useful directions is one of the functions of such group experience.

As the leader works with his group to locate and define its objectives he must be equally aware of the surrounding social setting of which it is a part. The types of groups and activities customary in the particular social class, ethnic group, age or sex grouping to which the members belong will play their part in determining how the group organizes. The social-distance patterns, products of their social setting, will act to determine membership policies as well as group objectives. This is very obvious in groups like the Y-Teen Club, where the agency is attempting to introduce a new concept of social acceptance which crosses established racial taboos. It is equally clear in the struggles of the newspaper group to determine its relation to the Jewish and Gentile communities. It appears in the attitudes of the Mike Club members toward Negroes in a nearby area, and in the class consciousness of the R.R.C.'s toward the lower-class boys whom they reject. As any new social entity comes into being it must start in terms of the participation habits and social-distance attitudes current in the social setting. Patterns of social acceptability seem to form an area of probable grouping within which actual grouping takes place. Here, as in the formulation of objectives, the function of the leader may often be not to accept the status quo as socially desirable but to help the group to move toward establishing its place in the community on bases consistent with the respect for all groups and co-operative relations between them. As indicated in an earlier chapter, agency purposes are likely to contain in some cases formulations which give direction to such modification of social attitudes.

As he understands what the group actually wants, not merely what they say, as he sees how they are related to their setting, the group leader can help them by his knowledge of types of groups and program activities. The intimate social club, the larger acquaintance club, the class with rather formal teaching, the informal interest group, the special interest club, the team, the short-time project group, the committee, the canteen and lounge programs—all these and others are tools of the group leader. They are in fact patterns of social relationships. These familiar group forms differ from each other in terms of certain characteristics of the relationships assumed to exist within them. The major differences lie in the type of purpose that binds them, the method of determining membership, the way indigenous leadership is developed and its relation to agency leadership, the degree of organization and its method of control, the implied intimacy involved in membership, and the expected duration of the group. Out of these elements many different types of groups can be built to serve different ends. The R.R.C.'s and the Jokerettes with their need for a secure person-to-person relation create the typical friendship club, with its membership determined by congeniality, its "natural leaders" who serve to focus the group feeling, its relatively slight organization but rather rigid controls over its members, and its expectation of immortality. This contrasts sharply, for example, with the Social Action Committee with its impersonal objectives, its membership determined by representation from other groups, its formal organization, its lack of any assumption of personal intimacy, and its limited duration. Both of these differ from the interest-group pattern of the newspaper staff with its avowed emphasis on the interest in journalism, its shifting membership, its indefinite form of governmental control, its reliance on the group leader as an expert, its lack of intimate bond, and the assumption by the members of its temporary character so far as each is concerned. These elements of group structure can be combined in many ways. The group leader as an expert craftsman in social organization should be able to help the group to clothe its purpose in appropriate social forms custom-made to suit its particular shape.

Interpersonal Relations Within a Group

THE GROUP LEADER, AS HE WORKS with a group, is aware not only of the individuals as they participate in the multiform aspects of the group life. He will also become aware of certain discernible processes by which individuals are related to each other.

Perhaps the most obvious to the observant leader are the affectional relationships established between members of the group. It is this pattern to which the study of sociometrics is opening the door.[1] These might be described as a kind of horizontal pattern of emotional interactions. The emotions that create these links between individuals include the whole gamut of which human personality is capable. There are mutual friendship pairs, and in heterosexual groups courtship pairs in various stages of development. There are pairs of enemies in some of which the ambivalence of attraction conflicts with partial enmity. There are triads often consisting of the rivalry of two for the affection of one. Dependency and domination pairs are found in which at points elements of the masochism of the dependent meets the repressed, often unconscious hostility of the dominator. Occasionally there are sets of four as for double-dating with varying relationships crossing the sex lines.

In addition to these groups expressive primarily of affection or hostility, there are subgroupings indicating in part leadership, producing admiration and influence though not always mutual affection. A star formation of a leader and satellites is familiar and in some groups, especially larger ones or smaller ones which are in revolution as it were, two or more rival subgroups headed by indigenous leaders. The leadership influence runs along a chain in certain situations in which the members are linked to each other but not all of them to the focal leadership person. Within the choice process between individuals there are, as Dr. Jennings has pointed out,[2] some individuals more frequently chosen, more sought after by others; there are the underchosen, including the isolates, who hang on the fringe of the group with little acceptance from any.

These personal choices or preferences and the functioning of leadership produce in any group the emotional pattern shifting with the ebb and flow of interpersonal response. In this each member makes his own place, in some way fitting his contribution to the needs of others and of the group-as-a-whole and drawing from others and from the whole such social nourishment as he can get to meet his own needs. Giving and taking, they produce the group in its intricate mutuality.

In addition to these affectional and leadership relations, members of a group usually arrange each other, as it were, perpendicularly. They "rate" each other using in the process value scales often held in common so that a collective rating is reached on each person.[3] This collective evaluation gives what we term status to each within the whole.

The nature of the rating process varies greatly between groups. Highly competitive situations produce a rating process of great intensity in which status is eagerly sought and where the emotional stakes are high. For some individuals the need for high status is especially urgent if it is required to meet deep insecurity or to compensate for previous rejections. For other, more secure individuals even failure in a highly competitive setting can be accepted with relaxation.

In addition to a recognition of the intensity involved in the rating process it is highly important to the group leader to understand what scales are being used by the group on which to rate its members. In many cases these scales will be different from his own and he may at points be blinded to their existence by this unfamiliarity or by an emotional rejection of their values. In some groups the scales for rating are antisocial. They represent a perversion of the values currently held by society as represented by the agency. As indicated in an earlier section, value scales differ widely in various population groups according to economic status, ethnic affiliation, age, sex, and many minor factors affecting limited sections of the community. Such value scales will be influenced in any group by the community values already imprinted on the members, by the values held by dominant and influential leaders within the group, and by the function of the group which give particular merit to certain forms of contribution.

A third element needs mention here if we are to understand the dynamics of group interaction. The interplay of individuals in a face-to-face group tends to produce in some cases well-recognized roles which are bestowed on certain of its members. The leadership and administrative roles representing the organization of authority will be discussed in a following chapter. In addition to these there are occasionally roles reflecting emotional needs present in the group and projected upon one or another of the members whose own personality needs prepare him to accept the projection. The scapegoat upon whom the collective hostility can be vented without too much fear of retaliation, the clown who wins a limited acceptance by offering himself to be laughed at, the pourer-of-oil-on-troubled-waters who can be relied on to smooth down the irritations, the idol who incarnates the group values and satisfies them by identification with him—these are familiar roles. The leader needs to be aware of the role making of collective emotions and to understand what this process may do both to the creators of such figures and to those who accept the group's projected needs.

From all three of these types of relationships—the affectional pattern, the rating scales, and the role-making process—the emotional structure of the group takes its form. Created as it is by the abilities, interests and drives of individuals, the collective results can be seen in dynamic currents and pressures on individuals, in esteem and stigma bestowed by the group, and in the place each holds within the web of interactions.

In order to illustrate these relations in the concrete we shall take three of our sample groups and put them, as it were, under a social microscope where by adjusting the lens we shall be able to look intimately into their dynamic life of feeling and response into which we step in fact whenever we open a clubroom door or stroll casually into the canteen.

The following material attempts to describe these interactions diagrammatically as well as by descriptive analysis. The sociograms included here were not obtained by the use of sociometric tests but it seems useful to include them even though they are—like all the illustrative material—based on estimates made by the leaders. The value of such material lies not in its claim to full scientific accuracy but rather in its ability to assist the insight of group leaders to become aware of such relationships. Since the relationship between members and between leader and members is of prime importance, it has seemed more practical—at least at present—to adapt the sociograms to the regular agency situation by using them as descriptive devices supplemented by narration. One of the defects of the sociogram in any case is that it has only three dimensions to describe an intricate process of many dimensions. It can signify direction of response and can indicate whether it is mutual and whether it conveys hostility or affection. It cannot convey intensity or describe the qualitative aspects of such responses. We have used it here to describe both status and affectional response by putting those with higher ratings at the top of the page. In each case we will introduce sociograms representing relations at different periods in order to indicate change. We have relied more on verbal description than on diagram to give a full picture.

The analysis of the value scales that influenced rating included in the following material was arrived at by observation of evidences of "looking up to" or "down upon" others in terms of common social factors. This is admittedly a hard process to observe accurately. It is, however, a common human practice to rate people by such factors and however imperfect this instrument of measurement it seemed important to include it. It should be clear that the status each attains within the group is partially the effect of personal characteristics, such as positive response to others, self-centeredness or defensiveness, as well as his place in a social rating scale. Some individuals low in one scale but high in the other will achieve high standing in the group, and vice versa. The functioning of social value scales of this kind plays its part not only in interpersonal relations but in program making and group control, considered in later chapters. With these explanations let us turn the lens of the microscope and look down into the dynamic interaction of three of our sample groups.

We shall take for our first description of interpersonal relations the Jokerettes. It will be remembered that this is a close-knit friendship group, formerly functioning as an autonomous social club in a lower-class Negro area. Because of the impact of the area and of the class lines within it, it seems necessary to begin with the discussion of the value scales effective in the group and reflecting their environment.

From the standpoint of a group leader this type of observation of group interactions points up several elements of importance in the leader's relation to them. An understanding of what is acting to give status gives a clue to the currents of esteem and stigma that play on each individual, and which will affect the response of the group to the leader's and the agency's purposes. In the second place, the analysis of affectional response clarifies for the leader what she no doubt recognized more dimly before—the position of the inner circle and the relation of the isolated members.

The leader describes this situation as follows:

"The Jackson District in which the Jokerettes live is well known for the pathological features of its community life. In the first place, there is an extremely high incidence of family breakdown, with children living in broken homes where one or both natural parents are absent. Sometimes this is due to inability of the family to be a going economic unit, mostly because of employment discrimination; sometimes to the lack of continuous cultural tradition regarding the cohesion of the natural family. The matriarchal family structure of slavery days, which has been continued through easier but limited employment opportunities for Negro women, the dislocation of the family unit through migration and difficulties of adjustment to urban living and crowded living quarters destroy privacy and healthful conditions for marital adjustment. Discrimination in employment not only affects family breakdown but the lack of upgrading and skilled jobs means that rewards for learning and for inhibiting aggressive and impulsive behavior are lacking. The housing situation is deplorable. Ninety per cent of the housing in this district is considered by housing experts to be substandard. Health in the area is of a lower standard than in other sections, and there is high incidence of tuberculosis and venereal disease.

"With this as a background the leader has tried to evaluate eight types of social factors which she has observed as elements which affect acceptance of individuals by the Jokerettes.

"(1) Status with respect to location of residence seems to come to those living 'farther out' than Lincoln Street. Ruthie, Eva and Bertha live in this desirable area, and both Ruthie and Eva have moved 'farther out' this spring. Four live in the housing estates. Housekeeping standards here and equipment vary among those in the estates. Elsie and her mother, for example, actually have a luxurious middle-class apartment. Clarice on the other hand, lives with her step-father, mother, aunt, and two small children in a three-room apartment where the children have to sleep in the livingroom. At the bottom of the scale come six club members who live in the slums surrounding the housing estates. In these cases the homes are in dilapidated, alley-surrounded, dimly lighted sections, with trash and debris constant reminders of the slum area. Inside, the homes vary from Eva's which is fairly comfortable to Lottie's apartment, which is shared by eleven children and the mother, with little furniture and with sections of the wall unplastered. There is much doubling up in sleeping arrangements in most of the homes in the last two categories. One night at Elsie's the meeting was delayed several minutes while Nora and Lottie, who came from dilapidated homes, explored delightedly the various features of the bedrooms and bathroom. Lottie is very self-conscious about her home, and once asked that when her turn came to have the club at her home that she be allowed to use the House for the meeting.

"It should be noted that the housing projects are considered by the neighborhood to be on a higher status level and the most desirable sections of this area. However, the leader believes that the girls and their parents feel it even more desirable to live as they say, 'farther out.'

"(2) Occupation of parents seems to be an important factor in rating. Of the thirteen girls, two have both father and mother living together amicably. In both cases the parents work. It would seem that having both parents contributing to family income would offset the lack of having the mother at home, and apparently the girls with two working parents occupy a top position. The mothers of seven others are working in factory or 'day' work. At the bottom of the scale in this respect are three whose mothers are at home tending large families and entirely or to some extent supported by Aid to Dependent Children grants.

"(3) Family financial status seems to be subdivided in their feeling about it into three classifications: At the top are the three girls who are fairly comfortable, next seven whose families have a continuous financial struggle. At the bottom the three girls whose mothers receive Aid to Dependent Children grants. The group leader feels the club members attach stigma to being Aid to Dependent Children recipients.

"(4) Number of siblings in family is a matter which affects status also. The girls seem to be envious of the privacy, additional income, and exclusive parental attention of the only-child cases, and although there seems to be a general liking for babies among the girls, they would rate a girl coming from a family with less than four children higher than one coming from a family of eleven like Lottie.

"(5) There seems to be some prestige attached to the point of educational progress which the club members have reached. Six of the girls have reached Senior High. Two are in the last year of Junior High and five in the eighth grade. Actually the status of each girl with relation to her attained grade should be considered in relation to her chronological age. It is the leader's impression that there is a decided wish on the part of the parents and of the girls themselves to finish high school. This would seem to be a middle-class pattern or evidence of striving for such status.

"(6) Behavior controls by families are recognized by them in rating. This factor, like the next, is more difficult to evaluate. These adolescents in the Jokerettes are in a period in which they want to break away from family controls and to take on an adult role, but at the same time are demanding some controls.

"At the top of the scale the leader has placed those families which might be called permissive but somewhat controlling. In these cases she has observed that the girls in this group are permitted to choose after-school activities without consultation with the parent, can usually go to the agency and other dances without permission, are allowed to go to shows when they choose and are given show money, associate freely with boys, and have some home duties. Emphasis on staying at home to do homework is not marked, and club meetings can be held in these homes easily. Physical fighting in these families is frowned upon.

"The girls tend to resent and look down on girls with stricter family controls. These include such restrictions as staying at home for studying, inability to have club meetings at the home, rules regarding the hours the girl is to return home or the nights she may go out, punishment for staying out late by forbidding attendance at club, dances, or shows. Four of the girls fall in this category.

"With some doubt the leader has placed three girls at the bottom of the scale in this respect. Clarice, Lottie and Nora, for example, come from family situations where the home is overflowing with neighborhood children, and where there has never been any evidence of housework to be done before pleasure or restrictions as to activity chosen by the girl. The leader feels that the status of these three girls is somewhat lower in this respect and that they would consider the stricter controls of the first group somewhat desirable.

"(7) Relationship to boys is, of course, difficult to evaluate. The leader has noted three patterns—the girls who have seemed to be on easy relaxed terms with the opposite sex, dancing, talking, and teasing the boys freely; the girls who are inclined to talk and act aggressively with boys; and three girls, Peg, Tony, and Betty who seem to be less at ease with boys.

"In general the girls with easy relationship with boys are the older club members. The group leader feels that familiarity and successful relationships with boys are factors of importance to the girls, and that Peg's status, for example, would be raised if she could adjust more easily in this respect. Their ideas about illegitimacy and promiscuity have not been clearly stated. Jean reputedly was married this year following pregnancy: the girls tittered when she has been mentioned, though they consider her a member of the club on sick leave. It is interesting to note that Clarice's status does not seem to have been lowered despite the fact that she was allegedly 'raped' in May following a dance.

"In several of the families the girls are familiar with indiscretions by parents or family members. In six instances in the group younger brothers and sisters were born without a legally recognized father. The crowded living conditions, exposure to sex behavior, lack of supervision from working parents, are all conducive to freedom in this regard.

"(8) Skills of various club members are important status factors. By skills the leader has meant ability to jitterbug well, and also to do other types of dancing; ability to sing, to lead meetings, to write articles, to make posters. The majority of club members have considerable talent.

"(9) A ninth factor which perhaps should be included although it does not figure largely is that of employment. Peg, Mary and Ruthie have had Saturday jobs. These have given them status, though Peg confesses, 'You make so little at these jobs and hand it to your mother, so you don't have much for yourself.'

"The Jokerettes in fact present marked range in many of the social factors which might determine class status—such as location of home, parents' occupation, financial status, number of children, family controls. The leader feels that with the exception of Elsie, Ruthie and Eva they are from the lower class, but that in the lower class category they vary between a lower-lower class—a group which includes Lottie, Clarice and Nora for example, to an upper-lower class, a position held by Queenie. That there is striving among the lower-lower group is indicated by Lottie's mother's wish that her children finish high school and Nora's mother's desire that her family might live in the housing project or have a 'cottage' farther east.

"In addition to these factors which seem to play a part in determining status within the group the leader notes also some ethical values that function to control behavior and establish esteem. The most important of these seem to be the following.

"Honesty is recognized as a general ideal to be followed in major areas; robbing a store would be 'bad,' but in smaller situations, such as carelessness about treasury accounts, or selling some dance tickets on the side for personal money, deviations are not considered reprehensible. With respect to lying, complete truthfulness is evidently not a requirement: on at least four occasions the Jokerettes have lied to their parents about where they were going after their meeting or whether the meeting was held.

"Aggression by adults or youth is frowned on. This seems to be borne out by the repeated criticism of fights at the settlement and by Queenie's quick clarification to the leader that her 'argument' with Clarice was not a (physical) 'fight.' On the other hand, the girls have openly admired youngsters fighting on the streets.

"The girls frown on drinking to excess, at least by youngsters; they have several times indicated there would not be drinking at places where they wanted to give a dance, as they 'were too young.'

"There has been fear of the law and of community pressure when it is disobeyed, but the concept that laws and police are to protect and advise the community, not merely to punish wrongdoers, is not accepted. Getting away with illegal activities if possible is considered acceptable.

"Loyalty is perhaps the most important value, and its application is not loyalty for the good of the whole, but loyalty to group members and to the Jokers. The secrets of the club are for club consumption only. Jean, though under a slight cloud because of her forced marriage, is a member still. The club attitude toward fights between gangs is interesting. They frown on fighting at the settlement but they seem to think if an individual in a club has been wronged by members of another club, then it is all right for all the members of the first club to fight the other 'to protect themselves.' Club loyalty tends to transcend other values, such as obedience to the law."

The affectional pattern of this group is in all probability similar to that found in most of the close-knit friendship groups of early adolescence.

"It seems that the club consists of an inner circle of seven strongly integrated members, plus Lottie, Eva, Ruthie and Betty of slightly separated emotional distance, and two isolates or near-isolates, Tony and Elsie. Of those who have been dropped or have stopped coming, Tony's and Elsie's absences may well have resulted from lack of acceptance, and Eva's and Ruthie's may be related to their striving more overtly for a more middle-class status than this group provides.

"Clarice and Queenie are the outstanding indigenous leaders, though according to her sister's reports, Peg has presidential aspirations. Clarice and Queenie, however, are close friends; Queenie reports that they have always played together. In meetings Queenie seems to be secure in her relatively minor official role as Sergeant-at-Arms, to be content to affect the group as an active participant, and supporter of Clarice.

"Both Clarice and Queenie embody to a great extent the group ideal in popularity with boys, physical prowess, ability to dance, educational aims, concept toward law, attitudes toward honesty, aggression, and loyalty to the group, though naturally in varying degrees in respect to each value. Clarice might seem to have a less strong aversion to physical fighting, and her aggressiveness was probably a reason for election last spring. Queenie might easily be the next year's leader, showing a possible change in club attitude on this point. These leaders are able to reinforce the values of the club. For instance, Clarice has lectured the club on 'decency,' meaning respect in the club for the president and club agenda, taking responsibilities, and attendance; Queenie on respect and quietness in meetings, and occasionally on standards of honesty (this is interesting, for Queenie has a Juvenile Court record of stealing a watch a few years ago).

"It is significant that of the members who are in the second circle of acceptance or indicated as isolates, Ruthie has a high I.Q. of one hundred and twenty-five, the highest in the club, and has considerable status strivings which eventually took her out of the group, while Lottie and Elsie have low I.Q.'s of seventy-three and sixty-eight respectively. The other club members have I.Q.'s ranging from eighty-two to ninety-five.

"Let us look more closely at two of the rejected members. Ruthie joined the club in November. She is an attractive, able Senior High School student with a quick mind, a teasing sense of humor, and a capacity to be serious and to contribute to the club. She is particularly interested in writing and wanted to interview the paper in connection with the Anniversary of the club. She was uneven in her performance as assistant secretary. At a number of meetings she demonstrated impatience and irritation which seemed to be a protest at the diffused thinking and time wasting of the other girls. Her lack of acceptance here may well indicate that her social status is too high to make her fit this group and in the late spring she moved 'farther out' into a middle class area.

"Elsie, the most rejected member, is fifteen and an only child. She lives with her mother in a very luxurious apartment in the Housing project. She attends Junior High. Elsie has an I.Q. of sixty-eight and had a hard time in studies last year so that her mother kept her in evenings; this year things have gone better and she is able to go out three or four times a week at night. The school secretary described Elsie as being a problem, 'a regular little devil, and very mischievous.'

"Elsie is a keen-faced little girl, short and stocky, with light skin and reddish brown hair. Although she often has a petulant, sober and absorbed expression in club meetings, she looks much more alert than such a low I.Q. would indicate. She appears well but has complained of a 'pain in the stomach' which has bothered her for two springs.

"Her mother is young, attractive, and talkative; she is much interested in the girls and has been cordial in having the Jokerettes come to her home and frequently offers suggestions in meetings. She apparently wants Elsie to have friends. While the girls are gathering her mother tends to talk to the leader over Elsie's head, but with encouragement Elsie talks quite freely. She seems rather dominated by her mother, part of the time accepting this and at other times showing her resentment by irritated or monosyllabic answers to her mother's questions.

"The leader has not observed her enough to see much relationship with boys, although at the first dance at the settlement she was very aggressive and autocratic as she kept boys from crashing the dance and ordered a boy around who agreed to get ice for the girls.

"Elsie seems to be quite isolated in the club. She wants acceptance, and takes criticism meekly from Clarice and Queenie, the leaders of the group. Actually their criticism seems to be for very trivial causes. In meetings she contributes rather infrequently but what she says is quite relevant to the subject under discussion. Her unpopularity may be due to envy of the girls for her more middle-class standards and only-child status. It is reinforced by her own insecurity and low intelligence."

The sociograms depict diagrammatically the relative position of these girls on two occasions. "In the first sociogram, Clarice and her older sister Nora, Peg and her older sister Mary, and Bertha are mutually friendly and accepting. These are in the inner circle of acceptance. One sees that Peg and Mary and Bertha vary in status according to the various factors, but hold a somewhat middle position. Clarice and Nora, from certain social status factors, rate lower, but such factors do not prevent their acceptance in the inner circle because personal characteristics overcome these handicaps. Lottie is not in the inner circle. She is accepted by the group but there does not seem to be such a strong bond between her and any individual as among the inner five at this meeting. The worker does not feel her rejection is due to her low social status nor to her slightly more aggressive behavior, as much as it is to her shorter span of interest and less adequate mental equipment (I.Q. seventy-three), lesser capacity to contribute to serious discussion and other club business, and her divided loyalty between the Jokerettes and another club with whom she plays around daily.

"In the second sociogram it will be noted that the inner circle of mutual attraction includes Queenie, who after a verbal argument with Clarice, subject undiscovered, during April is back and exercising her logic and loyalty with salutary effect. Ruthie is no longer attending; the girls say she is still interested but having moved has a hard time attending. It is probable that she has really left the club,

THE JOKERETTES

SOCIOGRAM I   MARCH 18

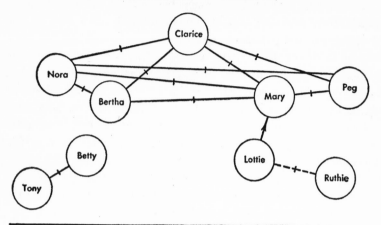

SOCIOGRAM II   JUNE 3

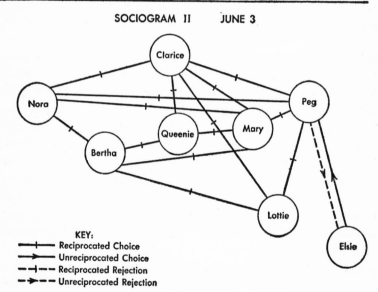

KEY:
———┼——— Reciprocated Choice
———▶ Unreciprocated Choice
— —┼— — Reciprocated Rejection
—▶— — Unreciprocated Rejection

for conscious and unconscious reasons in which status striving is important.

"In following the relation of the outer circle the following is evident: Tony attended only one more meeting after that of the first sociogram. Betty is absent on this occasion though she has been attending fairly regularly. Lottie seems to be on friendlier terms with the others though her divided relationships probably still affect her relationship with the Jokerettes. She has definite mutual attraction with Bertha, whose icebox she raided preceding the meeting with no obvious displeasure from Bertha; with Queenie; and is accepted to a greater extent by the president. The only evidence of rejection is Queenie's rejection of the isolate Elsie. At the meeting Elsie made several apparently logical remarks which Queenie thought were out of keeping with the business at hand, and at least twice Queenie told her to "shut up." Elsie looked hurt but accepted this criticism. The leader feels she is anxious to have Queenie's approval and has so indicated a positive attraction toward Queenie from Elsie."

Let us turn from the Jokerettes to the social relations of an agency-formed club which provides acquaintance rather than friendship plus some program emphases expressive of agency aims. In the Y-Teen Club previously described the interracial policy of the agency and the interracial composition of this school has produced a group of twenty-one Negro and white girls. As one would expect, the interpersonal relations here are considerably more complicated since social factors play a larger role than uninhibited personal congeniality. Here is the leader's interpretation of the relations in this group:

"Because of the interracial make-up of the group certain social factors which have no influence on other social groups do have a unique influence on this group. The major factors which seem to affect status are as follows: (1) Degree of color of skin. This is especially true in a colored girl's being accepted or rejected in the group. The lighter the complexion of a colored girl, the higher social status she gains from the group, all other factors being equal. (2) Father's education. This social factor is not so important in the white group, but is important in the Negro group. (3) Father's occupation. In the white group there is some significance attached to this factor.

It is noticed that all the fathers of the white members in the group are skilled workers. (4) Location of residence. This factor has marked influence on an individual's social status in the group. For the white girls, this is not so important a factor, although it does carry weight. For the colored members, this is very important and this factor happens to be better known than the other social factors. Members judge the financial status of a girl by the community she lives in. Some of the Negro girls live in Southeast Area, a mixed community of Negroes and Jews, and girls accord them much respect because of this one factor. (5) Religious affiliation and church attended. The Catholics rank probably the highest, and the Protestants are subdivided not according to sects but according to the church attended. For example, St. John's Baptist Church (which has a middle class clientele) would give a member more status than a small store-front church. (6) Ethnic background. Aside from the major difference of white or colored, such other factors as foreign-born parentage or recent immigration of parents from the South are not important factors. (7) Age and grade in school. Unconsciously the group considers that maturity comes with age, and so a slight emphasis is placed on the age and the grade in school of the member."

The biracial composition of this group shows up not only in slightly different bases of rating among white and Negro members but also as might be expected in producing a bifocal pattern of emotional responses. While acquaintance and mutual acceptance between all members are sufficient to keep the group alive and actively enjoying the program, spontaneous choice on a racial basis appears as one looks closely at the pattern of interpersonal relations.

In making these two sociograms club members are arranged with the white girls located on the left and the colored girls on the right. The second sociogram was taken at the third meeting following the first sociogram after a camping weekend trip and a number of cabinet and committee meetings. Two new members were added, Ray and Thelma; and two former white members, Agnes and Jane, rejoined the club.

Let us get a close-up of some of these members who occupy different positions in the group. The real test of this experience must of course rest on the meaning of it to its individual members. The group worker needs to be particularly sensitive to the varying situations on the individuals. The following short summaries of the attitudes of a few members indicate more fully what their place is in the group. We have here selected four such showing both accepting and rejecting attitudes.

"Julia, the club president, has reached a higher level of social maturity than many of her associates. This feeling is prevalent in the group, and is shown in her being elected the club president, although only a junior. She has a very charming and winning personality. Her outstanding social qualities are courtesy, co-operation, and ability to meet people. Julia came to the group with a definite need, to gain recognition and affection from others. Her family situation (she is a foster child) has given her a sense of emotional insecurity which is not outwardly shown in her relations with others. The leader feels that the group has already contributed to her emotional and social growth, and the status she has in the club as president has met her felt need. She has given generous time and effort to the club, adding a certain stamina to it.

"Julia is regarded with high esteem by cabinet members and club members alike. The good feeling-tone among the club in general is a very good criterion of her leadership ability. She does not dominate the group, but works democratically with them, and her willingness to assume difficult responsibilities has certainly added to her happy relationship with the rest of the club members. The white members do not show any resentment that a Negro girl is the president of the club. In fact they cooperate with her most effectively. Much of the self-confidence Julia has is due to her past experience as homeroom president last school semester. She is familiar with the procedure of conducting a meeting, and the members in turn indicate much faith in her ability. The leader has confidence in her being able to improve herself to the degree that she can become a discussion leader for some community or school study group on public affairs issues.

"Almost on a par with her in club esteem is Bernice, the leading

THE Y-TEEN CLUB

SOCIOGRAM I   MARCH 21

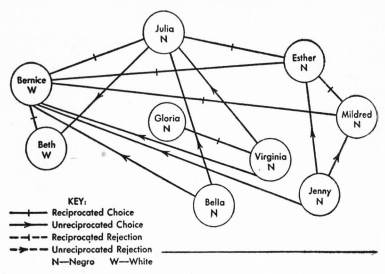

KEY:
──┼── Reciprocated Choice
──→ Unreciprocated Choice
──◄─ ─ Reciprocated Rejection
──►─ ─ Unreciprocated Rejection
N—Negro   W—White

SOCIOGRAM II   MAY 15

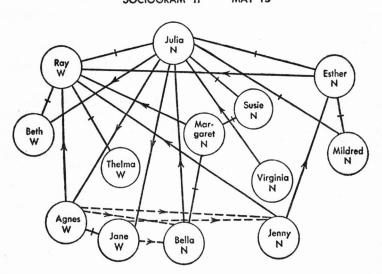

white girl in the group. Bernice displays superior intellectual ability. She does very well in her scholastic achievement, although not an honor student. She is alert and keen in her thinking. She has shown much analytical thinking on club problems, and has added much to the interracial progress of the club. Her intellect is known to the girls, and they value her ideas greatly. This was recognized immediately, for she was elected the vice-president.

"She takes a keen interest in problems of social concern, and with more stimulation in thinking about them can get wider participation. She speaks very fluently and her thinking shows much creative thought and high objectivity. Equipped with this intellectual trait, and other traits like willingness to learn, initiative, sense of responsibility, open-mindedness, she has real possibilities for growth.

"Bernice has probably made the most satisfactory and wholesome adjustment in our interracial group. She came to the group with some preconceived attitudes on race, but having functioned in an interracial cabinet and worked closely with the Negro president and other cabinet members and seen their ability, she has become very respectful of the colored girls. She accepts them and associates with them without being race-conscious. For example, she would skate hand in hand with a Negro girl or mingle freely in their cliques. The Negro girls like her very much and feel at ease in her company. She doesn't put on that 'I'm-too-good-for-you' air. Whenever it is mentioned that we ought to have a better representative committee or group, Bernice is almost always suggested by the Negroes. They realize that she is different from them because she is a white, yet she is one of them when it comes to working and sharing experiences together. The other white girls have a certain loyalty to Bernice and like and respect her very much. She has helped to make our interracial philosophy practical and meaningful to other members. Through her broad interracial views, she has been an example to the other white girls, and the colored girls have profited from her association and will be able now to accept more readily other white girls.

In contrast to these two outstanding members the leader notes of Agnes. "Agnes' social status in the community is in the lower-middle class. She lives in a Polish neighborhood where most parents are foreign-born, but in a better section of that neighborhood. It seems that her father's occupation and education have an equal status with other heads of families in the neighborhood, and she ranks on an equal status with her white friends.

"Although her parents are foreign-born, that is no stigma to Agnes' behavior with her friends whose parents were born in the United States. She feels equal to them, although there is some doubt whether she would adjust equally well to other white girls on a higher class level. She feels very superior to the Negro girls, but does respect their opinions, especially of those in the top social bracket. Because of limited past experience with the colored group, she is hesitant about association with them for fear that she might lose status with her own white group. She is studying the behavior and relationships with the colored girls of Bernice. Because of the wholesome relationship and mutual esteem that exist between the colored girls and Bernice, Agnes is following her footsteps whether she knows it or not. One expects a clash with her family when it comes to a point farther along in interracial experiences. Their background and probably unfavorable impressions of the Negro people since living in the United States would exercise much pressure on her actions, even though she might have some freedom. She has not reached a level of thinking in which she will or can interpret or educate her parents in interracial thinking. She needs help from outside and her family's thinking may change with the whole mode of thinking of the neighborhood. Agnes is respected by her white friends and their parents also show much respect and trust in her.

"Jenny, the Negro girl with the least acceptance in the group comes from a family with a high social status in the community in which she lives. Her family is making the transition from the lower-lower class in society to the upper-lower class, and with the higher educational status of the family members and moving away from the community, they will very likely attain this status in time.

"Although Jenny is respected in her community, that respect has not carried over into the club and she is not regarded with high esteem by the colored members of the club, much less by the white members. She feels, however, equal, perhaps superior, to the colored members in the group, and is anxious to secure a higher status with the white girls.

"Jenny has tried hard to adjust to the group and win recognition. She comes to the group with undesirable physical and intellectual traits, a dark complexion, kinky hair, and inability to realize her intellectual incapacity. The members cannot take her over-self-confidence.

"However, Jenny is a willing worker and the group takes advantage of it. She is the social chairman, having been elevated to the position following the resignation of Agnes. Her sense of responsibility is not consistent; at times she assumes responsibilities with much zest and real interest, and other times shows indifference in carrying out her duties. If she sees that she gains status by doing something for the group, she will undertake it. The cabinet is getting an insight into her social behavior, but accepts her because she will come through if thus stimulated.

"Jenny joined the club so she could, as she said, 'know and like other people.' There is some sincerity in this statement, and by knowing and liking people better, she hopes other people will know and like her better. She has met some rejection in the past, and is desirous of establishing a pattern in which there would be more acceptance.

"Being a member of our interracial club has been in some ways a valuable experience for Jenny. She is able to relate in a positive way to the white girls here, but it isn't reciprocal, as they do not respect her as highly as some of the other colored girls in the club. They like her out-goingness, however. She is a person, who in her desire to win friends loses sight of the fact that she must first strengthen her relationships within her immediate circle before permeating outside. She neglects to cultivate friendships with the colored girls first, but tries hard to win the friendships of the white girls.

"There are definite subgroups in the club, and these have tended to form along racial lines. Of the white group, there are: (1) the subgroup of Bernice and Beth, both seniors and both on the cabinet; and (2) the subgroup of the members, Agnes and Jane, who come from the same community. This subgroup has not adjusted favorably to the whole group as yet, but because of a positive reaction to the cabinet white subgroup, it may gradually work toward a more satisfactory group adjustment. Of the Negro group, there are: (1) the subgroup of the Negro girls on the cabinet, Julia, Esther and Mildred, and (2) the subgroups of Virginia and Gloria, and of Susie and Margaret. Other individuals in the colored group relate separately to the different subgroups.

"Because Bernice is the leader of her two-member sub-group and is very tolerant of the colored girls, that subgroup served as the unifying force in our interracial philosophy and practice. It is a very influential subgroup and generates much of the esprit de corps in the club.

"The committees were organized along interracial lines. The chairmen of these committees have worked themselves up to a high social status, so that now they form a subgroup in themselves, with the exception of the social chairman, Jenny. This subgroup might be called the 'power-behind-the-throne' for much of the club's effective program is due to their leadership. Susie, through her work on special club committees, has been admitted into this subgroup. Jenny, because of her lack of high intellectual ability, and because of her undesirable social qualities, is not a part of this subgroup, although she has a common tie with them as a cabinet member.

"There is some personal conflict among the independent colored members in wanting to be included in the cabinet subgroup. There is no unity among them, and they fit into the club sub-groupings as they can find a place from time to time.

"There are in this group several instances of individuals assuming certain roles consistently. Mildred, for example, is given the role of chief 'sour-graper.' There is a pleasant liking linked with her role, however. When the group meets any disappointments, Mildred without fail throws in a humorous comment with the sour-grape approach. The group appreciates her sour-grape humor, for it brings much esprit de corps and releases much uneasiness. Mildred gains much acceptance because of this role.

"Bella is the 'old fogy' in the group. She always has to have a different opinion, and often that opinion acts as a representative of adult approval. 'We can't do this because it doesn't look nice. Miss P., isn't this wrong?' But the group accepts and unconsciously shows need for Bella's role. Although this type of behavior can be aggravating and has made her lose much status with the group, still they prefer that to a quiet type. Bella is the eldest child in a large family of children. She assumes the role of a mother substitute to her younger brothers and sisters, and looks to parental approval for her relationships with the siblings."

The third case selected for discussion here is that of the Sub Debs. It seems pertinent to examine this as a contrast to the other two. Although the girls are only slightly younger, the institutional setting creates an environment which modifies behavior in major ways. It isolates them from social factors such as racial, economic or residential groupings. In spite of homogeneity on these points, the inevitable social evaluation goes on in terms pertinent to the institutional environment. The fact also that the group was artificially formed by the staff and that it contained without selection on their part all the girls of certain ages modified the affectional pattern. The relative inability of certain of these girls to establish meaningful relations is also an important factor to be considered in this material. The leader analyzes the situation as follows:

"Since the usual status factors such as nationality, school, finances, or location of residence tend to be eliminated in an institution, other kinds of factors take their place. At the Home, belonging to a group gives status in the institution. Hence all of this group have that in relation to the other children. Within the group, there seem to be five major factors operating which contribute to individual status.

"(1) Attention paid by parents and relatives. When a child first comes to the Home, the reason for his coming affects his status. The more socially acceptable his reason is, the higher he rates. For example, if a child comes because the mother has died, that is very acceptable. If he comes because the parents are arrested or have deserted him, that is much less acceptable. After a while, this reason for his coming is more or less forgotten but his contact with parents or relatives is constantly in the foreground. The status of every child in the Home is affected by his answers to these questions: Why did you come to the Home? Do your parents (or relatives) visit or take you out every Sunday? Do they pay for your support? Do they buy your clothes? Do they give you gifts? Do they give you spending money? How much? Are they divorced? Is there a chance that they may take you home? Probably all this adds up to 'How much do your parents love you?'

"(2) Conforming behavior. An institution has to operate within certain rules. By the time a girl has reached the age level of this group, she has learned a certain respect for conformity. Keeping clean, taking care of one's personal possessions, coming to meals promptly, doing required tasks seem 'right' even if not always lived up to. She has also learned that privileges are more likely to accompany conformity. If she avoids 'getting into trouble' she has a better chance to achieve acceptance with the institutional staff. All of these girls have been at the Home long enough to appreciate the value of 'getting along' fairly smoothly. Being a house mother's 'pet' does not add to one's status but an ability to co-operate in a general way does.

"(3) Ability to win attention and approval of adults. All of these girls have a basic need for adult love. They seek it constantly from everyone—from the cook to the superintendent. The nurse and the secretary are especially popular with this group of girls. Attention and approval from them adds much to status. Frequency of interviews with one's case worker is also important. The attention and approval of any adult on the entire staff counts. Approval, however, must accompany attention or else it seems like rejection again. This factor reciprocates to some extent with factor 2.

"(4) Standing with the Superintendent. The superintendent is liked and respected by all the children. She also represents the ultimate authority. She plays a maternal role to all the children but especially to the older girls. From about twelve years of age on, the girls seek her special attention. These girls are just at the age where this relationship is much desired.

"(5) Appearance and attractiveness to boys. During the past six months this has become an increasingly important factor to most of these girls. The three least mature are little affected by it as yet, but the others are approaching the 'boy crazy' stage.

"In attempting to analyze and understand relationships within this group, there are a few facts which must be remembered. In the first place, none of these children are at the Home of their own free volition. By being so placed, they have a choice among eighty children of both sexes ranging from six to sixteen years in age but none of whom is a free general choice. Some of these girls have their closest relationship with children much younger than they, children to whom they feel superior but to whom they show kindness. Secondly, because they are placed in an institution, these girls assume a kind of sibling relationship. This includes jealousy and rivalry. Thirdly, because of their deprived backgrounds, these girls feel individual needs foremost. Their need for love is on a much lower age level than their chronological age implies. Another factor to be kept in mind is that this is a formed group and not a self-selected grouping. In October, there was a general indifference in the group. With the exception of Florence and Gertrude, there were no outstanding choices or rejections. They were simply together. Sister relationships carried a little loyalty but this was pretty well outbalanced by individual rivalry between sisters. In respect to each other and especially in relationship to the leader, each girl was quite self-centered. Through more intimate association and group projects, relationships developed, but there has always been more tendency toward isolation than might be present in a more usual group.

"Sociogram I depicts relationships at about the middle of a regular club meeting in March. Relationships between these girls frequently shift during the course of one meeting. Between Florence and Gertrude, there is mutual choice and this has held steadily. Florence is the leader of this combination and pulls Gertrude along in her feelings. Elmira is seen as the leader with four followers. Edna is her rival also with three followers. Sarah falls in both groups as far as acceptance goes. Elizabeth, Dorothy and Lillian are isolates. At the time of this meeting the group was embroidering cushions which permitted participation and isolation at the same time. There was no strong rejection, but there was a great deal of isolation.

"Sociogram II attempts to show the development in group feelings within two months with the same activity. It indicates quite a different picture. A group of six find each other mutually acceptable and were able to share. When Sarah tried to join this group, she was rejected. There was no isolate this time. These two sociograms show progress in mutual acceptance which began to emerge in about February and grew slowly in succeeding months. Learning to accept each other and share was a basic need in this group.

"Sociogram III contrasts with Sociogram I. Feelings are more definite. There are several mutual choices, for example: Sarah and Elizabeth; Edna and Doris; Dorothy and Lillian; and Florence and Gertrude. Rose's choice of Florence is met with rejection. Gertrude likewise rejects her when Florence does. Edna is the object of a good bit of rejection. Dorothy and Elizabeth show mutual rejection. There is still much indifference and passive acceptance. Doris shows a passive acceptance of everyone except a choice for Edna. Doris was fairly new in the group and eager to be liked by all the old members. Hazel still shows no choice; this has been typical of her at most meetings.

"The changes in both status and choice are noticeable. They have come about through the intimacy of a small group and have been influenced somewhat by the leader's effort to encourage group feeling and to sublimate much strong self-centeredness. Acceptance and choice have shown some relationship to status as all of the diagrams show. Sociogram II especially shows the lower status members pulling together.

"In terms of role taking several instances were notable. Edna, for example, often deliberately plays the role of a clown in an effort to attain attention and approval from the group. She is successful if she doesn't go too far, for then the group becomes disgusted because her motive shows too clearly.

"Marion and Doris both tend to be imposed upon by the group. Both are quite mentally retarded and are eager followers who want to please the indigenous leaders. Again barring extremes, both of these girls enjoy their role. They like to participate in a way which shows their achievement. Serving food or sweeping the floor they know they can do well; being Master of Ceremonies would over-

THE SUB DEBS CLUB

SOCIOGRAM I   MARCH 15

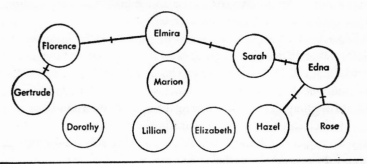

SOCIOGRAM II   APRIL 25

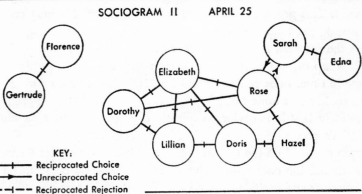

KEY:
—+— Reciprocated Choice
——→ Unreciprocated Choice
—-+-- Reciprocated Rejection
—►-- Unreciprocated Rejection

SOCIOGRAM III   JUNE 1

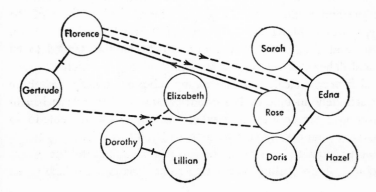

whelm them and they know it. The rest of the group do not look down on them for they appreciate the contribution these girls make. Only the very brightest girls (Rose and Edna) show any feeling of superiority toward Marion and Doris.

"At the beginning of the recorded period, individuals stood out alone rather than sub-groups. It was very difficult for the group to function at all. It seemed wise to choose activities which would permit individual work with individual satisfaction as stepping stones toward a group. This self-centered interest is understandable among deprived children who by their institutional living are forced to be part of a group all the time. A group with sub-groups gradually came into being. Elmira led a sub-group of four pretty steady followers. This group (Gertrude, Florence, Sarah and Marion) exerted the strongest influence on the whole group, largely because Elmira was the accepted indigenous leader of the whole group. Edna led a sub-group of two to three girls which varied in membership from time to time. Edna constantly bid for leadership of the entire group but could never quite make it. On occasions she led her sub-group in definitely hostile behavior completely opposing all other members. Elmira's group operated on a basis of personal congeniality; Edna's group operated on the demands of its leader. Florence and Gertrude constituted the only lasting clique. They frequently chose to be by themselves and excluded any others. This exclusiveness created some feeling against them but because of their comparatively high status, the feeling was envy and jealousy. This feeling was heightened by the desire of each girl to have one bosom friend, a desire typical of this age and emphasized among these insecure girls. Most of the time, however, Florence and Gertrude fell into Elmira's sub-group. Lillian and Hazel, and to a lesser extent Dorothy, tended to be isolated. They did not form a sub-group among themselves. Hazel found it very difficult to relate to any sub-grouping. At first, Rose was definitely an outcast. No one tried any 'uplifting'; she had to win group acceptance by her own efforts. She was finally able to do this and within two months no longer played this part."

Let us now turn from these concrete situations to the group worker's role in dealing with interpersonal relations of these types.

CHAPTER VII

The Group Leader and
Interpersonal Relations

AS THE GROUP LEADER COMES TO
understand the interacting pattern of personal relations he must find
his own place in it. What is his function in terms of these relations
between the members? What of his own relation to individuals and
to the group?

The group worker through his awareness of the opportunities
available through both the activities of the program and the relations
between people should be able to help the members fulfill their own
purposes more thoroughly. This means that they should have more
fun, deeper and more satisfying enjoyment, a chance to learn effectively if that is what they are seeking, or in administrative groups a
more effective planning and execution of their affairs. In all these
aims of the group the development of satisfying interpersonal relations will have a major part.

THE SOCIAL CLIMATE OF THE GROUP

One condition which predisposes to such relations consists of
what is sometimes called the social climate that pervades the group.
Intangible though it is, this atmosphere of groups is obvious to
every sensitive participant. One of the aids to fruitful personal relations lies in a warm, friendly and accepting atmosphere. In such a
climate the powers of each can more easily expand and become
socially valuable by contribution to the whole. The tentacles that
reach out for response to potential friends and companions have a
more auspicious environment for growth. A hostile atmosphere filled
with rivalry, retaliation and repressive leadership either prevents
these sprouts from breaking the surface or by frustrating them turns

them into aggression. The leader by his own warmth and interest in individuals has much to do with producing the social climate and determining the opportunities for growth of personal relations.

In every group, however, the leader must learn to accept the fact that all will not be amiability and mutuality. A certain amount of hostility is created by the group experience as well as by that which individuals bring with them from other relations. Aggression will select different weapons in various age, class or ethnic groups. Some, like Lottie of the Jokerettes, carry their knives in their handbags and others subtly wrapped in ridicule. By accepting the inevitable presence of a certain amount of hostility the leader may prepare himself to meet it. His own acceptance of its inevitable presence helps him to deal with it intelligently and not increase it still further by unnecessary repressive measures.

To accept the fact that hostility will appear does not mean that the group leader permits or encourages its unimpeded expression. In group therapy with unusually aggressive people a high degree of permissiveness may well be one of the best tools of treatment. But in groups of the kind here presented, one of the learnings from the experience is the discovery of ways of finding harmless or if possible useful outlets for the unavoidable hostilities of life. To learn to accept the limits that society places on aggressive expression is a requirement for every growing child. These groups can provide especially for youth an experience of self-limitation of aggressive demands in the interest of the larger good of the group. Much of the socialization of personality occurs in this learning. Within the experience of these groups many opportunities lie ready at hand for working out such feelings. The leader in such groups represents the authority of their enveloping society. While he needs to be understanding of the hostile as well as the positive feelings, he needs to incarnate without the spirit of retaliation the customary controls of aggression that their society expects. The fact that the leader in leisure-time settings is there to help them enjoy themselves and to do it by co-operative enterprises makes it easier than in some school or institutional settings to combine the necessary limitations the leader may have to impose at points with proof of his affection for them, and with the acceptance of social controls by the group itself.

THE RELATION OF THE LEADER TO SUBGROUPS

As the pattern of relationships forms within the group it is important for a leader to be aware of his part in this social structure. The inexperienced leader sometimes assumes that he can achieve an undifferentiated group without cliques. This attempt will almost certainly be unsuccessful. His function is rather to assist those relationships which are wholesome to individuals and the group and discourage the others. In the Sub Debs, for example, the ability to create a group of six able to work together showed increased capacity for co-operative behavior and the friendship pairs that appeared within the club were probably among its most valuable results. The group worker will need to recognize and accept these more intimate relations within the social structure of the group.

There are of course in some instances subgroups which represent malignant growths which may either threaten the life of the group or be injurious to individuals. In some cases subgroups represent values which the group leader is aiming to affect, as, for example, in the case of the racial subgroups within the Y-Teen Club. There is evidence also that a snobbish preference for "higher class" position serves to group together the low-status Negro girls. Evaluation and preference are, of course, inevitable in any group. The question is, on what bases is such evaluation made and are individuals "rated" not by their own characteristics but by classification as members of some larger social grouping? Within these small groups, as in the larger society, we get the effects of the social hierarchies, whether they be based on an economic, ethnic, age, sex or some other factor. To release individuals from stereotyped reactions so they can secure such acceptance as they can win for themselves ought to be one of the opportunities within these groups. To accomplish this the group leader must accept each person on his own merits.

Where disruptive or hostile subgroups appear it is important for the group leader to recognize that at times healthy conflict provides the way by which issues are worked out and new decisions reached either on leadership or on policy. This is illustrated in the following chapter in the R.R.C.'s. His function here is largely that of referee. It is when such disruption is rooted not in the reality of the group's situation but largely in the inner need of certain individuals projected on the group that he may need to assist the group to deal with it. At times this will require dealing with people on an individual basis, as we shall see in a situation within the Mike Club or as in the case of the Bulldog's diverting destructive energies into more socially accepted channels by means of program.

The Relation of the Leader to the Socially Inadequate Members

One of the most important functions of the group leader in dealing with the interpersonal relations of a group lies in his use of the group situation to assist the isolated member or those upon whom is thrust a role expressive of rejection or hostility. Persons of this kind are often referred by anxious parents or friends or by other social agencies in the hope that they can be helped to make friends or to have a good time which will lead to greater self-confidence and social acceptance. We do not know as much as we should about these difficulties in establishing relationships with others, but there is enough evidence to indicate that they are symptoms which require careful diagnosis.

Among those who are likely to turn up in this way in a recreation agency are some whose social isolation is a symptom of severe personality disturbance. To the inexperienced group leader such members may present themselves merely as peculiar, sometimes unusually untidy, lacking in energy, excessively aggressive, or absorbed in an inner world of daydreams. They often make little response to attempts to draw them into activities or to establish any relation to them. In some cases these individuals are in fact not ready for group experience and in some these symptoms may be evidences of such severe disturbance that the person should be referred for treatment to a psychiatrist or case worker.

Among those who find it difficult to establish social relationships are others who can be helped by a skillful group worker. Dr. Mary

Northway from her studies of "Outsiders" has defined two types of isolate behavior familiar to many group workers.[1] There are, as her observations indicate, some people who are socially uninterested often because they are absorbed in solitary concerns of their own—in music, in science, in art. If they can be encouraged to contribute their interest to a group they may find life more satisfying eventually. It is important, for the leader to understand the basis for the apparent withdrawal and to respect the right of each to develop his own interests, using group contacts as he may wish. Some of these people, however, are merely using this absorption as a shield to cover their social inadequacy. They have in fact a real desire for participation which with encouragement will lead them to become a part of the group.

A second type of behavior familiar to group leaders is that found among socially ineffective people driven by a desire for recognition which they try vainly to gain by noisy, arrogant or boastful behavior. Beneath the apparent self-assurance a deep insecurity leads them constantly into taking the wrong means to accomplish their desires.

From the sample groups discussed in the previous chapter it will be clear that some degree of isolation will be found even in the close-knit friendship group. What can the leader do, for example, to help Elsie, the outcast member of the Jokerettes, or to bring Bella, a rejected member of the Y-Teens, into a more acceptable position.

To an understanding worker an acquaintance with Elsie's home situation will help to give her insight into the insecurity that marks her contacts with her peers. It is clear from the record that Elsie is facing problems at school and at home so that her social inadequacy with her peers is not surprising. Her lack of experience with other children in the family combined with a dominating mother are enough to put her at a serious disadvantage, while her low intelligence in comparison with the other members further handicaps her. The leader with this understanding of her situation may be able to help her in several ways. The services of a family case worker to work with the mother were used in this case to relieve some of the pressures put upon Elsie at home. Individual attention from the leader within the group setting reassured her and increased her chances to contribute of herself, rather than by using the money her higher economic status provided. At the first dance Elsie assumed of her own accord the role of "bouncer" and with sharp aggressive comments and some pushing was able to keep out the unwelcome "crashes." It seemed clear that this occasion gave her the chance to work off some accumulated aggression in the service of the club. However, the leader may need to help her toward some opportunities for friendly and giving behavior as well. The popular positions at a refreshment table are often a good first experience for a shy and partially hostile girl. While Elsie's low intelligence rate and basic insecurity are serious handicaps to full acceptance, the fact that she is within even the outer fringes of so close-knit a circle means that she has some capacity for establishing relations. A sympathetic leader with this situation in mind can usually find opportunities within the group for building upon her positive abilities and attractiveness to help her win a place for herself.

A similarly rejected position is occupied by Bella in the Y-Teens as the sociograms indicate. Bella, it may be recalled from the previous chapter, has cast herself into the role of the representative of adult values, the reminder of how their behavior will "look." Unwise leaders are sometimes inclined to welcome this type of assistance. A closer look at Bella's situation will make the leader help her to give up this role for a more equal and co-operative one with her peers. Bella is in fact the oldest child of a large family for which she has had many responsibilities. Her father is away from home considerably and Bella acts as a companion to her mother and a mother-substitute to her younger brothers and sisters. There is much harmony and real love in the family, of which she receives her share.

Bella suffers from an unattractive personal appearance. She is dark skinned, which is a handicap here even with the Negro girls, and her face is marred by deformed lips and an oily complexion. She dresses in poor taste and lacks the "aids to beauty" so important to the adolescent girl. In spite of these handicaps Bella has assets. She is skilled in dancing, skating and volleyball, and speaks well in the group. Most of all she is accustomed to love and acceptance at home.

When she first entered the group she repeated the only group pattern she knew—that of her family—and attempted to act as a controlling older sister. This immediately precipitated resistance. In this resistance the leader was able to help her to see the need for a different approach and her relations began to improve. Assistance with physical appearance, as far as possible, with clothes and the accessories essential in her society have further helped her in adjustment. While she has never won acceptance with the white girls or with the Negro girls of higher social status, she has been helped to move from a bottom position and an unpopular role toward greater acceptability.

The attitude toward the socially inadequate individual suggested by these illustrations again demonstrates one of the elements basic to the group-work approach. In such instances the leader needs to see the behavior of the isolate, whether expressed in withdrawal, meekness, or overt hostility, as symptomatic and then try to help with the underlying motivations. There is little use in treating the symptom directly in the manner formerly adopted by annoyed adults, who approach the shrinking child by asking brightly, "Oh ho, so you've lost your tongue?" As we understand the desire for affection, the guilt over hostility, the deadening sense of insecurity that underlies the isolate's position we will no longer forget him and let him drop out of all the normal enjoyments of life through neglect. Nor will we ridicule or pursue him with exhortations to "be a good sport," "get up and dance with the girls," or similar advice beyond his power to use. Rather, we shall recognize that isolation is a sign of retardation in the normally expanding social relations that personality requires for its happiness and health. For such retardation, mild or severe, he needs sympathetic understanding by the leader and a warm accepting climate in the group.

The skilled leader will be aware at points not only of those who suffer from social inadequacy leading to isolation; at times it will become apparent that some individuals are being harmed rather than helped by the personal relations within the group. He may be aware, for example, that a dominant-dependent relation between two people is serving only to continue both patterns without helping either to move toward more positive or more mutual relations. At times he may find, if he has several siblings from the same family, that rivalry and disputes will reappear within the group setting in ways which reinforce the worst features of the family life. He may realize that one clique is acting to lead the group into serious antisocial behavior. He may discover instances in which the group scapegoat or clown is serving to establish habits of bullying, on the one hand, and of meek acceptance or repressed retaliation, on the other. At points the group exploits one of its members. The Y-Teens' use of the meek and hard-working Jenny as social chairman is a case in point.

In the Bulldogs, for example, the leader points out that Jimmy, an undersized younger boy, a continuous chain smoker, has gained admittance to the group only because he is a younger brother of a member of a powerful gang which the Bulldogs wish to emulate and appease. The Bulldogs are using him in the role of a lever to hoist themselves up in gang society. Jimmy would not on his own merits have been taken in, since he has no athletic skills to recommend him and little capacity for mutual relations. As the leader reports: "Jimmy is isolated by the group at its meetings. A part, and a major part, of this isolation stems from Jimmy's own insecurity resulting from his home life. He is an illegitimate child living with his mother who is known in the neighborhood as a 'widow.' His family has never been a group from which Jimmy could receive any amount of stable attachment. This had apparently made Jimmy wary of group attachment, because he is never sure how he will be received. A manifestation of this insecurity and need for acceptance that Jimmy has is indicated by his willingness to fight. Jimmy is not an aggressive boy, but he is lured into mischievous behavior by the prestige he can obtain in doing so. Building on his older brother's reputation as a 'tough guy' in a notorious gang, he feels his only way to acceptance lies in proved physical prowess, or in raiding exploits in the nearby markets." It is obvious to the leader in such a situation that Jimmy's membership in the Bulldogs only serves to reinforce the worst features of his family and community environment.

In the case of Jimmy the leader should consider whether he is misplaced in this group. He is not wanted by them and his hold on them builds upon antisocial habits on both sides. As a group worker, the leader may have some resources in the way of other groups of Jimmy's age in which he would have more chance to secure standing in his own right—not borrowed from his brother. His fighting abilities under the leadership of a good physical educator may become a socially acceptable asset. The family situation may prove to have some strengths to build on in spite of the poor start he has to con· tend with. In such a situation the leader needs to explore the resources available by which Jimmy can have a better time in ways more productive for him in the long run. If this does involve movement to another group or other opportunities in the gymnasium or consultation with his mother, Jimmy, of course, must be approached before anything is done. The leader here must act as an assistant who enables people to find their own ways to satisfactory adjustment, if they will and as they can.

These situations and others like them serve to point out certain basic principles upon which the group worker can build his approach. In the first place, the recreation-education activities are not occasions to which people come consciously for treatment or because they are in trouble in which they are asking for assistance. The leisure-time function of the agency must be kept clearly in mind. However, we recognize that there will appear inevitably in the normal course of offering such activities many individuals who obviously need and some who consciously want help in their interpersonal relations. The group leader, however, does not begin to "treat" people or to provide service without their knowledge or consent. He must be sensitive to individual need and to the effects the group is having on its members. Within the group itself he can often help people to work out their relations in ways that will yield greater satisfactions and more socially desirable results. Only when a person wants individual assistance can the leader enable him to secure it. It is at this point, as we shall see in a later chapter, that the leader can use the available resources, including his own relationship.

THE LEADER'S RELATION TO SOCIAL FACTORS AND VALUES

The intricate intermingling of social and personal elements mentioned in Chapter V appears again here in the understanding of interpersonal relations. Inevitably social factors, such as class position, occupation, religious affiliation, place of residence or ethnic background, enter into the evaluation and acceptance of individuals within such groups. These factors seem of increasing importance with age as society imprints upon the plastic material of youth the mark of its social barriers. In the social hierarchies within intimate groups the effect of social distance is constantly making itself felt. The congeniality of the inner circle of the Jokerettes, for example, consists in part of the comfortable sense of at-homeness that comes with similar social background. The leader needs to be aware that occasionally what appears to be isolation is a case of misplacement in which a person is too different from the group socially to fit in or may in some cases be on the way out of that particular social grouping. That, for example, is the case with Ruthie, who is found on the fringe of the Jokerettes. Unlike Elsie, who is a psychological isolate, Ruthie is a person of high acceptability. She and her family, however, are on the move upward in their social milieu. Her position on the edge of the Jokerettes can only be understood in the light of her social situation.

It seems probable in this instance that Ruthie was misplaced in the Jokerettes. Her superior intelligence and abilities make her dissatisfied with their rather restricted level of activities. The stricter supervision by her mother, her educational aspirations, and her change in residence are in this community characteristic of a family which is moving upward in the social scale. Her fringe position at the time of the last sociogram was followed soon afterward by her withdrawal from the club. The leader in this case needs to recognize the pull upward of her socially mobile family and the fact that Ruthie's intelligence and personal qualities make it likely that she can use more education advantageously. Her social contacts as she matures probably should be with youth in the middle-class Negro community to which her family aspires. The leader should therefore not try to encourage her continuance with the Jokerettes. She might help her make a connection, for example, with the Y-Teen Club that functions in the neighborhood to which she is moving. This would give her both interracial experience and contact with other middle-class girls.

As might be expected, social factors play an important part in the interpersonal relations of the Y-Teen Club. The attempt to bridge the racial differences by including Negro and white in a formed club is successful to the extent that both remain within the group.[2] Even this takes conscious planning, as the leader indicates, to keep in the minority (in this case the white girls). The less intimate character of a larger formed club with more agency determination both of membership and of program makes this more feasible than it would be if this were considered by the members an intimate group. It is quite possible that the fear, suspicion, and at points guilt that appear in both Negro and white when they break the community taboo and accept each other as friends is helped by the agency's approval of this policy and especially by associating the policy with religious sanctions, as is done by agency ceremonial in such groups. If we examine the interpersonal life within the club, however, we see that social difference—both racial and economic—do affect the personal contacts. While leadership is accepted across the racial line, intimate friendship does not cross it.

For example, the number of mutual acceptances between those of the same race as estimated by the leader in the two sociograms was thirteen as compared with four between Negro and white. While this is probably not exact in any sense it reflects what one would expect to happen in this area. The fact that these girls are capable of accepting mutual acquaintance and can work together on a varied recreation-education program represents for their neighborhood such a step toward positive racial relations that it may well represent as much as a leader would hope for in such a group. Since one of the agency's purposes is improved interracial understanding, the leader who recognizes the mingling of personal and social elements in these situations is better equipped to gauge the meaning of what is going on. Only then can she help each of these individuals to find in the group the fullest range of personal acceptance and the broadening of experience into appreciation of people regardless of racial factors. But she cannot do this effectively without understanding both the personal and the social factors with which she must work in each case.

Similar indications of the influence of social factors on acceptance can be found of every group which is heterogeneous as to social composition. In the Mike Club the one Protestant girl moves always under a social cloud. In the R.R.C.'s the group by common consent excludes boys from a lower income area near by. Within the children's institution, the child of divorced or neglectful parents faces as subtle a barrier, when she tries to gain a place with her peers, as does Jimmy, the bastard among the Bulldogs. These handicaps arising out of various types of social position function through stereotypes. To overcome them the individual has by his own efforts to break through the stereotype and gain the right to live as a person, not a figure hung with generalized characteristics. Leaders can recognize this stereotyping habit as it affects acceptance and assist in the process of breaking the crusts of prejudice so that individuals can step forth with what individual capacities they may have.

One final factor needs to be considered in terms of the leader's place in interpersonal relations. The status achieved by each member is geared to scales of values functioning within the group. These value systems are largely products of the complex social setting from which any group emerges. By the process of personality formation the values expressed in mores appear within each individual as the dictates of the superego, consciously formed into concepts of right and wrong and unconsciously functioning as well. Such value scales as determine status within such groups are of course only a small part of those held by individuals. It is their collective force brought about by group evaluation that gives them power to assess place to each person in the group.

The leader's relation to this process of evaluation is significant. In the first place, the values apparent in these scales have various relations to his own and those of the agency. In the case of the Rowdy Robbers, the newspaper group or the Gay Canteen Committee, for example, the values accepted by the members are those generally accepted as socially desirable by the wider community. They include sex restraint, personal honesty, educational ambition, responsibility for oneself, kindness to others, and courtesy to older people. Added to these are values held by the youth subculture of that area: athletic prowess for boys, feminine attractiveness combined with restraint for girls, and the desirability of at least a high school education for all. With these values the agency and the leader are in substantial agreement and the groups serve as a means of establishing them as a part of the behavior of youth.

In certain of our sample groups, however, some of the values held by the group are regarded by society as antisocial. This is most clearly shown in the gang society to which the Bulldogs aspire, in the disorganized, partially antisocial area of the Jokerettes, or in the somewhat isolated nationality community from which the Mike Club is drawn. In such situations the leader's values and those of the agency are antithetical to some of those held by the group. In fact one reason why settlements and public recreation centers are placed in such districts is to try to change these very attitudes. It is in these groups that leaders are forced to come to grips with this conflict. What can the leader do? What does he have to build on? How can he go about it?

He has certain assets to build on. To a considerable extent he shares and can support the values by which the group bestows status. For example, while he and the agency may aim at different standards in regard to fighting, sex behavior, or protection of property from theft and vandalism, he does share their interest in the masculine accomplishment in physical prowess and athletic skill, or for the girls in the improved skill in dancing or the creative arts. In supporting where he can he gains rapport with the group. He too wants them to have a good time and the shared enjoyment he has with them gives him an entrance to approaching the less desirable values they have learned from their environment. It is important for him to avoid moralistic exhortation, which merely identifies him in their minds with their natural enemies among the forces of law and order. On the other hand, they will not respect him if out of insecurity or desire to appease he condones what he himself actually disapproves. The answer lies rather in a clear hold on his own convictions demonstrated by behavior but without an aroma of either uplift or retaliation. If he is able to establish rapport with them his values begin to affect theirs by a kind of social osmosis. He may be able also to support within the group individuals with more acceptable standards and so shift the status accorded them. This is a long-range process in which agency influences from several leaders and various activities may be needed to effect change. It is only one aspect of the attempt to affect basic values which have been contaminated by pathological communities or distorted by personal misfortune.

Finally, it must be kept in mind that in those neighborhoods where the social environment itself is a constant source of individual deterioration "delinquency" is almost a "normal" reaction. The answers that must be found—while they may never be worked out in time for the Bulldogs or the Jokerettes—must lie in such long-range social improvements as will eliminate the gang life bred of poverty, insecurity and ignorance. The group worker, like the doctor and the case worker, unfortunately must face the fact of the untreatable character of some individual situations. This must make him redouble his efforts at the social action that, like the preventive measures of Public Health, will reduce in the future the diseases that affect the social body itself.

Achieving Democratic Control

EVERY GROUP, WHATEVER ITS purpose, develops some form of government, some aspect of leadership and authority, some control over its members. The necessity of government in small groups as well as in the larger society,[1] in recreation and education groups as well as in economic or political organizations, rests on the simple necessity for the control and pruning of individual impulse, the co-ordination of the powers and interests of each in the pursuit of collective ends. The group leader, who represents the authority of the agency and who frequently differs in age or social background from the group, must inevitably discover his function in relation to such group government.

His role differs widely according to the type of group he is working with, its age and capacity for self-government, the mores of its particular community regarding authority, the personal drives and needs of individual members.

Among the types of groups described in an earlier chapter the customary patterns of authority and control differ widely.[2] The most common perhaps is the self-governing club—a one-cell form of democratic society in which objectives, policies and program are presumably determined by the members, and officials are created to carry out the will of the group. Authority flows from such leaders to authorized subgroups in the form of committees appointed to fulfill functions of the group, co-ordination of effort is effected by such administrative officials. These familiar characteristics of the self-governing unit provide the structure for much of our recreation and education program. It is patterned in simpler form after the larger governmental bodies of our society, and the large organizations so important within it. It exists within the framework of the agency, which limits to some extent its complete freedom of control.

A different pattern of authority exists with the voluntary education group like the newspaper group or the Mike Club. Because the conscious purpose of the group is learning, the members voluntarily submit themselves to the authority of teacher, expert or coach. Control in such groups normally covers the arrangement of the subject matter whether it be some kind of knowledge or a skill and also such control of members' activities as is needed to make learning possible for all. In voluntary learning groups as distinguished from compulsory or credit-motivated education, such control rests basically on the capacity of the leader or teacher to provide a satisfying learning experience. Often such voluntary learning groups can and do take on some of the features of self-government, such as planning by committees or determination of subject matter by group decision.

Another type of governmental structure with which leaders will be working is that of the representative council or committee, such as the Gay Canteen Committee or the Social Action Committee, in which members act as representatives either of a membership body or for intergroup activity. In this case the group is self-governing within the limits of its charter but the authority residing in its members arises in part from their relation to their constituents.

Structure, however, is only the simplest and most obvious factor that the leader will have to understand as he assumes his relation to the group.[3] More important by far are the basic attitudes toward authority, the behavior by which those manifest themselves, and the capacity of the group for co-ordinated effort toward common goals. The leader needs to ask himself: What stage of development has this group reached in its capacity to control its members in the interest of accomplishing its purpose? What community forces or conditions affect its development of effective democratic control? What significant individual drives and needs are evident within the group which are determining its methods of dealing with authority? What regulations, limitations or controls are imposed by the agency within which the leader as its representative has to function?[4] In order to make clearer the relation between these aspects of the governmental process we shall draw from five of our samples, which present differing but characteristic problems in the development of authority during the age span between puberty and young adulthood.[5]

THE FIRST STAGE IN SELF-GOVERNMENT

The Rowdy Robbers Club is the youngest of our sample groups and it stands at the threshold of adolescence. Its roots in a middle-class community mean that patriarchal family controls are well established. Its members are subjected as well to the usual disciplines of the public school system. They are on the whole a group conformable to the stimuli and limitations of this environment. They are not rebels, nor delinquents. They are, however, like all adolescents, emerging from the shelter and guidance of the family life into the greater freedoms of a youth society set within a larger community. They are active, mischievous, noisy and aggressive like all normal adolescents. This club is probably their first experience with collective action which is not determined chiefly by adults, as is the case in school, in the family, and in the church. Here they must learn for themselves to control impulsive behavior, plan and co-ordinate effort, and create and accept leadership, not from adults but from their peers. Even under the relatively advantageous circumstance from which they come this presents them with some difficulties. Here is the leader's description of the process:

"The first meeting of the R.R.C.'s was characterized by wild behavior and the leader began immediately to point out that the club could accomplish nothing until the individuals were willing to devote their attention to the club's business. The group took no action on this at their first meeting and the leader exercised some authoritarian control, especially in stopping the boys from 'raiding' the girls' meeting next door.

"At the second meeting, using the development of the Raiders, a younger club familiar to them as an example, the leader suggested that much more could be accomplished if members raised their hands for recognition by the president. This was challenged by one member, Harry, as being 'too much like school.' But it was at this point that the real leadership of the group asserted itself—and the leadership did not at that time include Sam, the insecure and fortuitously chosen president.

"Seth, a rising power in the group, said the rule of raising hands for permission to speak was necessary because the members would not talk quietly among themselves as Harry had suggested. Bob and Ted, also well-accepted members, supported this view. The rule was adopted by the group, which then turned its attention to the penalty for infractions, since there was no question in their minds that punishment was needed to enforce the rule. Drawing on the Cub Scout merit system, Ted recommended a system of ten demerits before a fine was levied.

"Seth felt ten demerits were too much 'because it would be worth your while to break the rule.' He suggested two 'points' for a five cent fine and after long discussion and many votes this was accepted. It was assumed the president would assign the demerits and Sam began using this to punish other low status members.

"Next week the boys hid in the girls' meeting room, but when they wanted to repeat this the following week, the leader called them out and announced a flat 'agency' rule that any boy who went into the other meeting room or interrupted the girls' meeting would be asked to leave the building for that day. The group seemed to accept this adult-imposed limitation. At the same meeting, however, when suggestions were made for initiations that involved the girls, the leader suggested the group ask the girls whether they wanted to cooperate in this. The girls agreed and, with the sanction of legality, a very imaginative and amusing initiation followed to everyone's enjoyment. A week later Seth cautioned the club against bothering the girls without asking their permission.

"The rule of raising hands and the penalties for enforcement were carefully explained by the officers to new members as they were admitted to the club. In fact, the officers put heavy stress on this as the cornerstone of the group's method of operation. They were not so conscious that voting and majority rule had become part of their functioning from the outset. But this aspect of group control was so firmly entrenched that when Sam, then president, refused to come up for a meeting because he was waiting for 'winners' at ping pong, the group talked seriously of voting him out of the club. He was severely reprimanded when he did appear.

"One day after a meeting there was a cruel snowball attack on the girls. The leader asked at the next meeting what the boys thought about this. Guilt was written on every face and Sam proposed that fines be levied for taking part in the fight. Someone asked whether the club could control the behavior of its members outside the building. Bob insisted the club had this power and with little discussion the principle was accepted, though it was never mentioned or enforced afterwards.

"As the months went by and the boys became interested in activities and found the indigenous leaders capable of mobilizing the resources of the group to carry on these activities, discipline became much less of a problem. 'Points' and fines continued, however, and the group leader often had to step in to caution a member about disrupting a meeting.

"There have been times when the group leader has questioned the right of the officers to carry out certain punishments or make certain decisions without consulting the membership. Bill, an insecure and low status member, has protested against disciplinary action but he does not have the influence to press his complaints of 'discrimination.' On the other hand docile Tom accepts his disciplinary measures without a word of protest and Art (a deaf boy) converts them into a joke. In general, however, the group has worked out its own system of control and abides by the officers' execution of the system.

"The group has slowly accepted the rule against breaking into other meetings—and other meetings means the girls' club. They have learned that the agency prohibits rough-house within the rooms and know when it starts they will be asked to continue the melee outside. They accept the enforcement of these limitations by other members of the staff as well as by the leader. There is, in other words, no strong drive to rebel against the adult authority that the agency represents to these middle class boys."

The elements of self-constituted authority are obviously beginning to appear in this group. Unlike many groups at this age they not only draw up a system of penalties but, perhaps because they are in other situations accepting of authority, are able to enforce them on recalcitrant members. In more rebellious or chaotic groups the tendency to establish severe penalties is often noticeable and seems to satisfy the guilt they feel at their inability to control their own aggressive behavior. Having established such penalties they are not always able to enforce them except on low-status members or scapegoats. This group reflects a relatively mature attitude toward their own social control.

It is important to note here the role of the group leader. In agency-established rulings he is the responsible enforcement officer. This is a role well understood by these boys from other experience with adults and one to which they have little objection. While they will, like all normal adolescents, test him out to see if he is strong enough to fulfill his function as controller, they do not regard the rules as unfair nor do they feel his restraint as implying a personal rejection of them. In many less well-adjusted groups both these reactions are to be expected. From his point of view his purpose is to put as much control as he can into their hands as they are able to handle it without injustice to weaker members.

The experience of the R.R.C.'s indicates another aspect of the establishment of self-government, namely, the selection and training of indigenous leaders. Their first president, elected immediately after organization, was Sam, soon exchanged for Bob as experience showed Sam's relative incompetence. The leader reports this experimentation as follows:

"Sam, the first president, presented in the fall some very distinct personality difficulties. He apparently did not have any close friendships with boys his own age, but seemed to hang around with girls and with boys either younger or older than himself. However, his relations with his younger brother were healthy and mutually satisfying. He got real satisfaction out of his role as 'manager' of the younger boys' club, the Raiders, where he exercised a punitive role toward his brother's playmates. The invitation to join a club of his own age represented a threat to his position with the younger boys and verbally he resisted strongly at first. With reservations he joined the R.R.C.'s, and possibly by virtue of his close association with the agency, was chosen to be the first president. His status in the group was quite low at the time; he was both unable and afraid to exercise leadership. On the surface his attitude toward the leader and other adults was marked by a sullen, truculent air.

"As president Sam alternated between hesitancy in asserting his authority and impulsive, punishing behavior directed at other low status boys. He was far too insecure to handle discussion and disagreement within the group and very early Seth began to step in to straighten out the tangles. Seth, Ted and Bob emerged as the outstanding members. They made the suggestions that were finally accepted by the group.

"At his third meeting with the group, the leader suggested the possibility of producing a radio show for presentation at a Saturday night junior canteen. Bob moved into the leadership of this project so rapidly with his outpouring of suggestions for a Truth and Consequences program, that before it was apparent what had happened, he had literally taken over the chairmanship of the meeting.

"The leader gave Bob paper and pencil and he began going around the table asking for suggestions from the others. He showed immediately a sensitivity to the feelings of others that Sam had not been able to express. For instance, as he came to shy Dick, who could not make a suggestion, Bob quickly said he would come back later and passed on to the next.

"At the following meeting Bob presented a full report on the project: the outline of what they wanted to achieve and an analysis of the problems that would have to be solved. Members now turned to him for permission to speak. At the end of the meeting the leader suggested the formation of small committees to work on the various problems. There was no discussion or voting for chairman of the most important committee for Bob was actively functioning in that role. There was no question raised when he picked Seth and Ted to serve with him. The leader pressed for participation by everyone on one of the committees.

"The group however was not ready to function through committees. Little clusters of friends gathered to work on the project between meetings. Sam, the president, was on the fringe of these groups but was growing in his capacity to participate. In spite of some emerging leadership the group was still unable to hold a successful rehearsal without the leader and when he was not present complained that nothing had been accomplished because of the bickering.

"The radio program was produced and was a success. The boys were not conscious of course that their first project had helped the group to find itself by locating its indigenous leaders. However after the seventh meeting Bob told the leader confidentially that 'no one likes Sam and that's why Harry and Jim quit.' Bob made no overt move during meetings until after the radio program had been performed, but behind the scenes he was organizing the revolt against Sam.

"Before the ninth meeting Seth and Ted told the leader that they had heard rumors of an effort to oust Sam. Partly to consolidate their own leadership positions, partly to cover up the hostility involved, they suggested that a change be made not on the basis of Sam's failure, but as a normal rotation of officers. The leader said this was a good way of approaching the question.

"Bob with the ruthless frankness of his age stood up at this meeting, pointed a finger at Sam and said: 'You know you haven't been a good president and haven't held the club together . . . I think we should elect a new president.' Ted and Seth softened the blow by calling for an election of a whole new slate, which was approved. Ted nominated Bob for president and perhaps in retaliation Sam nominated Seth. The first ballot ended in a tie, but Bob, maneuvering skillfully, suggested two new boys be voted into the club to break the deadlock. He won the election. The leader suggested the old and new president shake hands and this established a precedent. Seth then became vice-president and Nathan secretary.

"Sam was hurt by his summary removal but he accepted the criticism and demonstrated his growth as a member of a group. The group soothed his (and their own) feelings by making him treasurer. This position was evidently within his power to administer successfully. As this process went on, the changes that took place in Sam, quite possibly through his group membership, were both rapid and basic within the last few months of the year. He came to accept the usual controls within the group and to subordinate his own needs to those of others. His relationship to the leader and other adults in the agency became much more friendly and he was able to establish relationships with boys of his own age. It was obvious that he was a happier person. The leader suspected that Sam's needs for social growth were being met to a far greater extent than was the case with the other boys.

"Bob took over the presidency with a strong sense of responsibility. He helped the group move logically from one point to the next and threw in solutions to problems without forcing them on the group. With an objectivity which indicated his growing maturity, he set another precedent at one point by fining himself for too much laughing."

The group leader's relation to the rise of such subgroups as Sam's, and to changes in control must be chiefly in his assistance to seeing it is carried on without corrupt political means. The experience in evaluating and shifting leadership is important for the group.

Here in the first experiences with self-government lie the sources of attitudes later used in political parties, trade unions, religious bodies, and other adult organizations. The leader can assist the group to deal with Sam's inadequacies and to find other opportunities for his abilities which make him better able to function with his peers. In dealing with Bob he can also help to develop obvious leadership talents but within the controls of the democratic procedures which if applied will limit domination and manipulation and encourage participation by all.

One of our most effective means of establishing the function of leadership at this age as distinct from personal friendship or pre-eminence consists in the procedure of rotation of office. When authority moves by rotation from one member of a group to another several important psychological consequences follow. In the first place, it symbolizes the fact that the authority is group-created and bestowed by the group for its own ends. Moreover, by the removal of power from one person and bestowal on another the ties are broken between one indigenous leader and the group in so far as they are mixed expressions of personal friendship and leadership. The friendships can then, of course, continue as such but the leadership tie is formed with another person and by that fact somewhat depersonalized. It is also a contribution to democratic functioning that there be returned to the role of member persons who have been leaders. They can increase the intelligent understanding of what is involved in leadership out of their experience with it and can fertilize and point up the critical judgment of the constituency. They often assume the role of the "leader of the opposition" in government. It is no accident that the ruling by divine right had to be superseded before democracy could function, by premiers or presidents whose authority obviously was bestowed by election. Not only was this necessary so that it could be kept in the hands of the people. By its very changing from one person to another the personal elements of attachment were obviously separated from the official function of leader. The experience of youth up to the point of adolescence is almost completely with authorities which he did not select and which he cannot depose or control.

In the case of parents, their authoritative function is normally intertwined deeply with affection. In the case of the teacher, the other predominant bearer of authority, some remote "they" selects the person into whose orbit of power a group of children is thrust for the eight months of a school year. The police, who represent the chief community authority with whom they come into contact, are equally beyond the scope of their control. If they are to enter upon democratic citizenship, however, they need to have a concept of the authority of our society as arising not by inherited right or mere traditional assumption but out of the consent and participation of the governed.

It is this essential concept which gives its most basic meaning to the self-constituted authority of youth groups. Within the compass of face-to-face relations and in dealing with interests in which they are then deeply concerned adolescents like the R.R.C.'s have the chance to experience the creation of authority and the investiture of certain selected persons with it.

Coming to Terms with Authority

To those accustomed to disturbed or delinquent adolescents it may seem that the behavior of the R.R.C.'s is not typical. They have, it is true, the advantages that stable, economically secure families and well-constructed neighborhood life can provide as scaffoldings to the developing powers of adolescence.

Many of our groups, however, demonstrate behavior toward authority far less constructive.[6] Let us take the struggle of the Bulldogs' leader in his attempt to counteract well-developed antisocial attitudes toward authority. Such attitudes had arisen in many instances from personal experiences with broken homes or ineffective parents, but in this case they had been reinforced by authoritarian and much-resented controls in church and school, and the neighborhood training in gang warfare against the police and all constituted authority. Although these boys averaged several years older than the R.R.C.'s, their level of social maturity is decidedly lower. The following material indicates these differences:

"The leader's relation to control in the case of the Bulldogs has taken several forms. In the first place they are still unfamiliar with the simplest parliamentary forms and have not in their minds any clear differentiation between the role of member and that of president. The group elected officers in order to give it status as a club. The officers were however very uncertain as to what their functions were and Henry, the first president, was unable to accept the responsibility for maintaining control. He constantly shifted back and forth between his role as president and his position as a contributing member. There were however occasions where certain members notably Jud and Red, asked for more control by the president. The leader therefore had as one of his first jobs with the group the interpretation to Henry of his functions as president. This was done as occasion offered in the meeting and also through several outside conferences.

"The group was transforming itself slowly from a typical neighborhood gang functioning by an informal process of selection and the following of indigenous leaders. To domesticate this form of government into even the slightly formal parliamentary procedure suggested by the leader required a long and arduous process. The aim of the leader here was by such means to give them experience both in conferring responsibility on elected leaders after some consideration and also in the acceptance of such responsibility by the leaders so selected. Within the few months of this first contact with the agency some slight progress seemed to be evident in this direction.

"The second problem that confronted the leader was, however, more fundamental. This group had through its experience acquired definitely anti social and anti-adult habits.

"The group instinctively patterns itself along the lines of the neighborhood gang formations. There is inherent in this a degree of aggressiveness, a show of masculinity, and of 'a way with the women.' Not only does the group manifest this type of behavior pattern in its collective behavior, but also in the aggressiveness of its individual members. Underlying this aggressiveness is their hostility to adults and adult-imposed limitations. They are accustomed to adults in the role of policeman and their behavior in the building at times demonstrates this expectation. Their major, commonly accepted value is their concern around the whole battle of survival among other individuals and gangs in the area. It requires of its members first of all that they know how to handle themselves physically in the area; they do not want 'sissies' in the group. To be dared into something is a part of this whole code of behavior. Along with this tough veneer is also the understanding of their place in the gang structure of the area. They are on their way up in the gang world. Among their peers this toughness is expressed in open aggressiveness and on it depends their whole line of succession in the area. To the older groups there is acquiescence, imitation and at times idolizing. These values are a part of their mores. The Bulldogs come from homes which have been a part of that area for many years and as such are steeped in its tradition. The leader realizes the strength of these values in providing security in the group, but the aggressive and destructive tendencies which a good many of the gangs in this area manifest are not, of course, consistent with the agency's or the leader's values. These aggressive values had to be recognized by the leader to begin with and have not been stringently opposed or suppressed. However, the leader and the agency are constantly attempting to develop more positive attitudes with the group, while at the same time trying to develop these values with all who use the facilities of the agency so that this gradual change in group values of the Bulldogs will not be isolated but will be a part of a changing community pattern.

"These standards which the group have relate directly to the selection of indigenous leaders. Henry, the president, is most advanced in his popularity with the other sex. He knows how to dance and, due to the fact that he works, he is on a financial par with older boys in the area which the group is attempting to emulate. Jud, on the other hand, embodies the aggressiveness of the group. He is the biggest, the oldest, is out of school and has served time at the State Industrial School. His leadership gives them the 'gang' toughness and fighting prowess needed in the area. The group fluctuates in the following of this leadership as the situation changes. In canteen or dances, it is Henry, and to a lesser degree Bernie and Tirky that the group follows. On the football field, in front of the corner drug store or in making secure a position in the agency, it is Jud and his satellite Pat that lead the group. The greatest enemy of the values that the group has established for itself is the inroads that 'outsiders' have made on the area. The aggressive and ofttimes destructive tendency which the group has exhibited toward the housing estate evidences the feeling that they have toward any institution that is a part of the outside influences that are destroying some of these old community patterns.

"The leader has dealt with this attitude in several ways. In the first place it was necessary for him to establish himself with them as a non-authoritative adult interested in their enjoyment and able to assist them in ways important to them. The agency's facilities for basket ball, and for the dances they wanted gave the leader the means to make clear to them his interest in them. He avoided verbal exhortations on their behavior and where possible helped them to succeed in legitimate and socially desirable enterprises in the agency so that they began to win the approval of other groups and of other adults. Since they had never before been popular with the powers that be, this new experience tended to soften their well established hostile attitudes and move them slightly toward agency standards.

"The leader also uses as a lever the program activity itself. In the time when they were in the agency it was necessary to have absorbing activity continuously available. Whether it was preparing for a dance, going over football formations, practicing a play or making decorations for a Christmas party, program had to be planned and available every instant. This gradually gave them an increasing experience with continuity rather than the random disruptive behavior previously their chief form of fun. Such absorbing activity proved to be the most effective means of immediate control and it seemed also to have value to them in lengthening their interest span and teaching them to plan and carry out the responsibility which their projects required.

"It was inevitable however that with such a group occasional conflicts with authority would arise. A specific instance of this happened at a meeting following a very successful dance. They had gained great satisfaction from carrying through a project more elaborate than they had previously attempted and had basked in the approval of the staff as well as that of their peers. When the leader reached the agency for the meeting following the dance, he was approached by the other worker and told that when she had arrived at the building the group was already inside and the building, to all indications, had been securely locked before the staff had left for supper. Later it was discovered that some hardware was missing from various doors. The leader requested the floor after the meeting had been started and asked the group how they had gotten into the building and informed them of what had been discovered missing. The boys looked at each other and finally Jud said, 'We got in the building by using a knife to get the side door open. Anybody can get in this building if they have a good knife. But, Mr. S., we didn't take those locks off the door. A couple of years ago we might have but we don't do that stuff any more.'

"The leader then opened up the question of the result of such behavior for other groups and for their own slowly improving status in the agency. Such discussion is unfamiliar to them since they are accustomed to authoritarian and punishing responses by adults to their usual depredations. The leader in approaching these incidents had constantly to demonstate to them his continuing interest in their activities and to get discussion going without the atmosphere of preaching, so familiar to them. Gradually there was some response to this approach. The relationship of leader and group had relapses in which they slipped back into customary attitudes toward the police-man-adult. These were fully discussed as soon as possible after they occurred in order to bring further insight into the role of the com-munity center and the workers' relation to agency regulations. While adult-imposed measures had at times to be used, care was taken to explain the basis for them and to make clear to the group their own interest in having the center well run. A gradually developed identi-fication with the center as their own seemed to be proof of some success in this direction."

In this type of situation, it is to be expected that it will take much patience and a long pull if this group is to emerge into the mature acceptance of authority as necessary and then acquire the ability to impose it on themselves in constructive ways. Certainly the only likely way to break this impasse is to provide experience with leader-ship which is understanding rather than punitive and to draw them gradually into consideration of the necessary limitations that must be imposed for the greater benefit of all concerned. No miracles can be expected but the successful establishment of rapport with an understanding leader marks the first break in their anti-adult, anti-society front.

The Jokerettes, growing up in another but equally unfavorable environment, also present their leader with problems as to her role with them. In their case, perhaps because they are girls, their con-flict in regard to authority may lead them into too great dependence upon the leader. She reports her experience as follows:

"The leader feels that the Jokerettes have demonstrated ambivalent feelings toward authority and self-government, sometimes showing rejection of authority and hostility toward agency controls and the leader, at other times wishing for control. Their initial reluctance at joining the settlement as individual members after almost a year of independence as an autonomous group, their hostility over certain agency requirements, were in part the result of rejection of adults in their unconscious need to throw off parental authority. In addition, however, the children in this section have hostile feelings and suspicious attitudes toward the police, because of frequent and painful experiences with them in their neighborhood; the school teaching methods are often rigid, and autocratic, judging from the aggressive behavior of many children following school hours; parents indulge in frequent if not wise punishments. These factors produce a hostile attitude to authority.

"Along with resistance to authority, there is from the same cause a pattern of submitting to it in most cases and at times in the case of the Jokerettes an obvious desire for such control from adults. Special caste factors undoubtedly enter in. Not only in the South from which many of the Jokerettes' parents have come but here in this city there is undoubtedly a caste acceptance of domination of the Negroes by the white caste. It is reported that white police have had less trouble than Negro in this section despite the frequent changes and insecurity of many of the young police briefly assigned to this district, because the lower class Negro still manifests attitudes of subserviency to the white officer which reflect caste position. The fact that the leader in this instance is white may therefore stimulate customary responses of deference. Since many of the Jokerettes lack fathers in the home, it is possible also that there may be a special dependence upon the mother parent which is here transferred to the leader as a somewhat older person. These factors along with the adolescent's need at times for adult support may account for the following incident.

"That the girls desire direction from the leader to a dangerous extent was evidenced at the March 4 meeting at which the girls came to the settlement to discuss their relationship with the agency. After the leader suggested frank discussion of how they felt things had been going after five months with a sponsor and sponsoring agency, Queenie said, 'Maybe you'll think I shouldn't say this, Miss D., but anyway. The girls like you and want you for sponsor, but we don't think you act like a sponsor should.' The leader said she'd like to hear how they felt a sponsor should act—this was just what she'd hoped they would talk about. Queenie continued: 'Well, a sponsor should be more strict. She shouldn't let the girls keep making a lot of noise and then have to ask them to explain things. And when there is something like asking for a room for a dance, you should do it and not make us do things like that. If you had asked we might have been able to have the room.' . . . Queenie compared the leader to Mr. M., the sponsor of the Jokers, who she said 'ran the boys.' They didn't speak until allowed, and he did many things for them. He protected them when they got into trouble, even when they went to jail."

In this demand for control, assistance and protection by a leader we have a need felt by many adolescents. Their conflict over adult-imposed authority, their insecurity in assuming mature responsibility mean that they need from their leader especially sensitive and flexible assistance. If she becomes too passive or too permissive, she increases their insecurity or their guilt over their own hostilities.[7] They want help from her in controlling their aggression and—in this environment—they also want protection and concrete assistance. They need her help in learning how to become self-governed. That, rather than the domination they seem to be asking for, must be her answer to this demand.

Self-government by Responsible Youth

If we turn from the Bulldogs and the Jokerettes to the Gay Canteen Committee we have moved not only from the Flats to the North Side. We have also moved to a situation in which youth of practically the same age have assumed with the co-operation of an adult sponsoring committee the responsibility for maintaining and controlling a canteen program for approximately a hundred of their peers.[8] As the elected officials this group has been given authority by the total membership to represent it in the community and to establish and enforce necessary regulations. The stable working-class community surrounding the canteen has come to believe in the need

for wholesome recreation but they believe it should be conducted
properly and within the standards sanctioned by the powerful parish
churches and the neighborhood mores. Even with these supports the
committee is confronted with problems in control quite typical of
canteens. The leader describes their situation as follows:

"The Canteen has a constitution which sets forth certain rules,
such as the prohibition of smoking, profanity, drinking and 'displaying of affection.' For the most part these rules are well obeyed
without much reminding necessary. Occasionally the boys have
lighted cigarettes while still upstairs, but a caution as to the fire
hazard has been sufficient, and smokers have adjourned outside until
the cigarette was finished or have put it out immediately. Now there
is scarcely ever occasion to mention the smoking prohibition.

" 'Displaying of affections' is the one rule which certain couples
have broken most often. These situations the young people find
hard to handle by themselves, and will either overlook them or come
to the leader with the whispered comment: 'trouble in the
lounge.' . . .

"As far as the Canteen Committee meetings are concerned, all
members abide by the rules well. Since it is a smaller group, there
isn't the noise and confusion that there is on Canteen nights. Much
of the orderliness is due to the fact that Herb, the president, has
gained a great deal in poise and in learning how to conduct meetings. At first he was hesitant about asking various members to pay
attention. Now, when he calls the meeting to order he means just
that; nor does he hesitate to say: 'Okay, now, let's quit the horse
play and get down to business.' Also he has adopted the policy of
calling on them individually for their opinions when the group as
a whole have failed to respond.

"A part of this improvement is, therefore, due to Herb's gain
in self-assurance; a part is also due to certain changes in membership
—the elimination of some less responsible, and the addition of
several new members who take it all seriously. There is not need
for too great control from the president, as individually most of
them have a pretty fair sense of what should and what shouldn't be
done.

"They have a rule on the respecting of 'authority of officers and chaperons.' This seems to be a further expression of the attitude of respect for authority and adults instilled into these young people in their homes. It is much more than just the keeping of this rule for the word of an adult is seldom questioned. In this respect the leader has had to be careful that her suggestions appear as suggestions and are not taken for commands. They simply do not question adults, and never have been known to defy them. Even in quarters where open defiance might possibly be expected in other groups, as with Harry in his occasional gang ringleader role, or with Jack and Tom with their drinking, these young people listen to the adult and at least outwardly accept what is said. It is true that subtle defiance is shown, for instance, on the part of Harry in later continued rowdyism—although this has abated to a great extent now, partly because of the pressure of group opinion. Even those taking part in occasional rowdyism will later express the feeling that it doesn't really 'go in the Canteen'—but once in a while 'a fellow just feels like it.'

"Their code goes beyond these written rules, too. As seen in a few incidents that have occurred, the person who admits to what he has done and accepts the consequences is more respected than the one who runs out. The fact that Jack on one occasion admitted to drinking and accepted the group's ultimatum raised him in the others' esteem. On the other hand an occasion when Harry ran out when he knew that he was going to 'get caught' for a minor breach of the rules brought forth expressions of scorn from several in the Canteen at the time.

"The area in which the young people themselves are at a loss is the 'necking' that sometimes occurs in lounge or dance room. In these instances it's always possible to put it on a basis of observing the rule in their own constitution which they signed on becoming members. One such occasion involved Jack and Betty, a girl who has a none too savory reputation, constantly seeks advances from the boys, brags about her boy friends, and is disliked by most of the girls. On this evening the leader walked into the lounge and found Jack and Betty alone on the sofa enjoying a 'necking party.' As she entered, Betty moved away from Jack, and the leader proceeded on into the office to see Fannie and Helen about something. When the leader returned, the same two were still on the sofa, and Betty had moved back. She stopped to talk with them and asked whether they thought what they were doing was in keeping with the Canteen standards. Both of them sat looking at her seriously, Jack shook his head slightly, and neither spoke. Tom, Jack's buddy, who seemed to have his weathereye out for Jack, came up to join the group—listening to what the leader was saying with a slight frown and a worried expression on his face. The leader reminded them that they both knew of the rule in their constitution, which they had agreed to abide by upon becoming members. Tom nodded his head and said, 'That's right, Jack.' Jack looked at Tom, back to the leader, and nodded his head. The leader suggested that they had a certain responsibility to themselves and to other Canteen members to keep those rules. All of the leader's remarks were punctuated by Tom with, 'That's right, Jack,' or 'I told you, Jack.' As the leader left the room, Betty moved away and sat down in one of the chairs, while Tom sat down by Jack. The boys obviously feared that Jack's membership was in jeopardy—inasmuch as twice Jack had come to the Canteen when he had been drinking and had been warned about the breaking of rules.

"Later in the evening Betty came up to the leader, looked her in the eye—watching her reactions—and said: 'I guess I owe you an apology—I don't know what was wrong with me.' The leader said we all did things on impulse occasionally for which we were sorry afterwards—it just meant we had to watch ourselves a little more closely. She then stressed again the fact that in the Canteen we had to obey the rules not just for our own sakes but out of loyalty to the group, in keeping the whole tone of the Canteen one of which we could be proud. Betty said she knew that and then said: 'I guess it's kids like me that need the Canteen.' The leader was a bit startled by her statement—it sounded like one she had overheard—and she said we *all* needed the Canteen because we all needed a place to go where we could have fun with others our own age—that therefore we wanted to keep it the best possible place we could. Betty agreed and voluntarily promised she would never 'act like that again.' The leader simply said, 'I believe you, Betty,' and the conversation ended. Since then Betty has always made it a point when in the Canteen to come to talk with the leader about school, her sister, and especially her boy friends. She is still not accepted by the girls, and in the Canteen she is an isolated member.

"A similar incident arose on another night when two of the boys, Jack and Tom, appeared obviously under the influence of liquor and when Fanny had been 'displaying affection.'

"The decision reached by the Canteen committee following this occasion was that Jack and Tom should have their membership cards revoked, and that Fannie should be warned as it was her first offense. Before the leader had time to say a word, the three were brought in individually and asked point blank whether the stories heard were true. Jack and Tom both said, yes, they had been drinking, and were both told by Herb that he was sorry, but they had decided the boys should hand in their membership cards. Both boys accepted the ultimatum, said, 'Okay,' and left.

"In Fannie's case, Herb said, 'Is this true—what we hear about Saturday night?'

"Fannie looked straight at him and without batting an eye, said, yes, she guessed it was.

" 'You know that's serious, don't you?' asked Herb. 'Jack's had his membership card revoked.'

" 'What are you going to do with me?' Fannie wanted to know. To this query she was given no direct answer immediately, but later was given to understand that this was to be considered a warning.

"Everyone involved in this episode was much in earnest, extremely serious and most desirous of being fair. The three involved accepted the decisions just as seriously.

"Later, upon Jack's request to be reinstated, the Committee decided that, since three months had elapsed, Jack's membership card might be returned to him. Jack had agreed to abide by the rules.

"The pressure of group opinion has a great deal to do in this Canteen with group control. The young people as a group are exceedingly jealous of the reputation of the Canteen. Anyone who jeopardizes that reputation also jeopardizes the existence of the Canteen. They have been on trial in the neighborhood and know it."

These incidents indicate the place of the leader as a reinforcement to officials even when they are as competent and responsible as this committee. It is evident that in this situation, in contrast to the Bulldogs, there is no tendency to regard the regulations as adult-imposed or to resent adult authority. On the contrary, the committee relies on the leader for support without, however, refusing to carry the share of which they are capable. In this group social maturity is well advanced toward full acceptance of social responsibility in accordance with community mores. The leader here is moving toward the position of an executive secretary, who enables the group to function as it decides. This is the relation essential in working with young adults who are ready to step up into citizenship, parenthood and jobs. As this group of adolescents move toward adult responsibilities this committee can help not only by providing good recreation but also in giving them concrete experience in establishing their own authority and in selecting and controlling their own leadership.

We have been discussing so far the learning of democratic attitudes partly in terms of their emotional components. There is need, however, to get clearly established the essentials of democratic methods as experience has wrought them out in our centuries of parliamentary government. In their simplest terms they can perhaps be defined in four common aspects of all group government: (1) the opportunity of members to take part in the formulation of major decisions; (2) the opportunity of minorities and opposition groups to present their case; (3) the insistence that officers are accountable to the members for the carrying out of accepted policy; and (4) the provisions for open and honest elections at regular intervals.[9]

These are the obvious and accepted methods through which democratic process has been established. But they require more than the bones of a suitable constitution to make them possible. They require in addition a certain type of relationship between leaders and members which can be learned only by doing. This relationship consists of the interplay of participation by the members, the bestowal of authority on leaders, and its use for the carrying out of the common goals. It is with this interplay of members and leaders that the group worker is most concerned if he wants to assist in making group government democratic.

GOVERNMENT IN REPRESENTATIVE GROUPS

We have so far been dealing with the process of control in the self-governing group in its simplest form. The council or representative committee differs in that the process is complicated by the necessity of co-ordinating not persons only but groups; and also in the fact that people function within a council not only as persons but also as representatives. The government of every representative body has to determine the framework and relation between these three parties. In the first place, the unit of representation must be established in such a way as to guarantee that the central body truly reflects the parts of which it is composed. This includes the determination of the basis of representation and the number to be sent proportionately to the central body. If significant subdivisions, for example of sex, race, or opinion exist within the constituent groups, provision may need to be made in planning representation to see that such subdivisions are represented adequately. The determination of significant elements or subgroups requiring representation in a central body is a matter requiring careful analysis in each case. In some situations the constituent bodies are clearly subdivided and it is plain that representation needs to be provided for obvious subdivisions. In other cases, especially where the subdivisions arise out of differences of opinion or other less tangible bases of subgrouping, the determination of the kinds and proportions of representatives requires careful consideration by the organization or by its leadership.

A major problem in any representative body lies in the powers given to representatives in relation to both their constituency and the body to which they go. Much of the difficulty in such bodies lies at this point if no clear definition of responsibility has been worked out. Representation as used in voluntary associations runs a gamut between the instructed delegate, on the one hand, and the casual sample, on the other.[10] In the case of the instructed delegate a close and binding relation is set up by which the representative is free to speak only as he has been told. If proposals arising in the central body differ widely from his instructions he can act only after new consultation with his constituency. In many instances, however, representatives are free to act within wide limits of policy already determined by their constituent groups and may in many cases freely express their personal opinion on an issue. The representative in such instances is able to use his own judgment in regard to the commitments he may make for his group, but he is responsible for keeping his group informed of actions taken and of including their reactions with his own in participating in the representative body.

At the other extreme are representative bodies made up of members of constituent groups who react almost wholly as persons in their own right and who act very little as a channel between their own group and the central body. Such representation is more nearly a kind of sampling by which persons presumably like those in the constituent groups are brought together for some common action. This type of representation sometimes develops where issues are not very significant to those involved or in other situations where the constituency is not organized and has no means of electing representatives.

The third party to any representative relation is the central body, committee, council or convention. Its powers obviously are determined by the make-up of its constituent bodies and by the powers given to representatives to speak for them in the creation of a new governmental body. Such powers and their limits need to be clearly defined in the original creation of representative groups and strictly adhered to if the process is to function successfully.

The creation of effective group government within any representative body will show certain effects of its representative character. This condition will arise because in addition to the usual complexities of interaction between persons, the members are functioning constantly in a kind of three-layer consciousness. They react in terms of their own feelings and opinions, in terms of the desires of their constituencies, and in terms of the issues, needs, problems of the representative group itself. The central body of course develops its own set of personal acceptances and rejections, its own esprit de corps, and its own program. Necessarily the cross currents playing upon it because of its complex character subject it to difficult problems. Pork-barrel tendencies on the part of some representatives, intergroup rivalries arising out of loyalties and well-established dissensions bred elsewhere, occasional conspiratorial tactics and unauthorized caucuses to gain control, are to be expected in most representative bodies. The achievement of common support for common projects requires leadership which can deal simultaneously with this three-way relationship along with the ever-present personality issues.

Among the groups selected as illustrative here is one which presents this type of representative body, the Social Action Committee. This committee is made up, with the exception of two youths from a settlement canteen, of young adults who have already attained the maturity necessary to govern themselves for which our other groups are still struggling. They represent another step toward social maturity in that they have developed a sense of social responsibility beyond their own personal affairs. In the ability to identify with broader social issues and to give time and effort to them during their leisure, they present the type of citizenship essential in a democracy.

At this level of development problems in group government appear but in different areas. For our consideration here we shall discuss them in terms of two familiar aspects of such groups—the functioning of representation and the attainment of full participation in control.

The Social Action Committee came into existence, it will be recalled, in response to an invitation to local agencies to attend a state-wide conference on social legislation. Each agency chose its own representatives. This resulted not only in a group very heterogeneous in age, education and experience; it also meant that the members of the committee came to it with widely differing motivations and concepts of their responsibilities. This appears, for example, in the cases of three individuals sent by various agencies.

"Robert Petro, for example, is a nineteen year old boy of Italian background who was sent as a representative of a canteen group in one of the settlements and who is also a member of the Mike Club. He had completed three years of high school and then quit school expecting to be drafted. He worked intermittenly in war industries and in casual construction jobs. He was later exempted from military service, the reason as reported by him being 'emotional immaturity.' He had been active in the House Council at the settlement, in various local athletic teams and has taken an active part in the productions of the Mike Club. There is some evidence that he managed the election of himself and his friend Tony, the other delegate, with an eye to the trip and the pleasures of two days in the state capitol. His parents suspected the conference of being 'communistic' but agreed after explanation by the agency to let him go. Robert when interviewed as to his relation to the conference said quite frankly, 'This was the first time I had ever been aware of social issues. The conference was boring. There were too many speeches and too few discussions.' In terms of his relation to his constituency at home, the leader reports as follows:

"The program of the Canteen Committee on May 9th was a symposium and discussion on the trip of two delegates and a staff member to the State Conference on Social Legislation. On April 15th the leader had introduced the discussion on the conference to the group. He had explained its purposes and some of the content which would be under consideration. After discussion, the group decided to send two representatives contributing to each twenty-five dollars, towards expenses, from canteen treasury funds. The representatives were instructed with regard to specific legislation. Prior to their departure for the capitol both representatives attended a city-wide meeting and reported back to the committee more details on the legislation under discussion. Upon their return, initial reports were made at the meeting of the Canteen Committee on Monday, May 6th. Robert the first delegate gave the background for the conference and told of their trip. He gave a report of the initial meeting with a woman member of the legislature. He stated that his group tried to pin her down to giving a definite statement but 'that she was a smart woman, she has a neat way of getting around things.'

He recommended that there was just one thing to do with her—write letters, and more letters, giving a viewpoint and your reasons for it. Tony reviewed the actual conference agenda. He went into the details of the various bills under discussion. He made some direct comments on an interview with one of the state senators. He stated that the Senator acted in a very aristocratic manner. 'He's a very intelligent man,' Tony said, 'it is hard to break him down.' Robert concluded by saying that he felt that the Conference was not unusually successful. He felt quite definitely that its result was dependent on whether or not those who came back could get their people to write letters and express their opinion on the legislation. He urged that continued interest by all was very necessary. After making this report Robert took no further responsibility.

"A second member who represents a different level of activity in her representative capacity is Mrs. Katherine Bruce, a young Negro housewife active in the Neighborhood Council. She attended as a representative from the Settlement Mothers Club. Mrs. Bruce is an intelligent, active woman with a high school education just beginning to take an interest in social questions. Mrs. Bruce's experience in visiting her senator was somewhat more favorable than Robert's. 'Talking to him,' she reported, 'was just like sitting across the table from your husband and discussing things. He's a smart man.' The group happened to arrive in the Senate chamber while a filibuster was in progress. This surprised and disturbed Mrs. Bruce considerably. It was her first contact with law making. As she said, 'We heard so much about absenteeism in industry and here I go to the legislature and a lot of senators aren't on the job.' She herself was particularly interested in the bill to establish a state F.E.P.C. but she was unfamiliar with the other types of legislation. In terms of using this experience with her constituents at home she was somewhat at a loss. 'It seems to me futile,' she explained, 'to try to get the common person interested in these issues. They are only interested at the point where the issues directly affect them. People need to be awakened to what is going on and how these bills will touch them.' Mrs. Bruce continued to attend the meetings of the committee following the Conference, but her skepticism and lack of experience prevented her pressing for effective action in the Mothers Club that had sent her to the Conference.

"A third member of the Committee is Mrs. Ralph Minton, a young married woman of about thirty with two small children. Mrs. Minton left school at sixteen to go to work in the garment industry. She became a skilled operator before she married at twenty-two. Her husband is an active member of the United Automobile Workers. At eighteen she became a member of an industrial club in the Y.W.C.A. and in time became very much interested in social legislation. After her marriage she continued to come to the Y.W.C.A. to a club for young married women most of them former industrial workers. She was made a member of the Public Affairs Committee and recently of the Board of the Y.W.C.A. and has been a delegate to national conventions. Mrs. Minton was elected by her club of young married women to represent them at the conference. In the delegation she was one of the most active members. She too saw the filibuster and interviewed the same senator with Mrs. Bruce. With her greater interest and experience in social legislation, she found the filibuster less disheartening and the senator less convincing. She was well informed on these issues from long acquaintance with them. On her return from the conference she felt responsible for informing her constituents of the results. She wrote a skit on the issues discussed in the conference which was presented in the fall at the general membership meeting of the Y.W.C.A. just before election. She made a talk in an industrial club and gave a short presentation at a meeting of the Public Affairs Committee. These were familiar channels for her where her experience and her status in the organization gave her a chance to function. A further result of the committee discussions following the conference was to arouse her to some neighborhood action. Just before the fall election she pushed doorbells in her own neighborhood because as she reported, 'people should know why the city welfare levies that are to be voted on are so necessary for the continued operation of general welfare agencies. We citizens must work harder to explain such issues to our fellow citizens.' "

It is obvious that these three members of the committee range themselves along a scale of experience and social maturity. These sketches are perhaps sufficient to point up the questions that need to be considered by professional staff of agencies in working with a representative group of this kind. In the response to the original invitation agencies must first consider which of their groups are at a level of interest and maturity to be able to participate in such a committee. The selection of Robert Petro raises the question whether either his group or Robert was as yet prepared for experience on so mature a level. Although he was relatively an outstanding figure in his age group within his rather enclosed community, he was thrown by this selection into a group of more mature and experienced people functioning on a level beyond his grasp. He was given little preparation for his role as representative either in terms of getting the opinion of his constituents, which in this case he obviously could not do, or in terms of his responsibility to use his experience effectively with them on his return. The agency attempted to open the doors for him so that he could fulfill his role at least as a reporter. He was, however, too unprepared emotionally and intellectually to be able to do more than that.

Mrs. Bruce was obviously in a much more advantageous position to use this opportunity. She already knew what it was to be a representative (in her community council). She had an active sense of responsibility and was moving into the ability to deal with social issues as evidenced within her agency. She understood her role in relation to her constituents. The place where she needed assistance was primarily in understanding the legislation other than the Fair Employment Practices bill, the only one she knew about to begin with, and in seeing how she could take hold of the problems. Her discouragement as to both the process of lawmaking as she saw it and the inertia of her friends and neighbors needed to be met by further contacts and education through the committee. Realistic facing of the difficulties of effective social action can be accomplished with less danger of complete discouragement if it is supported by an active friendly group containing some experienced persons like Mrs. Minton. To Mrs. Bruce also the opportunity that this committee afforded for interracial experience in co-operative effort with congenial white people contains the seeds of hope perhaps sufficient to overcome her sense of the futility of attempting to arouse her neighbors to interest.

The organization that sent Mrs. Bruce and the staff members who know her there will need to take responsibility for helping her to make successful use of this experience in her Mothers Club and in the Neighborhood Council. The pleasures of some success here may be enough to carry her on to further experimentation with active citizenship.

For Mrs. Minton the experience was one more expression of her consistent and well-informed concern with social issues. Her problem lay rather in the securing of sufficient opportunity to present the conference issues to the appropriate groups within her organization. If a representative is to function effectively it is clear that channels must be open into the constituency so that the flow back of experience can be full and unhampered.

One of the most significant and least understood aspects of group government lies at the point of the meaning of representation. In setting up representative bodies it is important for their efficiency and for what they can afford in learning democratic practice that the relation between representative and constituency be clearly defined. The channels for the flow of opinion and mutual demand need to be marked out and the representative must learn how he is expected to function to convey action to and from the central body.

The effective assumption of the representative role is more than a matter of organization mechanics. It involves both an intellectual distinction between one's own views and the wishes of the constituency and also an emotional ability to act in their behalf. How early this capacity to act in behalf of others does appear is not yet known. It is certainly apparent in all leadership but representation differs from direct leadership in that the representative has to act for others in their absence and in relation to other representatives. Both of these factors seem to require a developed social sensitivity and mature judgment. It demands also an ability to hold the desires of others as it were suspended in time so that he can project what they would want if present and see how a decision will act upon them in the future. It necessitates a constant gauging of the issues within the delegate body itself against their effect on the constituent parts.

Observation of individuals both adult and youth functioning as representatives will reveal uneven and fluctuating behavior at these points. Some people function in only one dimension, giving their opinions or voting as they individually think best with no awareness of a constituency to be considered in the background. Others seem to function sporadically, fluctuating from individual to representative role without apparent awareness of shift. Others consistently carry their constituency as a control within them. This does not mean they become merely the voice of others but that they integrate their own opinion with the desires of the constituency. A study of a number of representative youth groups in settlements seemed to reveal the tendency for them to lose their representative role altogether and become social clubs rather than councils.[11] This was obviously a social regression to a simpler form of group relation involving more immediate personal pleasure and less responsibility. This tendency to revert to the simpler relation may come about in part because of lack of vital activity and real responsibility given to the council and partly because of personal immaturity. It is, however, frequent enough to mean that adult advisers need to become more conscious of what is expected of representatives and more skillful in helping youth to learn the art of acting in that role. This suggests that representative bodies in middle adolescence should deal with simpler, more immediate projects not involving complex action from constituent groups. Interclub parties or city-wide festivals may be the first step of which they are capable. With increasing maturity, however, the more complex forms of representation need to be developed which would involve more interaction between council and constituency and on more advanced problems of the organization. By the early twenties youth will be called upon not only to elect their representatives in Congress but also to send delegates—or perhaps to be one—to groups like the Social Action Committee, to conventions of labor bodies, political parties, and similar organizations.

The Social Action Committee illustrates one further problem in group government common to young adult groups of this kind, namely, the securing of true participation and control by all its members. This committee, with the variation in maturity and experience described above, contained one member, Mr. Toby, who was already active in the local political scene. He was an energetic young man belonging to a youth group in an agency and also to an outside political body actively interested in several of these bills. As the Committee got under way in its preparatory meetings it was clear that Mr. Toby was better informed than many of the other members, already had definite opinions on the issues, knew the records of the legislators, and was familiar with local politics in his area. He gathered a following of two others of somewhat similar views from other agencies. The professional leadership soon became aware that this subgroup was taking the lead because of their greater knowledge and enthusiasm, and there was some evidence they were working on the basis of a preconceived plan to obtain control. The results were that less sophisticated or informed members were being moved faster than they fully understood and at points in directions they did not comprehend. The heterogeneity of the Committee and their lack of acquaintance with each other made this easier to accomplish.

What is the role of the staff member working with this committee when he observes this type of activity? Obviously his long-range objective is to secure well-informed action by all members of the committee in which the legislation they consider is thoroughly understood and evaluated with the best knowledge available. The implications and connotations of joint action by the agencies in support of it need also to be known to all representatives and not only to a few.

The problem of manipulation within government is no new one. The tactics for it have been formulated since Machiavelli and are familiar in many organizations. They include the running of candidates for office without making clear the program or ulterior purpose behind their candidacy, the holding of secret caucuses at which plans are made for determination of policy, the refusal to allow members other than their followers to have access to financial statements, the use of the steam roller and of patronage in the form of committee appointments. Its practice is as old as government itself.

It is not surprising that it should occasionally appear in varying degrees within groups like the Social Action Committee. The ancient controls established by the wrought-out democratic procedures are one answer. The professional worker can rely to some extent on open and honest elections at regular intervals, on free expression for minorities, on the opportunity provided for all to participate through freedom of speech. Beyond the procedures, however, lie the more basic elements in personal integrity and eternal vigilance. There are no substitutes or short cuts to these if democratic procedures are to work. The greater knowledge and social interest of Mr. Toby can be a spur to the group if it is used to initiate the less experienced into intelligent and informed activity. The committee, however, must move at its own collective pace, with growing understanding from the less experienced, if it is to achieve the actual participation of all which democracy requires. To produce this the staff member must be both informed on the issues and skillful in the methods of producing sound integrated decisions. Thoroughly informed leadership of the caliber of Mrs. Minton who also understands democratic procedures is the best antidote to manipulative tactics when they appear. Within this type of group is the opportunity not only to take social action on significant issues but also to do it with the full participation of all, upon which democracy must rest.

In all these situations, different as they are, the leader's function has in it a basic consistency. His objective in each case is to help the group to attain effective self-government based on democratic premises. Until adolescents have achieved the emotional stability and social maturity necessary, the leader must give them enough control so that they can find the enjoyment they are seeking through the program activities. Chaos and confusion, while at times satisfying part of their ideas of fun, are not as a continued diet enjoyable even to the most mischievous or destructive. More than that, however, adolescents will develop their own capacities for control best in an atmosphere of secure and understanding authority. Where adults evidence either inability to control them or confusion as to whether they should, the result is to increase their guilt and their own insecurity. Learning to control themselves in a group, like learning to walk, needs supports at first. These, adult leadership at times must provide. However, because it is consciously used with a recognition of its purpose, such supporting authority does not mean personal domination over the group nor the production of continued dependence. As far as possible, groups should assume responsibility so that they are competent increasingly to establish their own leadership and govern their own affairs. The authority of adults over children as first experienced in the family needs a large admixture of affection to guide the child without connotations of rejection in his own growth. The necessity to get free from parental control in adolescence in order to win self-control throws up in adolescent groups much of the chaos, confusion, dictatorship and disorder that appears even with normally developing youngsters. By the late teens this is usually worked through into more orderly if not always democratic procedures. As the group worker recognizes the stages of emotional growth to be expected in working out the relation to authority, he will see his role in assisting toward responsible participation by all and the assumption of leadership by those with such capacities. When he is dealing with groups whose normal growth has been retarded or distorted by circumstances he must recognize that such pathologies require even greater understanding and the expert use of his own authority as leader.

As he deals with young adults in whom such maturity has been achieved he comes to grips with the perennial and universal problems of democratic government. He needs at this point a firm conviction of the essential values of full participation by members and responsible leadership by officials. He must be familiar with democratic procedures. He must use his relation as group worker to see that the group moves increasingly toward the full assumption of democratic responsibilities.

As youth achieve the capacity for well-informed control of their own affairs they should when possible be given larger scope within the organization. This will not only open new avenues to them but will be valuable for the organization in the fresh viewpoint and democratic relations it will produce. The desire of people to control their own recreational facilities is evidenced by the creation of the cellar clubs and other nonaffiliated youth groups, and by the very vocal demand in some of the teen canteens for a place that is really their own. It is unlikely, however, that either the financial resources or the administrative experience of youth is going to make possible adequate provision for leisure-time activities without adult help, even if this were desirable. Some method needs to be found, therefore, for a joint administration of adults and youth in which full participation of youth is encouraged and realistic recognition is given also to the necessity for the more mature and more stable contribution of adults.

There are at present two major devices for promoting participation of members in the administration of the organization. The first is through the councils or other representative bodies discussed in this chapter; the second, through the inclusion of the more mature and more outstanding members on the boards and committees of the organization where the structure of the organization makes it possible.[12] It seems likely that in matters concerning financing and staffing, provision of equipment and its maintenance, that the main responsibility will rest with adults. In questions of program planning, intergroup activities, protection of equipment, and control of behavior in activities a large share of responsibility can rest with members.

In addition to the representative council many organizations can democratize their administration by the inclusion of more mature youth on governing boards and committees. This may of course not be feasible with adolescents but it is quite possible with young adults. It is structurally perhaps easier in the membership organizations containing many young adults since the election of the board by members makes it possible for youth to elect representatives of their own choosing. In agencies with self-perpetuating boards this would have to come through the action of nominating committees. As elsewhere, the mechanics are less important than the desire which such inclusion would indicate to make the organizations self-governing. There is no doubt that such participation might at points change the regulations and customs of the organization. Even its reputation might suffer for the time being. But if through active sharing in control more members come to regard the organizations as their own, it will eventually be worth the cost. With the older adolescent and young adult, where independence is naturally desired and should be developed, the increasing share in control should entail responsibility in the more difficult aspects of organization management.

In addition to the inclusion on boards and committees of participants where the structure of the organization makes it possible, there is the necessity to demonstrate the democratic character of these organizations by having on the governing bodies adults who represent the parts of the community from which the membership is drawn. A great change has come over the social and economic scene since many of these organizations were born. A higher standard of living and of education, the assimilation of immigrant groups, the rising power of organized labor, all are producing a shift in the relative position of the providers and the receivers of the various social services.

Among the leisure-time organizations recognition of all these trends can be found. Representatives of labor or leaders of nationality or racial groups appear with increasing frequency on agency boards. In agencies serving neighborhoods more effort has been made in some places in recent years to get the leaders of the neighborhood into active participation. The question is, however, whether any of these efforts are moving fast enough or going far enough to meet the changing attitudes of the community the agency exists to serve. Unless the organizations prove that they can meet the test of the new democratic demands, they are likely to become outmoded and to give place to newer models more suited to the modern temper.

CHAPTER IX

The Art of Program Making

THOSE WHO HAVE READ THIS FAR may well have an impatient sense that we have been killing the reality of the groups by dissection and that we have not yet reached the major question—namely, what kinds of activities are appropriate and satisfying, how the group leader gauges success in terms of what the group is doing.

As stated earlier, the group worker is always concerned simultaneously with what the group is doing and how it is feeling. In this chapter we shall therefore try to draw into focus the strands of the previous chapters around the question of the group life as expressed in and through its program of activities. As the group comes into action, all the attitudes and feelings described in the previous chapters are brought to bear in the selection and carrying out of program activities. If the reader will glance back in retrospect, he will, we hope, see, as a group leader must, what is actually in process within the club, the interest group, or the committee. He will understand behind the eager and relatively well-controlled behavior of the R.R.C.'s the same search for affection and group acceptance that binds the turbulent Bulldogs and the deprived and insecure life of the Jokerettes. He will understand the groping toward maturity, the need for expanding interests, that drives both the Sub Debs and the staff of the *Teen Tattler*. He will sense the attitudes toward authority in all the range from the defiant aggressiveness of the Bulldogs to the more socially responsible Gay Canteen Committee. He will pick up the reactions to racial pressures, the struggle to attain security in relation to minority group status, the slowly developing evidences of a more mature social concern, as they appear in the Y-Teens, the newspaper group, or the Social Action Committee.

Like the expert group leader, we hope he is also able at this time to recall a few of the individuals within the group life on whom we have in the limited compass of these pages turned the spotlight. If he can recall them he will see Queenie jitterbugging smoothly into the ken of the "sponsor," bringing with her into the community house her attendant train of Jokerettes. He will remember Melvyn actively, almost anxiously organizing for his own security the newspaper staff. He will recognize Rose, the isolated and rejected member, hovering anxiously on the fringe of the Sub Debs, Jenny, the scapegoat, trying with limited mental capacities to achieve a foothold by meekly accepting the menial tasks in the Y-Teen Club, and Jimmy, the restless chain smoker, fighting his way into a limited tolerance in his gang-ridden society. The group leader necessarily does not acquire immediately his understanding of the bases of the group formation, its value scales and pattern of interpersonal relations, its attitudes toward authority and capacity for self-government. He often does not see the individual members in his first meeting. They begin to emerge from the blur of the group as he works with them. As he can increasingly perceive both the relationships that produce the group and the needs and interests of individuals he can more expertly help them to determine their program.

Program in such recreation-education groups consists of the whole range of customary activities frequently mentioned in the preceding pages. It is not necessary here to deal with the activities available, since a very extensive literature on these subjects already exists. Moreover, it is clear that in fact not the activity but its meaning to those involved is the significant consideration for the group leader. One man's work is another man's recreation; one man's play is another man's poison. We shall therefore take a further look through the doorways of our sample groups, focusing this time on what they are doing and why. Since program is affected in certain major ways by the purpose and structure of the group we shall discuss this in terms of the types of groups described in Chapter IV.

PROGRAM IN THE FRIENDSHIP GROUP

In the closely knit friendship group organized often by the agency into a social club there are certain typical responses to program planning which are rooted in the very nature of the bond that creates them. They are primarily concerned with being together and activities become the medium by which this basic need is expressed. Sometimes, as group leaders well know, they resist any suggestion for activity even remotely "educational." What values can they have for the members? We shall here turn to the Buckeye Bulldogs as an illustration. It will be recalled from previous references to this group that it is a gang of ten boys fifteen and sixteen years of age. A former chapter describes their aggressive attitudes toward authority, their drive for status in the gang hierarchy of the neighborhood, their two subgroups incarnating their twin interests, Jud and Pat representing the athletic achievement, the physical prowess and toughness their milieu demands of them, and Henry and his followers who have the sexual sophistication toward which some though not all the group are drawn. As the leader reports:

"The group program of the Bulldogs must be measured in relation to the goals that the club is striving for. The primary goal was for community recognition as a corner group and a group that was ready to take its place as a member of the Irish-Slavic Community. One had the feeling that outside of this group their social contacts were limited. Even their participation in the Catholic Youth Organization in the nearby parish church kept them closely together inside the same community. As one knew this group one became firmly convinced that the group considered its main purpose as expressed in program as that of recognition—that recognition which comes from their peers and from adults.

"During group meetings, the leader came into contact with varying types of behavior from hostile aggressiveness to passivity. For the first several meetings, he did not attempt to inject himself into the manner in which various members were conducting themselves in the group, except at those times where the room and the furniture in it were in danger. There was however a constant observation of the various members in order to see the part the community center could play in the group.

"In the business meetings or subject discussions of the group, the quality of group thinking varied with the individuals involved. A good deal of the discussions were on the information level, such as 'when are we going to have an affair' 'why can't we come into the building at certain times' or 'how can we become a better football team.' The members who were interested in these particular subjects were the initiators and leaders of the discussion. The clarity of thinking in these discussions again reflected the individual. Red, Jo and Tirky evidenced in discussion their superior intellectual level in comparison to the rest of the group. Henry, Jud and Pat spoke explosively and tended to lead away from the point at hand. Jimmy was pretty much the isolate in discussions and only became vocal when prodded by a member who wanted him to vote on his side. Around those topics, such as dances or football, and their disagreements with the agency regulations they were a close and integrated group in their discussions. At points in the business of the meeting, they tended to take a more partisan stand lining up in their two sub-groups. As time went on the leader played a large part in these group deliberations around program. A good deal of it he initiated and much of it was requested of him by the group. The leader felt that the need which the group had for feeling that adults were not always antagonistic toward them called for a gradual approach until he was acceptable to them. Inasmuch as it was characteristic of the group to arrive en masse there was little pre-meeting discussion. However, that which has occurred revolved around girls, fights and their scholastic difficulties. The general social climate of the meetings was one of surface friendliness. The fact that the group had a common purpose—that of acquiring the neighborhood gang prestige—welded them together in such a way that those who did not conform were dropped by the group. Hostility was much more evident toward a member than was overt friendliness. Individuals who differed with others in the group soon effected compromises in order not to incur the general displeasure of the remainder. This was further evidence of the gang climate. The group's members had not been successfully suppressed by adults, and were usually free in their expression of opinions among themselves. At first they were slow to use such freedom in the agency because they did not trust the leader, but as they soon saw that they could speak without limitation in the club group, they expressed themselves much more readily and were much more at ease with each other and with the worker.

"Contributing to the group climate was the important fact that the group knew that their meeting room was theirs on the night that they wanted it. Even though it was used other times by other groups, nevertheless, the feelings engendered by their own club room was one that contributed to the development of positive relationships. Fatigue did not seem to enter into the picture with this group. Even though several of the members worked, they, nevertheless, were eager and anticipatory in their group life.

"Outside of the one week's meeting for football and the one meeting for making Christmas decorations, the major programming in the group was toward the presentation of something. First, it was a dance, then it was a play which was combined with a dance.

"The part that the leader played in developing programs has in a large part been determined by the group's initiative and carry-through on their initial ideas. The group was encouraged and has been free to express the ideas which they had in the area of programming. The leader was called upon by the group and sometimes interjected his own opinions as regards the practicality of these program ideas. The boys leaned heavily on the leader for program augmentation and though they were quick to initiate program ideas they also expressed need for help in attaining those goals for which these programs were aimed. The general results of this approach have been to establish slowly easier rapport between the leader and the group and though there were relapses in which the leader had to take direct command of some situation, this was accepted by the group fairly well.

"In this assistance in program the leader brought to play some of his own skills. The leader's athletic experience was used to augment the boys' interest in having new football plays and his previous agency experience with dances run by youth groups enabled him to help the group more effectively meet the technicalities that arise in putting on such a program. An example in which the leader has effected program can be illustrated by the inclusion of football practice during the time they were preparing their dance. After meeting one evening, the leader had heard some of the members discussing their chances of beating a particular neighborhood team. Several days later, he met one of the boys in the drug store and inquired about the game and said that he would like to come down and watch them practice. The leader suggested that they might like to include this as part of the program for their next meeting night and use the auditorium and that this could be done after their regular meeting at which the dance could be discussed. The group approved of this and the activity took place on the following Monday night.

"In putting on the play, the idea was suggested by Tirky. The boys joked about their acting ability and the leader said that if they were interested he might be able to bring them some scripts which they might like to look over and they told him to go ahead and bring them for the next meeting. From this beginning the play was developed.

"Programming has served not only as the function of activity in the group, but also has been the paramount catalyst in effecting control of the group. The development from a hostile gang to a friendly, but still aggressive group which came about through this period was in large measure a result of programming. Through this experience, the group constantly had to focus its attention on their interrelatedness to each other.

"The teamwork that a good football team, a dance and a play requires can bring individuals to see the relationship of themselves in regard to others. This was a need which the group had, for although they were formed as a group to meet a customary neighborhood pattern, they had not in fact learned how to work very well together on common projects.

"The educational results that have accrued from these programs have varied. The putting on of a successful dance illustrates the results to them. The group became aware of the implications of preparedness through this experience. They had set a time limit, the date for the affair, and this gave them the experience of knowing that there were definite limitations as to the length of time they could 'take it easy.' Secondly, there has resulted an appreciation of responsibility. At the dance, with the exception of Jud, the group members carried through their individual responsibility as regards the various jobs they had to do that evening and as they subsequently evaluated the dance the fact that they had each successfully done their job was made apparent. It was interesting to note that even Jimmy, who was a passive member in the group, carried through most adequately his job, which was that of taking care of the refreshments. The effecting of their pattern of relationships has been done by relating the individual and sub-groupings toward their striving for successful program. The dance, the leader felt, was a factor in demonstrating what group cohesiveness can do in obtaining their goals.

"The foremost function at this period of the group's development was a change in their attitude toward themselves as a group, after some of their previous negative experiences during their gang period. The leader's help to the boys which was in the areas of participation in such activities as the dance, the play, football, and making Christmas decorations, demonstrated to them how their interrelatedness as individuals could contribute to their common achievement, and also how as a group they could achieve the status they seek within the socially acceptable framework of the agency activities.

"There was considerable variation in what the group was giving to each member. This was tied-up directly with the stability which they receive from other group experiences such as those at home, school and church. Jo, for example, was not as attached to the group as the others. He came from a home where there was good parental understanding and a positive sibling relationship between him and his sister. He was accepted in the church and his absences from meetings were often directly a result of his participation in church activities. Henry, the president, who had a job, was ofttimes late for the group. Some of this lateness was caused by his attempts at dating other teen-age girls who worked in the same dime store in which he was employed. If he was successful, he would not show up for meeting. Jud and Pat and Jimmy, who came from relatively unstable backgrounds were generally the first to be at the front door and the last to leave and attempted to stay in the club meeting as long as possible.

"The leader had a direct relationship with these strivings of the individual members as they took part in the program. He attempted to encourage behavior which contributed to the group's status and achievement along the more acceptable values for which the agency stood."

Summarized as this description of the Bulldogs' program necessarily is, it is perhaps sufficient to indicate some of the potentialities that friendship groups of this kind offer if the group leader can see below the surface demands for football and dances. The possibilities for development that are latent in this and similar groups are numerous. Such groups provide the opportunities for working out individual needs as various members present them through the demands of the program. As the leader understands Henry's need to build his status upon his greater sophistication with girls and Jud's need to release his aggressive impulses in hard and successive football, the program gives the concrete materials in which each can not only satisfy his need but do it in ways which teach him to co-operate for the good of the group.

Moreover, the informal discussions before meetings and the bull sessions give the group the necessary ventilating experiences to blow off the aggression accumulated in the rather authoritative setting of the school and the new demands of first jobs as well as to thrash out their first experiences with girls. Their old gang experience no doubt gave them this same opportunity. The difference here, however, lies in the presence of a sympathetic and increasingly accepted adult whose contribution to such discussion is welcomed. It is only in such give-and-take that shifts in values can occur to the more desirable standards sought by the agency.

It is also true that in a group of this kind, already conditioned to antisocial and anti-adult behavior, the experience of co-operative effort with an adult who works on their projects—football, plays and dances—has implications for a new relation to the representatives of authority. If this can be maintained it may weaken their customary resistance to adults and win them eventually to a constructive position.

Finally, the values that inhere in a socially sanctioned outlet for their most urgent psychological drives can hardly be overestimated. As the community, through its representative, the group leader, helps them to achieve athletic skill and the status that physical prowess brings, as he encourages their interest in girls through the well-ordered and prepared dance, he opens to them the channels that lead freely into not only immediate pleasure but the pleasures also of social acceptance by the wider community.

It is essential for the group leader to recognize the real significance of such interaction. It is the means by which the capacity for mutual affection is developed; it is the act of socialization of the self; it is often the way in which an emotional ventilation of pressures and aggression can be harmlessly secured; it is at points the channel by which new values can be wrought out in the free intimacy not available elsewhere.

PROGRAM IN THE AVOCATIONAL INTEREST GROUP

The interest group presents on the surface at least a simpler situation. People have joined because of an interest in cooking, current events, ceramics, dramatics or some such subject and it can be assumed that one at least of their reasons for coming is their desire for increased skill or expanded knowledge. Even in such groups, however, the unavowed but sometimes powerful demand for interpersonal relations of certain kinds will shift the emphasis in program in order to satisfy that need. Status values attached to certain types of activity and likely to shed glory on the group as a whole must also be recognized as functioning especially in those groups where one purpose is to provide standing to its members. Unless the leader has an understanding of the nature of the bond that is holding the members together he does not know where to start with program.

Beyond that he will need to reckon on other factors significant to program making. These include for example the activities customary to that age and sex group in that particular community, the level of knowledge, skill and ability in the group, the personal needs of the more vocal and dominant members, and the resources available in the agency or the community.

Because of the variety of problems common to program making

in such groups we are here including material from both of the sample interest groups, the Mike Club and the *Teen Tattler* newspaper staff.

The "Mike Club" represents a group of this kind, where, although sociability is constantly sought, there is a conscious desire to learn something of radio script writing and acting. It will be recalled that the agency had an additional purpose in organizing the group in that it hoped to broaden the educational horizons of a rather enclosed nationality community and to affect anti-Negro attitudes prevalent in the area.

In order to see the process of program making more distinctly we shall in this case turn from the summary to a few specific occasions in the club's life. Here, for example, is the leader's first contact with the group.

"The leader introduced himself to the group and the group members to each other. Tom stated that he was very much interested in radio training and that he almost took it up in school. Butch said he had been to the radio stations in town and had been on the air. Lily said proudly that Butch had won a few singing contests.

"The leader asked if anyone had seen the evening paper. He brought it out and asked the group how the lead story in the paper, namely the execution of Laval, might be handled in radio. Nick said a news commentator could talk about it, and Tom added that it might be a play.

"The leader produced radio scripts on the main theme—Laval's Treachery. He explained that it had been written by Elmer Rice in 1943. Tom said, 'Didn't he write something else we heard of?' The leader asked how many had seen the picture 'Street Scene' in the movies? That was by Elmer Rice, too, the leader went on to say.

"Louis remarked with hesitation that he 'freezed up' when it came to reading lines. The others however spoke up with interest and assurance. Nick asked if he could play the part of General Benedict Arnold; Butch wanted Laval and Marie was very anxious to play the role of Joan of Arc. Tom took the part of the radio announcer. Louis took the part of a messenger. . . .

"The reading continued with zest and the playlet finished. Upon its completion the leader asked the group if it were too serious a play (a younger boy who had barged in had commented it was too much like school). The group emphatically said no though Fred added that it might be a good idea to do some comedies too.

"Tom acted as temporary chairman to get ideas for future meetings with Lily taking down the notes and names of those present. This resulted in rapid-fire suggestions. Tony suggested some musical programs might be done; Butch was in favor of singing groups; Ted and Marie suggested discussions on all kinds of topics might be a good idea. Louis was in favor of microphone techniques being given. Nick said he would write away for more scripts and asked the leader for addresses. Ted and Marie will meet the leader on Thursday afternoon for discussion of next Monday's meeting. Lily and Marie asked the boys to invite more friends into the Club, while Tony and Butch asked for more girls. Lily said she wanted it to be a swell club. After the club meeting a community sing was entered into with some twelve others as guests.

"With this kind of beginning the group developed each meeting with a variety of program centered around radio interests. The variety that this afforded is indicated in the following glimpse of one later meeting.

"The group was divided into two parts. One group stayed in the club room while the other group went into the adjoining room for rehearsal. . . . The other portion worked on a skit and musical number; in the club room the group worked on musical numbers and special commercial take-offs.

"Tom announced his group would perform first and hugged the mike bellowing forth thunderously and taking keen delight in performing. He introduced Two Jills and a Squeak. At this point several visitors entered the room for the performance. Attention to the play was excellent. The Jills and Squeak harmonized excellently and they got a hand from the audience. Tom and Butch did a Rinso-White song and announcement. Further harmonizing went on. Tom as Master of Ceremonies introduced those present—calling on them to say a word if they cared to. Although the program of his group was over he hugged the microphone for some time. the group pressure finally calling upon the second section for its presentation. A playlet was given. After it was over Tom called out. 'That wasn't original.' 'It was from a movie.' This was followed by a singing act. The leader then asked the group what they would like to have for the next meeting. Marie suggested commercials. Each member was asked to write a three minute commercial advertising some product for presentation at our next meeting.

"Interspersed with this type of performance, the leader took occasion to give the instruction in microphone techniques which they wanted and some assistance in the elementary type of script writing that could be done in the time available. As time went on he began to introduce scripts for reading which had more content and better literary quality. The device of a Forum Hour modelled on the familiar Round Table technique provided an opportunity to introduce subjects for discussion and to get some preparation done on them before the meetings. These Forum questions began with issues vital to the group such as 'Should College Players be Paid in Football' and went on to 'Should the Government Control Prices?'

"Around the edges of the radio activity discussion on racial issues raged at intervals precipitated by the fact that Negro families were moving during these months into an adjacent district and were appearing in the high school in large numbers. Late in October this typical incident occurred.

"In the pre-meeting a conversation between Tony and the leader on the subject of football led to the leader asking if any boys were on their school football team. Tony said, 'No. They won't give an Italian a break.' The other boys chimed in with him. Fred said that one boy had even spoken against the 'Wops' in class. The leader asked Fred what he did about it. Fred said, 'Nothing,' but that he didn't like it. The leader noted it was unfortunate that people should be judged not on their merits but for some totally unrelated reason. He pointed out that attacking one group didn't stop with that one group but that discrimination spread to other groups. He showed the German attack of the Jews was followed by attacks on Catholics and eventually on all religion. Bob stated he could see why they discriminated against the Negroes. 'They're filthy and you can't trust them,' he said. Lucy said, 'They put butter on their skin in the summertime,' and Sam added he wouldn't trust them, they'd do anything behind your back. Fred pointed out that they commit crimes. The leader suggested that newspapers played up the fact that some Negroes were criminals by their categorical reference to them as such but that the word 'white' did not appear when non-Negro crime was discussed. Lucy suggested they ought to keep the whites and Negroes separate—then there won't be trouble she said. Why not make one state of Negroes? The leader asked if she would approve of one state of Italians. Lucy said, 'Well how can you think of Italians? They're not different from white people.' The leader pointed out that people had no control over what color they are born and suggested that while there were some filthy Negroes as Bob had stated there were also some filthy whites and that we couldn't judge people on that basis. 'Would you want us to call all Italians gangsters because Al Capone was one?' the leader asked. Lucy said she saw the point. 'But many of them were dirty,' she said with finality.

This type of discussion recurs with all the usual stereotypes throughout the year. The leader is able to introduce among the scripts which he brings in some that deal with interracial and intercultural themes. The following excerpts show the way program combined these various interests through the scripts selected.

"On December 18 we find them engaged as follows: The leader produced two scripts, one which dealt with the possibility of world unity and a second script with a Catholic-Jewish theme. They were particularly enthusiastic about reading and wanted more lines. In the first script the role of a Frenchwoman was read by Lily and Ted whispered jokingly to Tom that they were all prostitutes. One line of the play was, 'White, yellow, black, the blood is the same! Christian, Jew, or heathen, the blood is the same.' Lily said following this, 'Even though I'm an atheist, my blood's the same.' The line following, 'All are brothers and today all stand together in peace forever! Peace forever!' was reacted to by Tom who said, 'Yes, we are all brothers—it doesn't matter whether you're rich or poor, black or white.' There was no further comment on his statement.

"These scripts proved particularly pithy as an excellent medium of intercultural and interracial education. Tom's reflection and the fact that no comebacks were registered when black and white were so closely linked at least shows the weight of the play. Lily's atheist reference is believed to be related to the fact that in a sense she feels herself an outcast because she is the only Protestant in the group. She drew comfort from the lines concerning the brotherhood of man.

"Again on January 15. Robert asked if the Orson Wells' play, 'His Honor, The Mayor' might be read. The group agreed it might be tried. Robert asked for the part of Mr. Knaggs the Mayor, Lily was to read the part of the wife, Louis reading the Orson Welles lines, Marie Mrs. Carter, a townswoman, and Nick, Mrs. Egenhorn a fascist. Louis also read the part of a Catholic Priest.

"The theme of the play is the preservation of the right of free speech and presents certain other social problems such as anti-semitism, labor unions, the relation of the church to social problems, and a Dudley Pelley fascist. At the conclusion of the play the leader geared the discussion of it to reality and the group participated actively."

The combination of acting, writing of scripts, learning radio techniques, and bull sessions around the margins continued throughout the year. The culmination of the group's program was the presentation of a radio play at an intersettlement meeting to which their parents were invited and which provided them an opportunity for wider recognition not only in their rather enclosed Italian neighborhood but in the wider community. At the first rehearsal the leader reports as follows:

"The leader explained to the club members present that the Mike Club had been invited to represent the House in a program to be presented on February 21st, along with several other settlement groups in a social evening. He further explained that it was likely we might have an opportunity in the near future to participate in a radio program. The leader asked the club if they would like to take part in these programs and there was unanimity of opinion favoring this. He then brought out the script selected by the group for the occasion. It included Italian and Negro roles. It was noted that Tony read the Italian 1st Generation man, Peter, with an excellent and assured accent; but when it came time for Lucy to read the wife's part, she Americanized it; Tony commented that she wouldn't talk that way if she were his wife; she had to do it in character; Lucy couldn't do this; so Lily helped her work out the dialect. Nick read the part of the Negro doctor; it was noted that no attempt was made to read this part in the traditional 'darky' style—nor was there any comment about his reading the Negro role. He was reading it as he would read any other part and expressed the desire to take it.

"Following several more rehearsals the play was produced at an intersettlement occasion at which people of many ethnic backgrounds, including Negroes participated.

"The group performed very creditably and the mechanics of the performance went well, with good team work and generally excellent support being given in the broadcasting situation. They were very well received by the audience which contained many of their parents. Tony's part of the Italian man was particularly well enjoyed by the audience. Mr. F., the announcer for Italian programs on XYZ was so impressed with the performance that he called the group together at the end of the program and asked if they'd like to do it on the air. The group was obviously thrilled with the announcement and went around the room to their friends, telling about it."

It is important for the leader to be aware of the individual's use of the program activities. It is not possible here to follow many of those who run through this record but it seems valuable to include the situation of a member who had particular problems of adjustment which he was attempting to work out during this year. The leader's account of Tony is as follows:

"The leader's first association with Tony was in the Mike Club. He was a regular and took an active part in productions. The Mike Club has given Tony an opportunity to take on a stellar-role with his contemporaries which has been very constructive to him, inasmuch as he is not an athletic participant and never enters into sports program. Because of this fact, he has not been given the acceptance others found so readily. This is reflected in the make-up of the Boosters, a group of boys who formed with a focus on parties for members soon to enter the service. Tony fell into the service grouping but was never invited to join, although several of the boys go around with him. This was a sharp blow and he found it difficult to understand. Several Boosters were in the Mike Club and it was quite apparent that Tony was one of the most talented in the group. This, however, did not win Tony a place in the Boosters. They are inclined to believe 'that he thinks he's just a little better than anyone else.' This attitude is reinforced by Tony's use of the word 'peasants' so frequently in referring to the more foreign members of the Italian community. Tony takes pride in referring to some of his relatives in New York who apparently are very well off. For several summers he has invited various neighborhood boys to accompany him to New York where his aunt had them as guests in a large and spacious home. Tony has not worked after school this year, but plans to work with his uncle in a tailor shop and he hastened to add, 'Of course it's just to get money enough for a trip to Canada. I'll get twenty-five dollars a week.'

"Although Tony has as a boy with ambitions to go to college not met with total acceptance in the neighborhood, he has been able to achieve some balance, in part through his contacts in the Mike Club. One will find him in the local pool room as an onlooker and he is a spectator at athletic events in which the local boys are participating. One will not find him involved in crap games on corners, or playing 'Mora' with gusto. Within the Mike Club, however, he was able to use his capacities and win real acceptance by his talent for acting."

By this means the leader can help Tony in the group. Through it he can meet his need for achievement in nonathletic pursuits and his tendency to isolation due to his intellectual ambitions to climb into the "college boy" level can be modified by helping him to keep relations with his own crowd.

The *Teen Tattler* staff presents a somewhat different picture in terms of program development. The reader will recall that this is a group organized to edit and issue a house newspaper in a middle class neighborhood with a combined Jewish and Gentile population. In a previous chapter (Chapter IV) the origin of this group is described and the central place in it of its editor Melvyn is indicated. This group is included in our discussion of program development because it illustrates two points primarily: the educational potentials available in such programs and the opportunity to work out through this experience problems related to ethnic identification and social action so significant at this particular age. It illustrates in two of its leading characters, Melvyn and Ruth, diverse ways of dealing with their own Jewish identity in a mixed neighborhood.

It is obviously not possible or necessary here to give a full picture of the activities of this group. The group had twenty-five meetings, all but one of which (a final party) were devoted to planning and discussion of content, production and distribution of the paper. We can here look in upon only three of these situations.

The first of these arose around a conflict as to the function and responsibility of the paper. The agency was engaged simultaneously in the organization of a council of youth groups in the neighborhood. Some of these were high school fraternities and sororities, some youth groups in Jewish organizations, some clubs within the agency. At an early stage in the organization of this council, while the problems of working out relations with such autonomous groups was still in process, Melvyn saw the opportunity for the paper to "scoop" the situation by playing up especially the criticisms and difficulties involved. The newspaper staff covered the meetings of the council as reporters which provided the necessity for determining the policy of the paper on the council development and whether it should become the official organ of the council. This led, as the leader reports, to the following situation:

"The night of the fifth meeting of the group another member of the agency staff spoke to Melvyn about the formation of an interclub council. Because this relationship of the paper to the Council occupied so much of the group's attention during the year and proved to be an exciting and valuable learning experience for the group, it is useful to follow this relationship through its stages of development.

"Melvyn appointed a representative to the Council and let the matter rest there. The leader posed the question of the relationship between the two groups. He pointed out the similarities in their scope and objectives since both were directed toward involving all Jewish youth groups in the community.

"It was not long after this that Melvyn told the staff that the Council was a failure and that its member organizations were dissatisfied. He said this would make a 'good story.' When the group looked to the leader for his reaction, he said the usual newspaper procedure in a situation like this was to collect comments and complaints and then give the Council adviser an opportunity to reply. The group accepted this and Alice and LaVerne were to collect the comments. Melvyn, guilty about offending the Council adviser, asked the leader to discuss it with her.

"The agency supervisor and the two staff workers involved discussed the proposed article and agreed that destructive criticism of the Council in the *Tattler* would be very detrimental to its chances of working through the problems it then faced. Alice meanwhile had collected a series of comments on the Council, some favorable and some adverse, and nervously read them to the group. The staff adviser was then invited to the meeting to discuss the matter, while Melvyn was busily dictating to Shirley a number of questions to be put to the adviser.

"The atmosphere of a trial prevailed when the staff adviser entered the room. Melvyn began on his list of questions. The staff adviser explained that the development of the Council had been slow and difficult, that an unsuccessful social affair had had an unfortunate effect and that the Council needed time to grow. The leader interrupted Melvyn's questioning to ask whether the paper should print 'charges' that could be disproved.

"The leader developed this approach and asked the group what they felt was the responsibility of a newspaper and posed for them the conflict between sensational, smearing journalism as against constructive participation in worthwhile projects. The staff adviser to the Council pointed out that as the article then stood, it could do real damage to the Council. She suggested holding off until the Council could move ahead with its present plans.

"The leader again reviewed the paper's relationship to the Council and ended by asking whether its ties to the Council should not and could not be strengthened. Bernard commented that full reports would increase understanding and support for the Council, but he felt the paper should retain the right to make constructive criticism. Bernard stayed on after the meeting and continued to discuss the problem of the social responsibility of journalists with the leader and Ruth and Elsie, the sub-group of high school graduates. This went far beyond their immediate problems and gave the group opportunity for discussion which it wanted so much.

"What meaning and value did this whole experience with the Council have for the group? The group had in the first place an opportunity to learn something of the problems of inter-group relations. By trial and error they reached a better understanding of the role and function of representatives from their own group to another and from an outside organization to their own body. They worked through the long and often laborious process of reaching joint decisions with another group and adjusting differences of opinion. In terms of the agency and the community, the discussions were part of the interpretation of the Council. . . . The newspaper staff was sharply confronted by the issue of its responsibility as a community force in connection with the proposed criticism of the Council. There was real growth in their appreciation of the values of constructive journalism as opposed to the irresponsible repetition of destructive rumors.

"The much-discussed article about the Council proved to be a realistic experience for Melvyn. His impulsive desire to rush into print with a 'sensational story' ran up against the necessity of considering more basic values. The group, by its final decision, and the adult staff members placed a firm check on Melvyn's wish to print 'hot news.' He did not agree with the decision, but the challenge to his standards was sharp and confronted him with a point of view he had not seriously considered before.

"In regard to the issue of sensationalism in relation to the Council, this problem opened up for Ruth, Bernard and Elsie the wider implications of the freedom and responsibility of the press in contemporary society. The post-meeting discussions with the leader on the daily press, books and magazines made them question the social desirability of much of what they had been reading. This in turn helped them to see new and larger social problems."

A second major issue arose out of the relation to a mixed Gentile-Jewish area of this wholly Jewish group within an agency with a distinctly Jewish program. This was precipitated by Melvyn's conflict over his relation to his own background and his ambitions for a wider scope. This conflict of the indigenous leader confronted the group with the necessity to work out its relation to both their own identification and the problems of the larger community. The leader describes this situation as follows:

"The group was learning more and more about the technical aspects of newspaper work and after a few issues Harry suggested and executed a two-color front page for the 'Christmas' edition. Christmas, however, posed a problem for the group members, standing as they were with one foot in the world of Christian customs and mores.

"Shirley suggested an article on Christmas, but Ruth objected that this was not appropriate for a Jewish publication and would appear to their nonJewish friends to be in bad taste. She suggested instead an article on Channukah, the Jewish Festival of Lights which also comes late in December. Melvyn quipped, 'What's Channukah?' and Shirley said no one would read such an article.

"Ruth insisted that precisely because so few of their contemporaries really understood the Jewish holiday, there was a need for it. She said it could be done with a light touch, not as a dull history lesson. She was given the assignment and brought back to the group an interesting humorously written account of the origin and meaning of the holiday presented in the slang of the teen-agers. It was enthusiastically received by the staff.

"Melvyn's uneasiness about being Jewish was expressed again when he asked the leader for a topic for an editorial and the leader said the approaching birthday of President Roosevelt might give him some ideas. Melvyn immediately asked whether this meant linking the FDR theme with Jewish political problems. He was relieved when the leader said that Melvyn might want to deal more broadly with Roosevelt's social philosophy, perhaps touching on problems involving Jews, if he chose. Melvyn asked the leader to give him specific ideas at the next meeting. The leader suggested Melvyn bring in a rough draft of his own to discuss. Melvyn did not do this but later wrote on the March of Dimes thus avoiding any reference to Jewish themes.

"After several issues had come out, Melvyn told the staff he was tired of printing the same kind of news, 'always about the Council, the canteen or the fraternities and sororities.' He wanted the paper to serve everyone, including the non-Jewish community, and he would like to see some Gentiles on the staff.

"Ruth said the paper should first improve and consolidate its service to the youth in the Jewish community, but she suggested inviting a boy from a nearby church canteen to write a guest column on a joint canteen then being discussed by the agency staff. Melvyn at once wanted to make this boy the canteen editor of the *Teen Tattler* but Ruth said flatly that this would be moving too fast. The group agreed and Ruth's suggestion was carried out.

"Nothing further was said or done concerning Melvyn's desire to involve Gentiles until he excitedly called the leader to say that the teen editor of one of the metropolitan dailies was interested in the *Teen Tattler* and wanted to write a column on it. This meant city-wide publicity for Melvyn and the paper and he jumped at it.

" 'I explained,' he said, 'that we're a Jewish and non-Jewish paper with some members of Demolay on our staff.' Without challenging the patent untruth of this last statement, the leader suggested that the agency staff might want to discuss it with the teen editor. Although the downtown paper never followed up this contact Melvyn would ask about each new suggestion, 'Do you think this will impress the editor downtown?' Gradually the leader tried to give Melvyn a sense of proportion about the proposed column and to help him see the shallowness of judging everything by its possible effect on this 'terrific publicity break.' These efforts brought verbal agreement from Melvyn but no basic acceptance.

"While this was going on Ruth wrote another feature article on a Jewish holiday, again in a whimsical, jaunty style. The holiday of Purim involved a story of the oppression of the Jews and Ruth led up to a conclusion in which she appealed for peace and democracy throughout the world. She read the article to the staff for comment.

" 'Now that the paper is half-Jewish and half non-Jewish,' Melvyn said, the last part was 'too much.' The group seemed to agree with him. Feeling that the view expressed by Melvyn and some of the others was a reflection of their insecurity about their Jewishness, the leader stepped in at this point to ask whether it was not necessary to be clear in their own minds about the Jewish orientation of the paper, its relationship to a Jewish agency, to a Jewish interclub council. He asked the group whether they were denying or running away from the fact that the paper was basically a Jewish activity. Ruth said this should be kept in mind and added that their Gentile friends would be interested in the story of Purim. Melvyn insisted that the first issue had not even mentioned the word 'Jewish' and while he said he recognized that the paper was written by and for Jewish people, throughout the meeting he stressed the importance of news about Gentiles.

"Some months after this, Melvyn and a small group went out for coffee with the leader after a meeting. A friendly atmosphere pervaded the group and conversation flowed easily on the way to the restaurant. Some comment reminded the leader of a number of old Jewish stories and jokes and he told them to the group. Melvyn participated in this freely and with no embarrassment or resistance to the use of Jewish words and phrases and the leader felt that somehow Melvyn had been able to overcome for the moment his insecure feelings about being Jewish. In the restaurant, Melvyn told the leader about a theme he had written for school, a fantasy in which different types of animals represented humans and their racial and cultural groupings. The story was essentially a plea for equality for Negroes, but there were characters representing Jews in much the same light. His ability to write it and talk about it seemed to the worker to represent a measure of progress in working out his feelings on the subject.

"A third aspect of program provided the group with a contact with broad community questions. The leader asked the group one evening whether they had heard of an ordinance pending before the

City Council to prohibit discrimination against racial and religious groups at a private beach and resort. No one had heard of the proposed ordinance. The leader presented the background of the legislation, which involved a series of anti-Negro incidents, and stressed the stake in such legislation that Jews have as a minority group and asked whether they would like to take up the matter in its next issue.

"Melvyn thought the idea was 'terrific' and immediately proposed that they take copies of the paper backing the ordinance down to the president of the City Council to get some publicity for the *Teen Tattler*. The leader challenged this and posed the question sharply: was Melvyn interested in the ordinance or in the prestige he hoped to get for the paper? Melvyn quickly agreed with the leader, who then recommended that the staff discuss the ordinance fully so that any action it might take would reflect the whole staff's thinking.

"Ruth thought this was just the type of broad social problem the paper should tackle. Harry wanted to discuss it first with his councilman and Elsie was very cautious about committing herself. It was voted unanimously however, to study the matter further.

"Next week the leader brought in some written material on the ordinance and the campaign for its passage. Ruth showed an interest in the legislative and political process. Bernard and Elsie were the only other members present and the talk turned to the question of prejudice against Negroes. Elsie admitted that she had such feelings. The leader, utilizing some experiences the group had had with some of the lower status Jewish boys from a nearby low economic area, asked whether their social and economic problems, like those of Negroes, were not part of the picture. Elsie's response, which reflected her feeling of guilt about harboring prejudices toward Negroes, and her desire to avoid the specific issue was to question the concern over the one little part of the problem involved in this ordinance when we did nothing about the fact that 'Negroes can't vote in the South.'

"Ruth felt it was wiser to deal with the immediate, local issues first. Bernard questioned the right of the paper to take a definite stand and said it should only present the facts on both sides. However, Ruth was so eager to pursue the matter that she was given the assignment. The leader suggested she follow up her interest in the attitude of Negroes toward the ordinance by visiting the local secretary of the National Association for the Advancement of Colored People. He also arranged to go with her to a session of the City Council at which the ordinance was to come up.

"Ruth's first written account of the exciting City Council meeting at which the ordinance was approved was coldly factual. The leader suggested she try to catch all the feeling that the crowd had had in the council chamber and her rewritten article won the enthusiastic approval of the group. Melvyn, meanwhile, had written an editorial backing the ordinance, and this, together with Ruth's feature article, were headlined in the next issue.

"This experience in social action was a valuable learning process for the group. True, it was injected into the group by the leader and came as something new and unfamiliar to most of the members. But the group took hold of it and learned about the mechanics of city legislation and the problems of political action. Perhaps more important was the forum it provided for a frank and full discussion of racial prejudice and the opportunity it gave the leader to show the similarity between anti-Negro prejudice and anti-Semitism. This latter approach had some positive effect on Elsie. Ruth got the most out of this because she was the most receptive to this type of experience. Melvyn again had to face a conflict in values when the group and the leader pointed out the importance of the basic issues involved in contrast to his concern over prestige and publicity."

In both these situations Melvyn's problems are clearly illustrated. The leader had to work with him within the context of the group and its problem. He describes his approach to Melvyn as follows:

"Certainly Melvyn was the leader of this group, but his leadership was a mixture of his strong interests, skills and needs. His intense interest in journalism, his competence in writing and his efforts to bring together a staff were the positive contributions which placed him in the leadership position. But it is equally true that his insecure aggressiveness carried with it the need to dominate the group and use it for his own tremendous need for status and recognition. Melvyn's lack of status as an athlete, his somewhat unattractive appearance and the repercussions of that factor on his relations with girls, his confusion about his Jewishness and very possibly some elements in his family situation of which the group leader was never fully aware—all these were part of Melvyn's feelings of insecurity and inferiority. These were expressed in his drive for domination and for recognition through giving the newspaper a community-wide circulation. The latter factor seemed to be more important to him than recognition by members of the group with whom he was working. However he did develop some ability to abide by majority decisions and made some small steps toward more comfortable acceptance of his own Jewishness. . . .

"The group gave Melvyn respect as an editor with a highly developed skill, but they never fully accepted him as a person. It is true that he attended a different school and that he was often in the position of exerting pressure on the staff, but those factors cannot wholly explain his lack of real friends within the group. He did not make overt efforts to form friendships. Perhaps this was a defense, but on the surface all his feelings were directed toward his girl, Shirley. The two of them were always in a hurry to leave and neither before nor after meetings did they spend time in friendly conversation with the group.

"Ruth, on the other hand, was given the group's acceptance as a person and as a leader. It was, in fact, largely through her that a number of them struck back occasionally at Melvyn and Shirley, albeit the revolution eventually took the constructive form of a reorganization, giving more authority to the group as a whole.

"The leader's role during the year was one of trying to interpret limitations to Melvyn and Shirley and helping them to direct their tense energies into positive contributions to the group, as well as attempting to divert the group's resentment against them into equally positive and constructive channels."

In considering the art of program making in interest groups like the Mike Club or the *Teen Tattler* staff the group leader has a different approach than that which he will use with social clubs. This difference arises out of the bond that underlies the group. In these instances the group is united in part at least by a conscious desire to learn some skill and to participate in the selected activity. Whether they are brought together around dramatics or journalism, ceramics or millinery, current events or foreign affairs, the common base of the acknowledged interest provides the starting point. If they have a really keen interest, the group to be satisfactory must, in the first place, through its program give them a chance to acquire new knowledge, improve skills and achieve both as individuals and as a group in the designated line. Just as the demand for sociability is the first prerequisite for a satisfying program for a social club, the pleasure of advance in skill or knowledge is a first requirement for most interest groups.

The illustrations given in this section, however, indicate a second requirement of the leader. He must recognize and provide for the unavowed but potent motivations that also play into the group's formation. They want not only to learn, but to enjoy themselves with their friends of both sexes, to use their leadership capacities, to achieve standing in their communities through this group or for some other unavowed purpose. While the leader realizes the inevitable and frequently valuable pressure of these motivations, he needs to help them to satisfy them in socially constructive ways. As they attach the pleasures of achievement, for example, to an acceptance of their cultural background—Italian or Jewish in these instances—they find some answer to an urgent and difficult problem that confronts young adults emerging into our highly stratified society. As they find a way successfully to play some part in a community issue, they take a step toward social maturity.

Intertwined with these rather widespread motivations, which are unavowed but obvious to the perceptive leader, there will be also a third opportunity related to the distinct personal needs and interests of each individual. Whether he is working out with Tony a way to achieve a much-desired acceptance previously denied him or attempting to help Melvyn curb his dominating leadership and gain security by accepting his Jewish background, the leader is using the varied potentialities found within the demands of the program activity. In neither case does he bring to consciousness through discussion the personality problem each boy is so obviously facing. This would precipitate him into a level of relationship outside his function to deal with and in which he could not carry through the necessary treatment. Within the interacting process of the group, however, he can assist toward solutions as the program situations provide opportunity.

A fourth aspect of program making in the avocational interest group lies at the point of the method used to produce advance in learning. While it is true that members want to learn or achieve skill, it is true also that in such groups the effort required for learning is not always easy to elicit. Without the goad of the truant officer, the fear of a low academic grade, or the lure of credit, how does one get people to make the necessary effort, to restrain the wandering or disruptive impulse, to delay the satisfaction until excellence can be achieved? It is this dilemma between superficial immediate pleasures and the deeper satisfactions of real achievement that has led some leisure-time agencies to turn to the conventional motivations for support. By dramatic competitions, exhibitions with prizes, by honors and awards, by various prods and lures, they have tried to produce the effort needed to get over the hump of inertia, triviality, or miseducated taste. Whether the program involves athletic skill, artistic standards, intellectual grasp, or the ability for effective social action the problem is the same. How do we stimulate toward excellence?

The sensitive leader is conscious here that he must steer a course between an educational Scylla and Charybdis. He wants to avoid, on the one hand, merely enforcing conventional values whether they are the middle-class manners to which he may be accustomed or the accepted artistic standards which determine excellence in aesthetics. On the other hand, he may be tempted sometimes in the name of a misinterpreted democracy to say there are no values. There are merely differences in taste or point of view. If the Mike Club prefers "White Christmas" to Beethoven, who is to say they should be urged to go further? If the Teen Tattlers feel qualified to speak on the city ordinance issue out of their own ignorance and prejudice, why struggle to get them to study the problem?

In the first place, the leader needs confidence in the pleasure of growth itself providing the necessary motivation. If he is aware that his prods or awards are liable to play upon the desire for adult approval or the self-seeking rivalry with others, he may be forced to use them at points but he will do so sparingly. He will not mistake hypocrisy for virtue, competitiveness for real love of the excellent, nor passive acceptance for actual absorption of the values into the self. He must, however, if he is to succeed in the delicate art of eliciting growth, put his faith in the inherent enjoyment that lies in higher and more demanding levels toward which he may entice the members. Excellence yields its own delights whether it is in the co-ordination of body and mind in physical skill, in the smooth symmetry and design of a piece of ceramics, or in the wrought-out solution to a social problem. The basis for such delight lies in the fuller use of the powers—that inner dynamism of life which seeks fulfillment through creation.

It is this growing of the powers toward fulfillment that provides the basis for that enjoyment which people are often seeking from their leisure-time experience. It is the leader's role to provide the setting and facilities through program activities and to enable, as he can, the delicate and groping process by which new strengths are born within the ego and brought forth into achievements which have social value. The true purpose of education, as Herbert Read has said, must be "to develop at the same time the uniqueness of each and the social consciousness and capacity for reciprocity."[1] Within the group-work setting these combined experiences can be found and utilized.

It is quite natural that it is from the world of art that there has come the greatest encouragement of this creative process. In the dance, in music, in the crafts, and in the fine arts, the opportunities lie readily at hand for some group members to find the way by which the deep and hidden roots of life can bring forth in unique outer form the meaning of life as each sees it. Whatever the medium utilized, the results emerge as a new and vitalized entity because, as Ruth Radir puts it, "it grows out of an absorbed self making visible an impelling idea."[2] When such experience is carried on in and through a congenial group, the necessity to communicate the impelling idea and to fuse it with others provides that deeper experience in mutuality which alone gives balance to individuality.

While the various art media can provide through such recreation groups for many people the most fruitful start toward a new expansiveness of the self, it is a mistake not to recognize that any collective enterprise has in it the same opportunity. The new twist to a throw in baseball, the first original decorations for a dance, the bright idea that vivified the dull committee meeting, and the rising concern for neighborhood improvement also contain the yeasty encouragement to growth.

It is the leader's function as he affects the program development to prepare the soil in which such sprouts as appear can be nourished to fruition.

Behind all such education, therefore, for those who act as group leaders must lie an underlying belief in the capacity of the people with whom they work and a deep desire for their development. Beginning with each as he is and respecting his capacities and his own inner direction, the leader can only assist in the process. The initiative, the control, the final answer to life must lie with each person.

NATIONAL AGENCY DIRECTED PROGRAM AND ITS USE

As indicated in the chapter on group formation, many agencies with specific educational goals in mind implement those goals by the way in which they organize their groups. To some extent any group existing within an over-all organization is partially at least determined by the purposes, methods and program of the sponsoring agency. In many youth groups, however, this determination is quite specific. It takes the form of setting up the focal purpose for such groups, determining their membership requirements, and establishing the organizational structure. Such agencies also express their goal by a direct influence on the program of the group. We are familiar with this process in the so-called national agency programs, such as the Boy and Girl Scouts, Camp Fire Girls and Hi-Y or Y-Teen programs. It appears also in other programs with older youth and in youth groups sponsored by churches, lodges, and political parties. It is most directly through the determination of activities that the goal of the sponsoring agency is expressed.

As we examine the methods used in such agency-directed program it is evident that there is considerable similarity in the means adopted although the goals vary. They often have these characteristics in common: The goals are formulated nationally in somewhat abstract and idealistic terms. Particularly in those dealing with adolescents these are often translated into codes of behavior, ritual and symbolism through which the inculcation of these values is expected. In the second place, the goal is further implemented by suggested activities. These are arranged by some agencies in levels of progression like an avocational curriculum. In the third place, some, though not all, such agencies encourage participation in the activities by means of extrinsic inducements in the way of honors, awards, prestige on completion of activities, and other crediting devices.[3]

Two other methods for reinforcing program emphases are commonly found. Many such organizations use representative conferences and councils, local, regional and national, to train and activate the leadership and to stimulate identification on a national or international basis. They also in many instances train volunteer leadership in the goals, methods, and program activities of the organization. This familiar pattern of program direction varies among the agencies not only in the goals selected but also in the flexibility with which group leaders are encouraged to use the suggested activities and in the inducements used to motivate the members.

It is well for such leaders to recognize the meaning that the formulated values of such program can have for their members if properly interpreted. In the adolescent and young adult period, many individuals are in fact in search of larger goals and broader concepts of life with which to meet the demands of maturity. This is the period of a re-evaluation of childhood values, an expanded emotional capacity, and the necessity to find one's place as a worker and a citizen. Many youth at this period have a capacity for wider social identification plus the need to find a philosophy of life and an emotionally satisfying tie to the adult society into which they are moving. The answer for both these needs lies for some in an affiliation to ideological groups which provide the security of collective action and goals which give them personal and social direction.

Obviously it is extremely important in the interests of the continuance of our democratic heritage what the ends are toward which the social attachments of youth are directed. This is the age group in which spontaneous youth movements in some societies or in some periods come into being and when youth respond to adult-sponsored social movements. It is also the age group that in totalitarian countries has proved most fruitful for the inculcation of their particular ideologies. These facts bear witness to the potentialities for collective devotion to social ends which exist apparently in considerable groups of youth. Such consideration involves the question of how to present the basic principles of democratic society in forms vital to particular youth groups and how to guide the collective experience itself in such a way that it encourages not blind following of leadership, itself inconsistent with democratic attitudes, but a consistent critical and informed acceptance of social goals which then become the basis for public-spirited, well-directed social action. We must avoid social indifference and absorption with personal concerns, on the one hand, and social fanaticism, on the other. We must prevent docile or emotional acceptance of adult leadership and equally the anarchy of complete individualism. The significance of the social ideologies presented to youth through such programs is of concern to the entire community, since in so far as they enlist support they train future citizens in certain social viewpoints and in the means of social action.

How does the group leader who works within an agency with such nationally formulated program goals and methods use the group-work approach? Is it inconsistent with the existence of such programs?

It is well for any group worker at this point to recognize the larger community process of which an agency of this kind is a part. Every society has means by which it passes on its social heritage to its youth and one of the universal and age-long methods is the presentation of aspects of its culture in the form of "ideals"—emotionally charged and often embodied in powerful symbolic form. This method of inculcation is characteristic of human society and we may expect its continuance. These youth agencies utilizing the leisure of youth and combining the collective ideals, whether religious or secular, with recreation and voluntary education are only the modern and more elaborate successor to the ancient rites of adolescent initiation to the church, to citizenship, and to mature and sanctioned sex experience. The questions that must be asked by the group worker lie at several points. Are these goals consistent with "the best" of our heritage? Are they being presented in effective form so that they "take"? Is the process of inculcation such that basic democratic attitudes of mind are encouraged? He will want of course to ask himself further whether or not the objectives of this particular agency are those which he wishes as a professional worker to promote. If all these answers are in the affirmative there is then the question, How does one work with the particular group under his direction?

It is clear that the group worker must approach such agency-directed program with methods consistent with his principles as a group worker.

In the first place, he must see the agency goals, whether the Boy Scout code, the interracial position of the Y.W.C.A., or the transmission of the Jewish cultural heritage, as a voluntary and not a coercive choice for individuals. While he offers the contribution of the agency as formulated in its program, he should encourage critical and informed evaluation of such goals, not docile or emotionalized yielding to authoritarian pressure. The basis for such an approach would lie in his aim to develop self-determining individuals and also citizens capable of evaluative judgments. The program goals and activities can then be used, but they become the opportunity to explore with intelligence, not to accept without question.

In the second place, a group worker therefore, working with such an agency group, must be free to adapt both goals and activities to the interests and needs of his particular group. Within the proposed range of activities, if he is to build soundly on the individual interests, he will follow not a prescribed pattern, the same for all groups of a certain age, but a selection according to need. The activities proposed by national agencies usually provide a wide field of selection and the group worker will of course also draw upon other program resources if those seem better suited to the groups' interests. Where such flexibility is allowed by the over-all agency, their program suggestions become a fruitful source of choice for the members. The fact that membership in such groups is always voluntary and withdrawal always possible usually acts to prevent a program's being imposed, which is contrary to the basic needs of the group.

One of the most important questions for a group worker to consider in using such program is the question of motivation. The place of crediting devices, such as honors and awards, raises basic questions as to the meaning of the educational experience itself. Are we stimulating competitiveness, rivalry, and the desire for the limelight along with what is learned more directly through the activity? This questioning had led in a number of agencies, as it has now in many camps, to a toning down of the honors and awards system and a shift to emphasizing the interest in the activity itself. The group worker in dealing with program making would always aim, in the first place, to relate program to the individuals in his group. If he is using any motivation of this sort therefore, it would be in terms of its effect on specific persons. For some, such an incentive may provide a needed spur to achievement, for others an overstimulus to aggressive competition. He would in all instances approach the question with the capacity to see below the symptomatic behavior to the underlying emotional results. Not the winning of a badge as such nor the acquiring of a skill, but the place of this experience in the life situation of the member is his concern. His decision as to whether or at what points he would use these agency-determined inducements would rest on such considerations. He would tend, however, to hesitate to use purely competitive motivations outside the values inherent in the activity itself.

One final aspect of such programs may be of special interest to the group worker. It is characteristic of such agencies to use local, regional, and national gatherings to which outstanding members are sent. These occasions offer a great program resource if they are wisely used. They can serve to extend the horizon of a narrowly limited group, to bring the indigenous leaders into stimulating and broadening contacts and produce wider social identifications, to provide an advanced experience to members ready to move on to progressively higher levels of leadership. The selection of delegates or representatives must of course be related to capacity to use the experience; and assistance from the group leader may be needed to make the most of it. Such community-wide, regional or national conferences, available chiefly through nationally determined programs, may be a valuable resource in program making.

With such considerations in mind let us turn to the one of our sample groups which illustrates this type of program. Obviously one illustration can bring out only a few of the situations involved in such agencies. We have in previous chapters described the formation of the Y-Teen Club (Chapter IV) and also the interpersonal relations found within it (Chapter VI). This material gives us a basis for looking at its activities.

As we examine the formation of this club the agency's part in program determination appears at three points: the purpose of the Y-Teen Club, which is presumably accepted by the girls on joining, its membership policies, and the nationally proposed set of emphases —the arts, health, personal and family relations, problems of social concern, religion, and work. In this particular group the leader soon sensed the need for flexibility. Her first attempts to develop committees around these suggested emphases had to be modified because of the inexperience of the girls with organization and the fact that their prime objective, as she points out, is to make friends, enjoy recreational activities with boys and girls, and learn certain recreational skills. She did succeed in developing a cabinet or executive committee, a public affairs committee, and a membership committee and some committees for social events as needed.

The program throughout the year included the usual types of social club activities, business meetings with games and singing combined with them, a Christmas party, a Valentine party with boys, an initiation ceremonial, a weekend camping trip. The significant factor in this program lies in the way in which the national program purpose is interpreted at the point of the interracial character of the group which grew out of the membership policy. The national purpose includes a phrase, "to grow in friendship with people of all races, religions and nationalities." National policy further inter-prets this to mean the development when possible of interracial groups. This group is the result of this deliberate intention and is advertised and recruited in a mixed white and Negro school on that basis. It is as the club works out the results of this policy that the purpose gains significance.

Obviously this is not all smooth sailing. As indicated in the material on interpersonal relations, the result of this membership policy is to produce in the group a diverse pattern of relationships. Two divisions are evident, between colored and white and between higher and lower economic levels which, however, differ in the two racial groups. It is on these psychological foundations that the leader has to plan with the group their parties, ceremonials, and camping trips.[4] The following excerpts from the record show in concrete forms a few of the resulting activities. The business meeting on December 13 reflects some by-products of the interracial policy in the early stages of the club's life. This is its second meeting, at which twenty-two are present and which is primarily devoted to elections.

"When the leader sensed that the majority of members had arrived, she suggested that the group might start the business meet-ing. Since the last game played had been a circle game, the girls pushed back the chairs in order to face the blackboard, yet sitting in the same informal style. The leader noticed that with the excep-tion of three white girls who shifted places in order to sit together, the rest of the girls unconsciously retained their same seats that they had in the circle game, so a general glimpse of the total group showed white and colored girls interspersed together.

"Before the meeting, the leader wrote the agenda of the meeting on the board, which included the names of the candidates for the various offices. Eve (N), temporary chairman, presided over the busi-ness meeting. For each office nominations were taken from the floor. Votes were taken by a show of hands with candidates putting down their heads, when voting. This method was employed for the following reasons: (1) The leader wanted to learn distribution of votes, whether individual members voted for best candidates without being race conscious or not; (2) Unsuccessful candidates could be nominated from the floor for other following positions; and (3) It saved time. Results of voting read as follows: President, Julia (N) and Vice President, Bernice (W); Secretary, Bella (N); Treasurer, Ethel (W); Interclub Council Representative, Eve (N); Program Chairman, Millie (N).

"The increase in enrollment at this meeting was a boost to the strength and morale of the group. Most of the new members who joined had heard of the group previously through publicity fliers, but could not attend the first meeting, last week.

"Three of the white girls, Agnes, Peggy and Jane, seemed to hold themselves aloof from the others. A check over the records shows that all three girls are in the same homeroom and have the same sports interests and joined the Y.W.C.A. in order to take advantage of the gym facilities and resources. Since two of them are on the cabinet, probably something can be done to widen their limited acquaintances.

"It was interesting to note that even with three strong candidates for the top position, Julia was nominated from the floor. Being the only Negro candidate, she received all her votes from the colored girls and was elected the president. The other colored girls favored Bernice. The group of elected officers was thus quite interracial; two white and four Negroes. More white girls will be appointed on the cabinet posts to balance the quota."

The next event of significance in the carrying out of the purpose was a party with boys on February 7. For this occasion a group of Negro and white boys had been secured through the Y.M.C.A. They were not members of one club but were selected by the Y.M.C.A. secretary at the request of the leader. A speaker also had been secured, a psychiatric social worker who talked informally on relations between boys and girls. She did not deal with questions related to sex education but rather with more superficial aspects of social etiquette and the attitudes of boys and girls toward each other at this age.

The leader reports this occasion as follows:

"As agreed upon, members arrived right after school, which gave them over half an hour to prepare the meal and set the table before the guests arrived. As the members arrived, they 'pitched in' and worked. About seven boys came half an hour before time and because the girls did not have time to entertain them, the leader asked whether they would like to help set up the games in the recreation room. They responded with spontaneity and enthusiasm. As they worked, they engaged in friendly chats with the leader, and the leader was impressed with their good manners. More boys kept arriving. The girls were quite excited as they learned of the great number of boys, fifteen compared with eleven girls. The problem was: how to accommodate that number. Probably there was more concern for the social hour after supper than for the supper itself.

"When the girls finished preparing the supper, they assembled in the recreation room. After a brief welcome speech by the president, to the guests, the speaker was introduced by Bernice.

"Miss Thomas' talk was excellently presented in a carefree, interesting style. It was obvious that everyone enjoyed it and found it quite stimulating and educational. During the discussion period following her talk, the boys asked her incessant questions. She answered them frankly and honestly and with an unusual understanding, the leader thought, of the psychology of boys. It seemed that there would not be an end to the discussion period, and because of limited time, the leader asked Bernice to close discussion. The group gave her a warm applause. As we moved on to the supper room, some of the boys swarmed around her and pressed her with further questions. The other boys carried on interesting small-group conversations with the girls. Even in the supper room, the boys continued to monopolize Miss Thomas at one end of the room. At this time Mr. Guthrie, the boys' adviser, arrived and he was favorably impressed not only with the large turnout of his boys, but also with the congenial spirit of the whole group. Before the leader spotted him, several of the boys encountered him. Later, when the leader mentioned that he had a fine group of interested boys, he remarked that the remarks made by the boys who greeted him were: 'She's okay. She knows her stuff, all right, Yeah, she's good.' They were thanking him in just those terms for encouraging them to come.

"It was surprising to note how lively the group was throughout the meal. Even our shy girls were making conversations with the boys. Conversations hinged on the list of traits boys liked in girls, and vice versa. Some of the boys had to leave early for their basketball game, but as they left, they thanked Miss Thomas, the girls, and the leader. Through quiet smiles and appreciative looks, the girls apparently liked this friendly gesture.

"Following a two-minute clearing-off of tables, the rest of the clean-up to be done after the social, the group moved to the recreation room. Chairs were quickly pushed back against the wall, and the leader led the group in doing the grand circle. Following this social mixer, the group was left on their own to dance. Since the percentage of boys far outweighed the percentage of girls, fifteen to eleven, there was very little need for the leader to persuade the boys to ask the girls to dance. The leader noticed that the only two white girls in the group were conversing with three white boys. Several colored boys went up to these girls and asked them to dance, but they refused. In an unobserved fashion the leader approached the group and asked whether they wouldn't like to dance. One of the boys replied that he had been persistently asking, but the girls wanted to talk instead. Toward the closing time, the leader suggested to the white group that they dance. One of the white boys asked Bernice to dance. Seeing that the remaining two white boys were not making an effort to ask Beth to dance, the leader suggested to one of the more outgoing colored boys to ask Beth. He did so willingly and obligingly. Beth accepted, and during the dance the leader noticed how congenial both were.

"As the group dwindled to a small number, for members and guests had made other engagements for the evening, the leader thought it would be better to close the evening affair while the group were apparently still having fun.

"Several points might be considered in evaluating the event. Although there were not enough opportunities for the two racial groups to mingle freely together for the leader to make a reliable statement, still there were a few evidences such as eating together, which showed much friendly spirit between the two racial groups. However, it was noticed that following the social mixer, most of the white boys left for other evening engagements while the colored boys remained. It is probable that they excused themselves because of the relatively few white girls present. The colored boys did not show outward feelings of inferior status to the white girls, and the fact that several of them approached the two white girls and asked for dances was significant and indicated some degree of their security in this situation. These same boys asked the leader to dance during the course of the evening. The girls showed a greater sense of responsibility, freedom, and social grace than on previous occasions. It is interesting to note how this great need of winning popularity with the opposite sex could so stimulate the individual girls. That drive brought forth added interest and initiative and added in no small measure to the high-pitched group spirit."

Since committees played such a part in the program of this group, it is perhaps of value to look in on one committee engaged in planning the initiation ceremonial.

"A meeting of the committee was scheduled to plan for the service of recognition and world brotherhood as discussed in previous club and cabinet meetings. At the last regular club meeting, the leader gave ceremonial material to Bernice, membership chairman, to familiarize herself with the form and content of it so she could make more of a contribution.

"Members arrived together, the two white girls and the one colored girl. The leader opened the meeting by giving a preliminary talk on the order of worship services and how to plan ceremonials. Application of the material presented was made in working out the ceremonial. Bernice remarked that her sodality meetings followed a very similar order of worship. The leader commented that different religions have the same fundamental philosophy and often carry out their means of communion worship in the same fashion. There was no formal chairing of the meeting, the leader and committee members merging their ideas together. The leader had to check herself several times, not to introduce her own ideas in her desire to work out a model service of world brotherhood and recognition.

"A variety of materials was provided from which the girls could choose. Within a period of half an hour the girls were ready to share their thinking on some of the material, having themselves gotten into the mood. Before beginning to work out the ceremonial, the leader stressed the importance of originality pointing out that although great thoughts in the form of music, and poetry have been expressed in the past and these should be incorporated into program, there still remained more to be expressed in terms that would have meaning to the girls. One piece of material the girls liked was a poem. The leader picked up the thought and related that she was on a verse-speaking choir for the reading of that poem during a Thanksgiving Service. Asked whether they knew what a verse-speaking choir was, they answered in the negative; so the leader went on further to explain how a poem could be dramatically worked out in parts and in unison to create an aesthetic effect. The leader saw the opportunity of giving some club members experience in speech and dramatics. The girls seemed tremendously interested. It was not easy to select what we thought the girls would like. In fact we found ourselves wanting to include more than what the girls could take in at one service. With much careful planning and thinking, an outline of the ceremonial was made."

It is obvious that this Y-Teen Club illustrates only partially the use of nationally suggested program as discussed above. It does indicate two major points of those mentioned, the necessity to look at the actual, not supposed, motivations of members who join such groups, and flexibly to adapt suggested program emphases to their particular situation, and secondly, the necessity to translate ideological purposes and the procedures developed nationally into concrete situations, even if that involves the inevitable difficulties reflected here and produces very slow movement toward such goals. Only as these aims have reality to individuals involved and are freely accepted by them do they actually become effective.

PROGRAM IN ADMINISTRATIVE GROUPS

The administrative group as described in Chapter IV of course has a program geared to the fulfilling of its specific responsibilities. This often involves analysis of responsibilities, division of labor among individuals or subgroups, co-ordination of effort and the relating of this group and its functions to others in the agency setup. The meetings are typically business sessions for the presentation of problems, hearing of committee reports, and making of decisions. These are such familiar accompaniments of our highly organized society that it is not always recognized that young people have to learn them through experience and that in the course of such learning are many significant opportunities for growth appropriate to their individual capacities.

The two administrative groups included here, the Gay Canteen Committee and the Social Action Committee, illustrate different levels of maturity as well as different functions. Both, however, have certain of the common problems of all administrative groups.

One aspect of program making in such groups consists of the group's acquiring the elementary procedures of administration. These include learning the art of presiding, the mastery of the elements of parliamentary procedure, the keeping of minutes, the making of reports when required, the handling of money. It is necessary to mention only these to make it clear that in a group of youth like the Canteen Committee the group worker needs to assist the officials who are often awkward and ineffective in their first attempts at these responsibilities. As the leader of the Gay Teens points out, this has meant individual work with committee chairmen and help to Herb, the president, in his role as presiding officer. This calls for sensitive handling to keep the responsibility in Herb's hands and yet to see that the control is increasingly democratic. As she says:

"In discussions the leader has tried to keep from expressing her opinions as much as possible, but she has also tried to throw into the discussion certain aspects of it which she feels they have overlooked. She has felt that educationally it was far better for them to work out their own ideas and come to their own conclusions. Many times when Herb has issued his decisions as ultimatums, she has asked whether he didn't think it was a matter for group consideration, or whether some of the others might have ideas on the subject, or whether the matter didn't call for a vote. In this she has had two things in mind—to help Herb to learn what chairing of a committee involves and to draw out the others in giving expression to their ideas in such a setting.

"On occasion the leader has felt it has been with good results—more members speak up, a greater ability to see more aspects is evidenced, and without prompting on her part, Herb has called for a discussion and put the question to vote. At other times however she has wondered as decisions are again 'handed down' autocratically or there has been failure to let the Committee in on issues that have come up outside. Then, all over again, it has called for suggestions and prompting from the leader. It is a rather slow process."

The handling of the treasury in youth groups is often a crucial issue, in which special help is needed. The funds of the group can prove at times considerable temptation to a youthful treasurer and it is also true that the skills in accounting and handling funds have to be learned even when no misappropriation is involved.

Even the Gay Canteen Committee, on the whole a responsible group, suffered from an incident not unfamiliar with inexperienced officials, in this case a situation in which the leader acknowledges her own mistakes. The leader reports:

"The only actual rejections that occurred were between Herb and Fannie, the treasurer. The situation arose over Fannie's books. A shortage in Canteen funds could not be accounted for, and Fannie's books were out of balance. Too many people had been handling the cash in making Canteen purchases without leaving an accurate accounting. Herb was in part at fault on this, as he frequently had made floor wax purchases, etc., without jotting down the items. Fannie was therefore unable to account for all expenditures. Fannie's fault lay in the fact that she was too often absent from the Canteen and therefore not on hand when the need arose for certain items. Although the leader had continually cautioned them on the need for exact accounting, the fault was hers, too, in that she had not checked on the books earlier.

"When the shortage was shown up, both Fannie and Herb felt the other at fault and in turn felt himself accused by the other. The leader therefore called both of them for conference and attempted to explain that it wasn't a matter of blaming anyone—that it was a case of too many people handling the funds without explanation of where they were going. The leader assured them that there was no hint of suspicion of funds having been used for anything but Canteen affairs—rather it was a matter of putting down for Fannie, by all of us, every item of income and expense and making sure she got the information. For Fannie, it was going to mean a greater assumption of responsibility in being present to check on all these things from night to night—for, as treasurer, one was handed a very ticklish and very important responsibility.

"The leader called the conference of the two of them together as she felt that meeting with each separately might indicate accusation of the other. In the talk she assumed her full share of the responsibility for not having checked the books earlier. Handling such financial matters is a ticklish business and feelings ran deep on this score. Candidly, the leader thinks there was a feeling of guilt in each of us—Fannie, for not having kept her books straight; Herb, for the slip in keeping items straight for Fannie; and on her own part, for not having seen to it that such items were getting to Fannie. She believes that the talk together did clear the atmosphere, although there was still a coolness existing between the two."

These incidents illustrate an important part of the learning available in administrative groups, the discovery by experience of what it means to be an official. An official is in fact a kind of two-layer individual, functioning for others and carrying responsibilities in more than an individual capacity. This requires a disciplining of the self which is a step toward mature social relations. It does have to be learned, and the group worker must recognize his part in assisting in this process.

A second aspect of program development in such groups consists of the setting up of official subgroups in the form of committees with assigned functions. Experience with youth groups would indicate that here too learning must come slowly. It may be recalled that the elaborate set of committees recommended by the national agency for Y-Teen groups turned out in this instance to be far beyond their capacity. The Gay Canteen Committee on their own volition set up a similar elaborate structure of five subcommittees, only to find it impossible to keep them working. Few and clearly essential committees, often with short-time functions, are likely to prove more feasible. While it is valuable to spread participation, it is also wasteful of time and effort to develop elaborate machinery. The leader and the officials need again to keep in mind why people have joined and build program here as in other groups on those underlying motivations. The Gay Canteen Committee had first and primarily to enjoy itself as well as carry its responsibilities. Only such machinery as fitted that need could be made to work. In the work of a more mature group, such as the Social Action Committee, with a serious purpose in mind most of the members had attained enough maturity to accept responsibility through committees.

A third major aspect of program in administrative groups lies in the adjustments necessary between the subgroups based on interpersonal reactions (as described in Chapter VI) and the carrying out of administrative functions. This problem is of course not confined to youth groups. Should the president put his friends in as chairmen of important committees? Should committees be built on friendship groupings? How relate friendship groups to the process of reaching joint decisions? These are perennial problems of every organization. Youthful administrators still unfamiliar with the distinction between official and personal relations are confronted with this question in critical ways. Herb finds himself torn, for example, between two such subgroups.

"One group comprised of Fannie, Lucy and Josie, Herb's sister, felt itself superior to others and friction, clashes of opinion, and an undercurrent of criticism had resulted. This has not been brought out in the open in committee meetings except as the above group retarded the handling of business through giggling and 'fooling' around with boys. Of the three, Lucy was the most stable and businesslike and seldom entered into these distractions during meetings. Other groups outside of meetings were critical of this group, particularly of Josie and Fannie. They sensed the girls' feeling of superiority, resented their affectations, felt that many of their ideas were too 'hi-falutin' ' and impractical, and criticized their behavior and the fact that they had rearranged furniture and thrown away furniture covers without the others' knowledge.

"Chick, Herb's girl friend, Helen and Betty now formed the other subgroup and were for the most part conscientious, serious, and capable of clear thinking. They numbered among their closest friends in Canteen membership those who were the most stable members and the most willing workers—ones who were in on the beginning of the Canteen.

"Herb at the beginning of the year was in the rather awkward position of having his girl in one group and his sister in another. His sympathies for the most part were with Chick and her group, for he could control them more easily and got his greatest cooperation from them. However, he seemed able to deal with both, depending on which side he felt had the most practical ideas. For the most part he was able to keep peace between them—partly through overlooking the cleavage."

In such situations, the presiding officer has to acquire an objective and impartial attitude which makes him able not to swing with conflicting currents but to control attachments irrelevant to the business in hand. Here again the administrative group provides many opportunities for growth toward the maturity needed for democratic leadership.

The fourth aspect of program making in such groups consists of the making of agenda for the meetings. Agenda making for administrative groups of any age requires a special skill and judgment in leadership. Obviously the selection of items for the agenda is determined primarily by the immediate issues involved in fulfilling the function but within that is a wide range to be determined upon. For example, in a group representing as great diversity of age, interest and education as the Social Action Committee, the method of presenting the legislative material in a form suitable for all is a major problem. What will get the attention of young Robert Petro is liable to be too elementary for the more mature Mrs. Bruce or the better informed Mrs. Minton. Mr. Toby, with his tendencies to manipulate by presenting only one side of an issue, has to be met by seeing that necessary material or speakers are available to round out the picture. The type of written material used, the speakers introduced, the handling of the discussion need to be geared to the interest and information levels of participants.

Agenda making requires also the breaking up of the problem into smaller units appropriate to the issue and providing handles by which to take hold of action. This division of function into compassable problems and then their distribution and co-ordination in the business session is the central point of administrative program. Where a group worker is assisting officials the working out of agenda becomes an important part of planning before meetings. If officials are young and inexperienced, this will require more than the usual time and skill in preliminary conferences. Here as in all groups the leader must keep in mind the complex motivations that tie people in such groups as in others. They too are often seeking sociability, status, or the sanctioned outlets for aggression. They too are bound by ties of interpersonal relations and rated by accepted scales of value. Here too, as in the three types of groups previously discussed, the program must be built upon and relate to the whole person who brings to the committee meeting not only his interest in its function but his hopes and fears, his capacities and his lacks, his insecurities and his aspirations.

A major problem sometimes confronts group leaders in dealing with that part of the program which touches controversial social subjects, as in the case of the Social Action Committee and to a lesser extent some of the other groups. If a leader in contact with young people is capable of picking up and following their interest today, he is bound to come upon social questions in which they are involved. He is not likely, however, to find much well-developed social interest. Since it is essential for training in a democracy that citizens be alive to public issues and that they learn to think for themselves, the leader must accept the responsibility for helping youth to deal effectively with the problems that confront them.[5]

The leader who is dealing with these questions faces several issues. In the first place, he must be sure that he has located the interest at their point of concern rather than his own, and that he encourages its development in ways adapted to the age and capacities of the group. The awakening social interests of youth may first appear in connection with their local playground. As he develops, the adolescent may find his hot spot of interest at the point of race relations or his own employment. Whatever it is that awakens the individual's wider interest needs to be developed into program adapted to his capacity and not the result of the adult's conception of what needs to be done.[6]

In such groups where controversial social questions are being discussed, the group leader faces the same problem which is familiar to the teachers of the social sciences. The leader will need to keep a balance between his function as teacher and his own position on the question. The effective teacher is not one who has no opinion and is so open-minded as to be unable to reach any conclusion. Such a position only serves to teach futility and incompetence. The leader will therefore need to have and make clear his own position on the subject under discussion. This is not the same, however, as becoming a propagandist. As an educator the teacher's function is to practice the art of creating and using intelligence for the improving of human living. His object, therefore, is not to produce agreement in his students, but to produce the capacity for critical evaluation.

He will therefore welcome disagreement and express his own opinion not as authoritative statement, but as a point of departure for the discussion. He will value and encourage in the group all the evidences of independent judgment and sound criticism which he can find. In many cases he will need to bring in representatives of other points of view than his own in order to ensure the encouragement of critical thinking. Unlike the schoolteacher, however, the group leader is often dealing with groups whose thinking leads to action. This may take the form of the expression of opinion to their legislators, as in the Social Action Committee; the sending of contributions to some local organizations; or the participation in a campaign for passage of a city ordinance, as in the case of the *Teen Tattler* staff. Such collective action on wider social questions has value both as a test of the thought arising out of the discussion and as experience in community participation. The leader whose group is involved in social action will need to clear with his agency on the policies involved about such group action.[7]

In dealing with such policy on action, agencies will find themselves confronted with the same issues which inevitably arise around academic freedom in schools and colleges. In a period when democracy is at stake it becomes of increasing importance that the right to think clearly on controversial questions should be protected at every point.

In this interacting mesh of life, whatever the content of program, teaching and learning are a mutual process. If the leader is himself achieving his own guiding values, his own delight in excellence, his own deep sense of the validity and meaning of life, his own ability to function as a part of the social whole, that achieving by a kind of delicate osmosis is likely to be his most significant contribution to his group. He will at the same time, if he is perceptive, learn from them how life appears from behind the eyes of a Tony or a Jenny. To give and to take in mutual awareness is the underlying condition for an educational experience.

The Group Leader and the Individual Member

THE PURPOSE OF THE GROUP worker in attempting to help all the individuals within his group to secure from it the maximum enjoyment and growth of which each is capable is obviously not done by a one-to-one approach in which he concentrates first on one and then on another. He has to develop a kind of peripheral vision in which, while he is aware of the group interactions, the esprit de corps and the progress of the program, he is also able to take into his consciousness those of the individual members who for one reason or anther require his special attention. There is considerable variation in the ability of leaders for what Dr. Jennings has called "social expansiveness" or "the social contact range an individual establishes between himself and others."[1]

This relation between the leader and his group calls upon him for a sensitivity to the varying reactions of individuals and for understanding handling of each within the context of the group. To illustrate this we have selected the case of the Sub Debs. It will be recalled that this is an instance of a deprived group hungrily seeking response from a sympathetic adult. This material illustrates, however, not only their need at this point but that ability on the part of the leader to individualize need which is essential in the other types of situation as well. This leader describes the varying needs of each girl in their relations to herself as follows:

"Everyone of these girls would be happy to monopolize the leader during a club meeting. The basis for this is their need for love from an adult as well as the status such a reaction from an adult brings them. At first the leader was quite definitely a maternal figure to all of them. With time she has been able to shift this relationship to one more like a big sister with the more mature girls but she has remained much like a mother to the emotionally younger girls. Some of the noisy, show-off behavior has been a direct demand for the leader's attention. Some of the helpful behavior such as cleaning up the room has been to gain the leader's approval. Even a quarrel between two girls inadvertently attracts the leader's attention. Specific instances may illustrate:

"When the group was learning to make bracelets and the leader was the teacher, everyone wanted individual help at once. The leader started with the person beside her and took turns around the group. Dorothy would have been sixth, but she was so provoked not to be first, that she flounced out of the room. She returned in about five minutes but she felt angry with the leader for the entire meeting. Lillian uses tears to get the leader's affection.

"Those who are helpful and co-operative are often motivated in much the same way. They, too, want reassurance and approval from the leader. Again some specific illustrations may be helpful: In preparation for a party, Marion got a bucket of water and scrubbed the woodwork on her own initiative. She beamed when the leader was pleasantly surprised by her actions. Elizabeth volunteers for more responsibility than she can carry through. She promises to 'take care of things' so that the leader won't have to worry about them. She always has an excuse for not getting them done so as to check any displeasure on the part of the leader.

"On a trip there are always quarrels about who may sit, walk or associate most closely with the leader. All of these instances illustrate the rivalry within the group and tend to endanger the effective functioning of the group. At first this behavior bothered the leader considerably and she wondered how to handle it in such magnitude. Through experience she learned to relax in the midst of it and not to be too upset by the device each girl used to force her attention.

"Even though the individual girl sometimes gets angry with the leader when her own will is frustrated in favor of the group, she is unable to stay angry because the leader is too important to her and she recognizes the fairness in what the leader is doing. Anger like this seldom lasts more than a few minutes and is followed by anxiety until she realizes that the leader is not going to retaliate. The leader has consciously tried to be consistent and non-punitive because she appreciates the reasons for this behavior.

"The leader feels that she has attained a warm, friendly relationship with all of these girls and has been able to meet their needs to some extent in the group with the possible exception of Hazel. . . .

"Hazel felt rejected by the leader in the formation of this club. She is a very inhibited child anyway and could not reach out for a relationship which carries with it the fear of rejection. Consequently, the leader has taken some initiative in building the relationship. Both she and the case worker explained to Hazel why she was asked to leave the club during its formation. (She had slipped in before reaching the age set for the group.) Intellectually she understands. For several months, however, after she reached the necessary age and was admitted, she was stand-offish with the leader. The leader used every occasion both in and out of the group to be kind to her. She realized that there was progress when Hazel finally began testing her out. She became very demanding in the club meetings, even requiring the leader to thread her needle for her. Then she asked for privileges like straightening up the cupboard in the recreation room. (This meant a privilege to her.) Very slowly this testing period was passed and then Hazel made shy but affectionate overtures like touching the leader's hand. The leader feels that a warm relationship is emerging, but it has taken six months to attain it.

"The leader does not mean to overemphasize the importance of her role. Yet she does feel that with these disturbed children, the adult figure represents stability and strength and, if she is liked, a person with whom to identify. The leader sees many imperfections in the job she has been able to do, but she does feel that the leader of a group like this has major responsibilities in constructively helping to shape the lives of these children—responsibilities which usually belong to the parents and the home environment. Hence she has used her personal influence in trying to meet group and individual needs within the group itself."

The reaction of this group is obviously immature for their age, but their lack of normal family life has produced an unusual need for adult affection. In lesser degree this need will be found in many adolescent groups, and even among older groups there will be some individuals who seek in more disguised ways to get the same response the Sub Debs so overtly demand. One of the values of group experience is the ability to accept the limitations inevitable when desired persons must be shared with others. If the leader handles this wisely they can draw much from the warm accepting atmosphere of the group as a whole, they can learn to share affection when necessary and many can learn to turn to their peers as we see these girls doing in time for the more intimate mutuality necessary for mature emotional satisfaction.

Most sympathetic and approachable leaders are constantly having contacts with members outside of the meetings. Some of these are casual and fleeting and can do no more than convey the general interest the leader has in the group. However, some of them involve individual conference and at times continued contact outside as well as inside the group. The bases for such contacts include all the needs and interests of human relationships. We shall consider here several varieties which illustrate the leader's relation to different situations.

There are certain points at which a group leader may need to help individuals who are having difficulties in establishing themselves in the group. These may arise, for example, out of physical handicaps which have had such effects on personality as to make social relations difficult. This, for example, was the situation with Art, the deaf boy who was taken into the R.R.C.'s. Without individual help from the leader and assistance to the parents, Art would probably have been dropped by his peers into social isolation or active rejection. The leader describes his attempt to help Art overcome his handicaps as follows:

"Art, aged fourteen, was born practically stone deaf and there has been no improvement in his hearing as a result of his attendance at clinics. Art, tall and chubby, attends a Special School and, though his intelligence test score is far above average, the school considers him behind in reading ability and limited in vocabulary, 'immature and willful.'

"Art enunciates so indistinctly that only with experience and careful attention can his speech be understood. He is able to do some lip-reading, but for much of his communication both he and the person with whom he is speaking must resort to writing notes. Contact with the family and observation of his behavior characteristics present a fairly clear picture of parental rejection of Art, whose emotional development is at the seven or eight-year level.

"He began coming to the community center soon after it opened and played ping pong and checkers whenever he could find someone to play with him. He joined an evening photography group, in which he showed a great deal of interest, occasionally working in the dark room alone during the day. Although he was not able for many months to establish very meaningful relationships with other individuals or groups, he came more and more frequently, with the active encouragement of his parents. At the junior canteen he played games and danced. He confided to a member of the staff that he had 'a girl friend at the canteen.'

"Art often joined in the running around and usual rough-house before club meetings, but he complained bitterly that he had no club. As the staff found it necessary to limit his demands for constant attention, his frustration was expressed in anger and occasionally in tears. The staff and through them some groups developed the practice of giving him small jobs to do, such as stapling, sealing envelopes and lettering signs. This was a source of satisfaction to him but was not enough.

"One day some of the R.R.C. group brought him to a meeting to become a member. The leader asked the group to think very carefully about inviting him to join in terms of their willingness to meet some of the difficulties that would arise. His sponsors insisted that he could read lips and that, above all, 'he needs social life.' The leader told the group it was a fine thing they wanted to do but cautioned them to consider that it might not work out successfully and the effect this might have on Art. One boy suggested having a pencil and pad for Art at the meetings. Another volunteered to repeat to Art what was being said. He was voted in. A few days later the leader was able to meet with Art informally and discuss his club membership. Voting, elections and the business of the meeting were explained and discussed. The leader tried to help him accept the fact that sometimes the boys talked too fast for him to read lips and that it might not always be possible for someone to repeat everything that had been said. He said he would try to be patient about this. The leader in a subsequent club meeting then turned to his major interest, ping pong, in which he had developed a high degree of skill, and suggested a tournament within the club. It was pointed out that Art might not only like to play, but that he could help by taking care of the scoring and records involved. This seemed to open up to him the possibility of making his contribution to the group, and although the project never materialized, Art was later able to make suggestions to the club on such things as fund-raising techniques.

"However, it became apparent soon after his entry into the club that he could not follow either the words or the meaning of the rapid action. He fell back on participating as a clown. With the solicitous help of some of the boys and with the leader's written explanations during, before and after meetings, Art has grasped some of the meaning of the democratic process and has advanced in understanding the limits group membership imposes on him. The group offers a rare opportunity for making some contribution, however limited, to his social growth. This requires however a constant process of adjustment by which Art is helped individually by the leader and the group is ready to modify its activities to suit his situation.

"The relationship of the agency to Art and his family also merits some explanation. It will be recalled that he began coming to the agency both afternoons and evenings as soon as it opened and long before his admission to the club. Another member of the staff not the leader visited his home and found his mother very happy about his association with the center. When the worker suggested, however, that Art come on only two nights a week, the mother became visibly annoyed and the father hastened to point out that they were not shirking their responsibilities as parents. The worker began moving in the direction of having the family make use of case work service and after considerable hesitation, the mother arranged for monthly interviews with a worker at the Family Service Society. Her contact with the case worker was sporadic and she discontinued it after several months.

"Both the visiting group worker and later the case worker found that Art's mother felt at his birth that she had been 'punished by God' and was to be a martyr because of his deafness. Later she began to be more hopeful about his ability 'to take his place in society,' as she said. There was a strong element of guilt in the mother's feelings and the case worker thought she used the interviews to 'relieve her feelings.'

"Soon after he joined the club the leader telephoned Art's mother at his urgent request to explain the club's dues and the disciplinary fines. The leader took this occasion to suggest that Art's mother help him to understand and accept the limitations of group activity. The mother said that he had been thinking about going to camp and that despite a 'bad camp experience' previously he might want to go again because some of his friends in the club were going. She later came in to discuss camp and to urge the whole staff to persuade Art to go. When it was pointed out that the staff would not subject Art to pressure but would help him reach his own decision, the mother quickly agreed that to do otherwise might give him the idea that 'we are trying to get rid of him.' When Art learned that his leader and the agency supervisor, as well as some of his friends in the club, were going to camp, he decided to go. The question of his camp attendance provided another opportunity for joint planning with the mother and more assistance to her in a more sensitive dealing with his problem."

It is noticeable that here the leader talked both with Art and with the group in order to facilitate his acceptance. With such help and concurrent interpretation to his family he was able to hold a position inside an intimate group which would otherwise have been completely closed to him.

At times the introduction to a group requires some assistance from the leader. An interview at the intake point may be helpful for many reasons. In the Y-Teen Group such a need arose in the case of Ray, an Austrian Jewish refugee girl, who had just arrived from England. Her harrowing war experience in both Vienna and England and her

unfamiliarity with American youth, made it seem advisable for the
leader to have several interviews with her at the point of her entrance
to the group. The leader describes her first contacts with Ray as
follows:

"Ray is a Jewish refugee, who came over to the United States from
England about two months ago. Because of her past enjoyable club
experience as one of the younger members of the English Y.W.C.A.
she sought out the Y.W.C.A. here and inquired about activities
for teen-age girls. Since the worker was advising a high school club,
the Program Director sent her name and phone number to the leader
for contact and possible membership in the club.

"A preliminary interview was arranged with Ray on April 21,
during which time the leader outlined the membership policy, and
past and future program activities of the club. Not wishing to commit her to joining the club without first giving her the opportunity
to observe the club and meet the club members, the leader asked her
to drop in at a club meeting the following Wednesday. Pertinent
data gathered at this preliminary interview included the fact that
Ray was of Austrian Jewish background; that her family was not
affiliated with any Jewish temple yet, due to lack of knowledge of
any; that she was a sophomore in a senior High School; that she was
fifteen years old and the only child in the family; and that she lived
in a Jewish neighborhood near the meeting place of this club.

"Ray attended the club meeting on Wednesday and won much
interest and attention from all the members. They were keenly
interested in her past experiences in England and were delighted
with her English charm, simple and unassuming manner and English
accent in speech. The girls expressed their enthusiasm for having met
her and invited her to come again.

"The second interview was planned to gain more knowledge and
insight into Ray's family background, her past experiences in Europe,
and her personal interests, so that the leader could help her to adjust
to the club and contribute to it.

"Ray seems to have a very interesting family background and close
home relationships. She is the only child in the family and has
perhaps over-protective and solicitous parents. As a starting point,

the leader planned to use the club registration card, which requested such information as, occupation of father, mother, country of birth of father, mother, education of father, mother. The leader wished to know Ray's feelings toward her parents' close supervision, whether she felt frustrated at lack of freedom and independence, or whether she accepted the parents' role in guidance, since she did not wish to create a conflict with the parents in urging her to participate in the club. . . .

"Ray was waiting for the leader in the office when she arrived. She seemed all aglow with enthusiasm and youthful vitality, and greeted the leader with hearty and warm response. We moved to the adjoining room for more personal freedom in talking.

"The leader again commented on how pleased and happy she and the other campers would be to know that she was going on the camping trip. Ray said she was, too, and proceeded to ask the leader what articles she needed for camp. After supplying her with the list, the leader gave her a general picture of the camp program, which included a Spring festival of folk dances, games, and songs, and asked her whether she wouldn't like to teach the group an Austrian folk dance, game, or song. She laughed and said, 'We speak German. I can't teach anything German, but maybe, I can teach them an English song . . .

"The leader explained the program in the Y-Teen club. She emphasized that they planned programs to suit interests of girls, and that because Ray came from a different background, there might be some club activities she would like to see included in the club program. A check-list of desired activities was gone over with Ray. She indicated an indifferent attitude on the topic of boy-girl relations. The reason for this attitude seemed related to the fact that she did not know social dancing. The leader mentioned incidentally in discussing religious club activities that the Temple offered very good services for young people as well as for older people, that the Rabbi had returned recently from a tour of Palestine and had quite interesting knowledge to give to members. Ray said that her Jewish girl friend in school had been encouraging her to attend the young people's group meeting, and that she might. When talking over activities in the field of the arts, Ray stated that she liked sewing and cooking. . . . She showed much interest in the sports activities, especially the out-door sports, and asked whether these could be included in the club program, whenever possible. It seemed that Ray is a very versatile individual, and has many varied interests, including such hobbies as photography and stamp collecting.

"As it was getting late and the leader did not want to detain Ray from dinner, the interview was gradually drawn to a close. Ray thanked the leader for giving up so much of her time for her.

"Much friendliness was created between the leader and Ray during the interview; and it is very likely that Ray was able to adjust more readily to the group out at camp, following this initial successful relationship with the leader."

This opportunity to talk with the leader before embarking on membership should increase the ease of Ray's entrance into the group. It also gave the leader an insight into her relations with the parents, the vocational ambitions of the parents for her, and her own abilities and interests which will be helpful in future contacts with Ray in the club meetings. It is important here that, while the group helps her to take on the American youth customs which will facilitate her relations with both boys and girls that the leader is aware of the pulls from parents and teachers perhaps in other directions at points. This understanding will help the group leader in assisting Ray to find a balance in these various demands upon her without creating a conflict for her.

The group leader who has established successful rapport with his group is almost certain to find himself consulted by members in regard to a great variety of personal problems. In some situations the request is one which can rather easily be dealt with immediately by the leader without committing himself to continued and deeper relationships than his leadership function permits.

The leader of the Mike Club, for example, was typing in the office when Robert Petro wandered in in a desultory fashion. After discussing his experiences in the state capital where he had recently gone as a delegate to the conference, conversation drifted to other things. As the leader reports:

"Robert peered at what the leader was doing. He seemed to want to assist, but didn't take the initiative. The leader went on with the typing. Robert watched for a while and then asked, 'Did you ever hear of the American Institute?' The leader said he hadn't. Robert said it was in New York and that he was thinking of taking correspondence courses. He said they were offering psychology and one or two other subjects. Robert said he had noticed the books up in the third floor lounge on vocational guidance but he didn't find anything on Personnel Work. The leader asked whether Robert had some idea of what personnel work involved. Robert replied that it was understanding people. 'That's psychology,' he said, 'and other things too, I guess.' Robert asked the leader what he knew about it. The leader answered that Robert had touched on an important point when he said 'understanding' people. He pointed out that in personnel work he would need to know about interviewing, office methods, labor-management relations and the problems of the particular industry in which he worked. . . . Robert said he would go to the library and see what other information was necessary, in order to go into personnel work.

"Since this incident, Robert has tried to get jobs without much success. The kind of job he wants is white-collar work, and he has found out that a high school diploma is an essential. The leader has now had several talks with him about school and has given him encouragement to return to complete his high school course. He has stated that if he is not inducted into the army this summer, he will be going back to resume the studies he quit over a year ago. He needs only fifty credits to graduate."

Obviously Robert is ready for educational and vocational guidance and the leader is in the position to see that he gets it. These opportunities with youth at school-leaving age or immediately after are frequent and leaders in recreation agencies are often in a good position to discover such needs and direct people to the available agencies. Unless they are trained in this type of guidance leaders should of course avoid attempting it themselves. They can, however, give not only the information on the resources of the community but also through their interest in the individual provide the additional impetus he may need to make use of the services available.

These contacts with members at times involve seeing people

through difficult experiences as a support representing the interest of the agency as well as the personal concern of the leader. Major misfortunes fall upon the group members and in some of the groups in less favored environments the incidence is likely to be high. When this occurs the group leader and the agency can often assist a member through the experience by a kind of supplementary support even when a case-work agency, the juvenile court or the church is involved in the major handling of the case.

Reference has been made in previous excerpts to the fact that during the program year of the Jokerettes here described their president Clarice was allegedly raped on her way home from a dance. When this happened the sponsor of the group necessarily came into the picture as a support even though the case had gone to the court. Some background on Clarice is essential to the leader's understanding of how to deal with it. The following states what she knew of Clarice and her family when this situation arose.

"Clarice was born in this city fifteen years ago, and is the fourth child in a family of eight children. Her parents were born in the South but have lived here since marriage. Her sixteen year old sister Nora also is a member of the club.

"At fifteen Clarice is in the 8A-2 class at the Junior High. She is described in school reports as dependable and outgoing, her adjustment to the teacher is fair, to children and work good; her school work is fair. The leader has not heard of any active interest in church in the family.

"The family lives in a six-family run-down brick apartment house, which except for Lottie's house is the most deprived of any club member's. While she and Nora were small eight children shared the same bed with her mother before the family moved downstairs from the grandparents. Even now the sleeping arrangements are very inadequate.

"Clarice's parents have been separated for almost ten years. According to the records, her father, a steady railroad worker, could not stand the bickering, hot temper, and laziness of his wife. He is supposed to be living with another woman. He contributes fairly regularly to the family and is generous with presents. Aid to Dependent Children gives a large grant. Although the father filed for divorce in December, 1946, he is apparently around the house a lot. Clarice came in arm in arm with her father during a home visit after Clarice's attack, smiling shyly at her father as she introduced him. According to records the mother once said she'd like to marry again and the children protested saying they already had a father.

"The mother is an immature person and the leader has found her to be an easy-going, pleasant woman in her early thirties who is permissive and affectionate to the children and allows many teen-agers to come in daily or cluster on the front steps much to the irritation of the neighbors. The mother feels she can supervise her children better this way. Once she told the leader she felt like one of the kids.

"With boys Clarice is on moderately easy terms, though she flares up sharply if she feels anyone is putting something over on her. She does not date steadily but is interested in boys in and outside the Jokers. On May 7 after club meeting and spending the rest of the early evening with other club members at a dance, Clarice was allegedly raped while walking home with a Joker by Tom B. who was accompanied by two other boys. Tom told Clarice she and the Jokerettes had been involved in a fight last summer in which his sister had been beaten up. Clarice disputed this and agreed to walk home to his sister's to verify her statement. At one of the school yards Tom beat up the Joker and had intercourse with Clarice, Tom's friends walking away in some protest, according to Clarice's story. She and the Joker, a quiet, dull-looking little fellow, returned to Clarice's home and the family called the police. The other girls told the group leader about this situation and after the next club meeting she stopped in at Clarice's home.

"She found Clarice's mother and eleven-year-old Jane asleep on the same couch for the night, another girl lying on a chair with a coat over her, and small Tony in process of undressing. Mrs. D. looked very tired and sad. She said Clarice had gone to the movies with her oldest sister since it was felt she should go on just the same as before.

"Mrs. D. reviewed the incident. She said that Clarice and Sam

had arrived home about 11:00 p.m. at night but that it had taken
the family some time before they could regain composure and call
the police. Clarice had identified Tom B. as the boy who had attacked
her and he had been picked up by the police that night. Sam, who
had been with Clarice, had been beaten up to some extent.

"Mrs. D. said Clarice had been quite ashamed but that she had
told her that this could have happened to even an older person like
herself. The leader thought this a very wise attitude and suggested
that Clarice be urged to talk this out as much as she could so that
it could have as little lasting effect as possible. The leader wondered
if Clarice had seen a doctor; Mrs. D. said she had been seen by a
doctor that morning where she had been treated against possible
infection.

"Several days later Clarice asked that the leader come with her
and her mother to the hearing at the Police Court the following
Friday, May 16. On Friday the leader met Mrs. D., Clarice, Sam and
his mother and the group went by street car to the court for the first
hearing.

"A week later Bernice called and announced that the hearing
before the Grand Jury was to be held today, expecting the leader to
go with her and her mother. The leader agreed to come and met
them at the courthouse.

"During the long wait, Sam was silent and worried; Clarice
retired to a back bench and slept; Mrs. D. talked with the leader for
a while, especially about police help, and their desires for better
housing. Later the leader joined Clarice and we talked at length
about school, track which she likes, the baseball team, summer jobs
and especially the Placement Bureau of the Urban League which was
just opening, etc. The leader suggested the girls discuss at the meeting next evening their desires for leadership during the summer and
fall, and under what sponsorship the club might be next fall."

The importance in Clarice's life of her relation to the club makes
it doubly significant to her that the sponsor should give her support
at this time. The traumatic experience itself, from which she perhaps
escaped by sleeping in the court waiting room, the element of constant threat in the gang warfare of which this incident was a part,

and the court hearings all combined to make a supporting relation-ship necessary. No other resource in the community offered as easy and natural assistance as that of the club sponsor with whom she already had established a relationship through the group. It is obvious that this family needed long-range assistance from a case-work agency but in this time of crisis they turned to the group leader, whom they knew, for support which obviously she had to be prepared to give. In time she may be in the position to refer them for further assistance since she has stood by them as a sponsor through this situation.

In some situations the resources available in an agency and in the community can be focused to help a group member who is confronted with a personal crisis.

In the Settlement House of which the Mike Club was a part one of the outstanding older boys who belonged both to the club and to the canteen suddenly became a ringleader in an epidemic of disorder and vandalism. The leader describes the problem that confronted him as follows:

"Mike is a nineteen-year-old second generation Italian. Mike's heavy frame and solid physique give him the appearance of a man in his middle twenties. He gives a distinct picture of virility. Mike graduated from High School a year ago and then went into the business world, starting as a stock boy and later working into the factory set-up where he is now employed on a piece work basis in an automobile plant. Mike's unusual physique and a natural flair for sports, made him a star throughout his teens. Excellent at football, baseball and basketball, he attracted all the boys to him, and was a popular hero to the girls. He participated actively in the parish athletics. Father F. who has known Mike for the past ten years has said of him, 'He leads a dual life. At times he is very boisterous but he has also a peculiar conscientiousness. He wants to be a leader, but will not take the trouble to do what leadership involves. As a boy he served Mass and as long as he could head the show, he took an active part.' The House had known Mike for ten years and he has belonged to a number of groups whose focus was athletics.

"A little over a year ago while playing baseball, Mike slid into second and suffered a severe ankle fracture. It had been set four or five times and he was still taking treatment. For many months he wore a cast and hobbled about. He was scheduled to be inducted at about the time of the accident, and the result was a 4F classification. This was very frustrating to him; he became very aggressive and sought to prove his masculinity in a series of episodes in which he was the definite ringleader. In the House Canteen he would enter the room and his cronies would begin to applaud after which he would start to make a mock speech; no sooner did he begin when they started the applause again. Then suddenly at a given signal from him, the folding chairs would 'hit the decks' and pandemonium would ensue. This behavior was carried over to an outside group. His gang created a constant disturbance at a canteen in a nearby neighborhood. They would start crap games going and in general carry on in an objectionable fashion. Their presence was not desired but they continued to come.

"This behavior reached a point where it seemed likely that Mike would be arrested in order to protect the nearby canteen from the raids of his gang. At this point the House stepped into the picture. A neighborhood Council organized by the Settlement and consisting of the parish priest, the agency head and influential local leadership was brought into play and his case was brought to it. The priest undertook to talk with Mike and his parents. The agency contributed by providing him with part-time work in the physical education department through which he could win back his standing as an athlete and display his masculine prowess. This responsibility served to put him on the side of law and order and the vandalism ceased in the canteens. The prominence secured and acceptance indicated by the agency's action helped to redress the balance of the 4F classification. A temporary upset that might have led to serious involvement was staved off by the use of agency resources. The leader's part in this was to set in motion the various forces that cooperatively worked out the solution."

In some groups a leader will find himself becoming the object of an adulation which arises from somewhat different needs than those of the groups so far described.[2] In certain groups of the ages considered here there are responses from members of a group to an acceptable leader which are reflections of their stage of emotional development. In early adolescence before heterosexual interests are consciously expressed or for those who find it difficult to grow into them, there is the familiar phenomenon of the idolizing of an attractive leader of the same sex who is usually ten to fifteen years older than the members. For some adolescents this is a part of the re-evaluation of the attractive and desirable which goes on as they outgrow their early childish identification with the parent of the same sex and seek in the beginning of mature masculinity or femininity as the case may be an object to love, admire and emulate. For many adolescents such a relation serves without great emotional significance to bridge them over into the adult world and the idolizing attitudes pass normally as heterosexual interests develop.

There are occasionally instances, however, where this relation takes on an intensity which may indicate that the member is using it to meet emotional needs of a deeper sort. These may occasionally be rooted in homosexual tendencies brought into action by the conflicts of adolescent tensions. The leader who finds himself the object of such demands must of course deal with them with understanding and skill. It is well for leaders to recognize that in adolescence apparently extreme demands for affection from adults or peers are often found in the course of normal growth. As the leader becomes aware of such intensity of feeling either toward himself or among members of the group he may find himself inclined to reject and rebuff because of his fear of his ability to deal with it. This will not help. He should not indulge in amateur diagnosis nor should he undertake to "talk it out." Rather he should reserve his judgment until he can secure psychiatric consultation or expert help from a case worker. This will help him both to understand his own reactions and to see what his place may be in helping the individuals involved. Certainly he will not himself pry into a situation which he suspects has deep emotional roots any more than he would undertake an operation for appendicitis, since by the very nature of his function he will not be able to follow through into the treatment which may be required. Moreover, his relation to other members and to the group process as a whole is likely to deteriorate if it becomes evident that an intensive relation to one member is being carried over a period of time. Referral to a psychiatrist or case worker, where that can be accomplished, not only secures the necessary help for this individual but relieves the tension in the group by shifting it to an outsider. The group leader obviously will need in such instances to maintain a steady helpful relation without elements of rejection or retaliation and most of all with an understanding of his part in the emotional problems involved. Co-operative carrying of the case by the group worker and the psychiatrist or the case worker or con-sultation with a case worker if referral cannot be accomplished may also be the best available way of meeting the situation.

In certain other circumstances also the agency and the leader will need to call upon expert services, such as medical care, family case work, child welfare service, or psychiatric consultation. Behavior within the group or direct request for assistance from group mem-bers may indicate the need for more expert and continuous individ-ualized service outside the function of the recreation-education agencies.

The close working together of group workers with case workers has now become accepted practice in many agencies. In some cases, as in the Children's Home, both are on the same staff. In others referral is necessary to an agency where the specialized service is available.[3] While it is not possible within the scope of this book to deal fully with this subject, it seems valuable to illustrate by one instance, which occurred in one of our sample groups, the way in which such joint working together with a case worker can help some individuals to use the group for learning how to adjust successfully with their peers. The instance chosen here is that of Rose, a twelve-year-old girl who had been known as a truant from school. She had been picked up for shoplifting and finally placed by her parents in the Home where the group leader meets her.

"One of the children whom the group leader noticed first at the Home was Rose. Surrounded by eighty children and a new staff that first day, no one took on much individuality, but the leader does remember a rather large, blonde, attractive girl who smiled at her and said, 'I'm interested in the Y and in dramatics. Don't forget me, will you?' In the succeeding days, while the children were still not very much individualized, Rose always spoke to the leader politely by name and smiled in a charming manner.

"Soon the leader had an opportunity to sit at the table with her for lunch and Rose directed much conversation toward her. She spoke quite intelligently and expressed herself well although somewhat dramatically. The leader noticed that the two youngest children at the table listened attentively but that the children nearer Rose's age tended to ignore her more or less. The leader could sense a rather hostile feeling toward her.

"The first direct group contact with Rose did not come until the first of November. However, before that time the leader had time and opportunity to observe many of her characteristics as well as to discuss her history with the case worker.

"Rose's immediate problem was an inability to get along with the girls who were near her own age. She was hostile toward them and they would not accept her. As the case worker and group leader attempted to analyze this situation, they came to the conclusion that it was Rose's almost complete lack of conformity to the institutional routine and accepted behavior standards that roused the hostility of the group against her. For example, Rose would come drifting home from school thirty minutes to an hour late; she would return to the Home late after her Sunday visits home; she would glorify her own home and rave about the wonderful meals that had been prepared especially for her; no other girl's account of a weekend could surpass hers. She would deliberately antagonize the other children by biting, sarcastic remarks on such tender spots as the disgrace of their parents' being divorced or the fact that their parents failed to come to see them. She would make derogatory remarks about the Home to which the others objected.

"Another form of behavior to which the girls objected was Rose's exhibitionistic attitude. She liked to show off her ability to do acrobatic dancing or to flaunt her superior knowledge. When Rose first came to the Home, the girls were inclined to appreciate her performances, but they soon came to resent it. These actions took place in the playroom which all the girls must share and there was no opportunity to get away from Rose and her antics. Consequently fighting and many verbal barrages frequently took place and stirred up the entire girls' department.

"The other children likewise resented Rose's habit of playing up to adults. She could do this beautifully and could always make a good first impression. The leader's first contact with Rose has already pointed out her technique. Since all of the children want to be liked by adults, they could see through Rose's acting and did not appreciate her dramatic approach.

"In October the Sub Deb Club was organized. At first it was to include only thirteen and fourteen year old girls. However at the first meeting, three twelve year old girls also attended. Since it was not possible to include all the twelve year olds this had to be discussed with the club.

"That evening when the leader met with the girls, she asked them to sit down at one of the tables with her and talk over seriously a situation which she felt needed all their thinking and opinions. She then brought up the matter of three twelve year old girls being included in the group while there were several other twelve year olds who apparently had not been considered. One of the twelve year olds present shouted, 'I'll bet it is Rose who is trying to get rid of us!' This remark set all the girls off. The leader tried to explain to them that no individual was responsible for the situation, but they continued to blast Rose. 'She's always causing trouble.' 'She's the worst girl in the Home.' 'She lies and cheats.' 'She is an old show-off.' 'She's stuck up.' When they cooled down enough to think more calmly, they seemed to be able to understand and accept the validity of restricting all twelve year old girls during the formation of the club. The three younger girls returned to the playroom. The others did not seem disturbed and went on with their meeting.

"The Sub Debs continued until November 4 before we again dealt with the problem of membership.

"October had been an especially stormy month for Rose. Her tardiness had increased. She had refused to cooperate within the department. She had fought with the housemothers and the other children. In the case work relationship, Rose had always tended to

view things from one extreme or the other. At one time, everything
was fine; her home was the best in the world; her family loved her;
she had been in the wrong as far as her family relationships were
concerned but now she had completely changed; if she could go
home everything would be perfect now. At another time, everything
was impossible; she hated everybody and everybody hated her, but
she said she didn't care. No amount of reminding her of past experiences could help her to keep a balance. During October, her attitude
had been the latter and all she had wanted to give or accept was
hatred. She had been able to recognize that she had difficulties with
the Home girls but she had projected all the blame on them. She
could accept none of the responsibility herself.

"Rose's general behavior became so bad that a staff conference
was called to analyze the problem and formulate a plan for Rose.
It was felt that Rose did need a firmer control to keep her more in
line with the group and what was expected of them since her lack
of conformity was so greatly resented by the group.

"At this same time, the leader discussed with the staff the possibility of admitting a few younger girls into the Sub Deb Club. We
considered all the eleven and twelve year old girls and finally our
judgment boiled down to three girls, who by virtue of high intelligence, general maturity, or natural grouping should belong to this
club. Because of intelligence, physical maturity, social skills and
interest, Rose was one of these girls. We were well aware too of
the other girls' attitude toward her but felt that if she could win
acceptance in the club there was a possibility of helping her learn
how to get along with other girls. With the support of the staff, the
leader was willing to approach it with the club the next week.

"Later that very day, the case worker had an interview with Rose
in which Rose expressed a great deal of disturbance about not being
included in the Sub Debs. She had already been sarcastic about it in
the girls' department and said that she would belong to the 'Diaper
Club.' Rose was obviously upset but she could not admit that she
was hurt. Instead she told the case worker that she would not join
this club under any circumstances, not even if she were invited.

"Before the next club meeting, the leader read Rose's case history, had a conference with the case worker, and we formulated a plan. We felt that these were Rose's chief problems before her admission to the Home:

"Rose was the least wanted of four children. She was born during the depression and her birth caused her mother to give up the job which was helping to support the family. Her father paid little attention to Rose except to yell at her in sudden outbursts for some misbehavior. Her mother is somewhat like Rose—overdramatic, projects her faults upon others, and runs away from her problems. There was a lack of cooperation between the parents and very little discipline in the home. Almost no attention was paid to Rose except in the form of punishment and then only when the situation got very bad and neighbors or outsiders got involved. Then it was extreme, including severe beatings. Once the father nearly choked Rose to death. Rose was extremely unpopular with other children in school and in the neighborhood. She felt this especially in contrast to her sister (one year younger) who was popular with other children and also conforming in the home. (It was discovered that the sister did this to gain favor over Rose. When Rose was removed from the home, the younger girl ceased to co-operate or conform.) Rose was often found wandering on the streets at 11:00 p.m. and had been involved in stealing incidents.

"From psychiatric examination and testing, it was found that Rose has an I.Q. of one hundred and fourteen with special ability in art and dramatics. She had strong narcissistic tendencies. Her stealing was motivated by a desire to get love and affection and was stimulated by the dramatic attention it brings her.

"After Rose spent thirteen days in a Detention Home on charges of neglect by her parents and after much interpretation to the parents of the need for placement, Rose was admitted to the Home in March. Since then she has had much difficulty in getting along and has run away several times.

"The case worker and group leader felt that if the Sub Deb Club would give Rose an opportunity and if she was made to realize that this was her chance, she might be able to adjust to the group with the assistance and acceptance of the leader. This situation would be in marked contrast to her home. The adult would not be threatened by any negative behavior, would try to give her steady support and would offer any necessary discipline without rejection. The sibling rivalry experienced at home would be different too, because of the adult's consistent attitude toward all the girls. Although the leader felt she was handling dynamite, her relationship with the club girls had grown secure enough that she was willing to try to carry out the plan.

"At the next meeting of the Sub Deb Club the leader brought up the admission of the three younger girls. To one of these girls there was eager agreement; to one a sort of indifference; and to Rose a strong negative reaction. The group became quite excited and some of them flatly refused to admit her while others said that if she belonged they would not come. They recited many stories of what they say is Rose's inability to cooperate. They didn't question her maturity.

"After letting off much steam, they finally began to consider letting Rose belong to the group. It was a quiet girl in the group, who is an undercurrent leader, who said, 'I think Rose does belong with us. Maybe we could make her over.' There was silence for a minute. Then a girl who is in the nucleus of the group said she agreed. Quite a bit of discussion followed on how they would *make* Rose cooperate—or else! One girl proposed letting her in on trial and making her live up to certain standards. However, when they considered making rules, they saw that the rules would apply to the whole club and they didn't want to place these restrictions on themselves. Consequently, that idea was dropped. The leader held her breath for Rose when the girls finally put it to a vote. All three candidates were admitted unanimously!

"The leader felt that the girls were exhausted and suggested waiting until next week to have these new girls join, but the club wanted to admit them at once. The president went to the playroom to call them, and they all appeared, beaming, immediately. A place for the most desired new member was made between two other girls. Rose sat at the end of the table and the one girl nearest to her moved a little farther away. The president required each new member to state that she wanted to join and would work for the good of the club. Rose was apparently sincere when she made her statement. The air was a little charged but the hostility was under control. Plans were made for the next meeting.

"The leader had a conference with the case worker on the preceding developments. We were glad that Rose had been admitted by vote of the club even though it was with a struggle. The case worker and group leader decided that the next step was to have a marginal interview with Rose to clarify for her the leader's position and support and to help her realize her own position in the group. Another purpose of this interview was to make clear to Rose that the group leader was aware of her situation. The case worker had found that Rose responded better when she knew that the adult understood her problem and when she was not bothered by conflicts in her own mind on this score. Her intelligence makes it possible to deal quite frankly with her.

"That evening after school the leader talked with Rose for about a half hour. She found that Rose did recognize the situation and had noticed all the little indications of the girls' dislike. However, she did not want to face the situation very squarely. She constantly tried to lead our conversation into more pleasant channels. She told of an adventure she had had coming home from school, how Christmas is celebrated in her home, and equally irrelevant things. The leader tried not to push the point too hard nor make her uncomfortable, and yet she did want her to accept some of the responsibility that she must assume if she is to win the approval of the Sub Debs. She agreed to try and wanted to cooperate with whatever plans developed. The leader appreciated with her the value of this cooperation but also tried to give her the feeling that she could assert leadership if she did so tactfully and if she won the approval of the girls so that they would accept her ideas. The leader thought she found her attitude supportive and felt that it was constructive for her.

"The November 11 meeting was devoted to planning and carrying out a Truth and Consequence program. One leader was chosen by the girls to think up questions and another to think up consequences. Rose was not chosen as a leader, but as the two leaders selected their helpers, Rose was the second choice out of six choices on the team working on consequences. This showed that the girls were willing to utilize her flair for the dramatic and give her an opportunity to work with them. She suggested several stunts and they were all incorporated by the group. She got a great deal of pleasure from having her ideas accepted and the girls accepted them because they were good. In carrying out the program, Rose was a good sport and performed for consequences willingly. Partly by chance, this proved to be an excellent activity to permit Rose to enter the group and make a contribution to it. One could not say that the girls were warm to Rose, but they did accept what she had to offer to the success of the meeting.

"At the next meeting of the club, they made pyrolacing bracelets to be used as Christmas gifts. To get started each girl needed some individual attention and each was impatient for her turn. Purposely the leader placed Rose about in the middle of the group and she bided her waiting time much better than many of the others. Rose and one other girl caught the technique more easily than the others; so the leader suggested their helping the others get started. The leader was a little afraid Rose might act out her superiority, but she co-operated very nicely. The girls likewise accepted her help. At this point the leader was perplexed in her own mind as to whether Rose was trying to prove to her that she could cooperate and thus win her approval or whether the slow but sure acceptance from the group was stimulating her toward better behavior.

"On November 20 the Sub Debs attended a Pot Luck Supper at the nearby Y.W.C.A. The leader was unable to attend with them; so they were very eager to tell her about it when she came to the Home the next day. The two girls who got home from school first gave the first report: 'Miss R., we had a wonderful time! We all got little favors and Rose won the big prize of the party. She gave a swell imitation of Bing Crosby and Lena the Hyena.' The pride in their voices was unmistakable, and this showed real identification of Rose with the club. Later Rose showed the leader the bath salts she had won and told of her good time too. From none of the girls could the leader detect resentment that Rose had received the best prize at the party.

"Rose's changed attitude during the next week seemed almost too good to be true. The leader was worried lest she was behaving for her and was perhaps expecting some approval from her. The leader had tried to live up to her role of being kind, friendly, and accepting of Rose, but she showed no partiality toward her. In conference with the case worker, it was decided that her behavior in the girls' department would be one criterion by which to judge. The leader conferred with the girls' housemothers and they said that Rose was much less quarrelsome with the girls in the department. After the meetings on Monday nights, she went along with the other girls in preparing for bed. These observations pointed toward a real adjustment on Rose's part.

"As a whole group we planned our Christmas party on November 25. Suggestions and objections to suggestions came from all sides. Rose suggested some elaborate and rather impractical ideas. Two of the girls especially would not tolerate her ideas and were somewhat insulting to her. These two girls are also bright and both are well accepted leaders. Possibly they feel somewhat threatened by Rose because she is just as capable as they. Rose restrained herself in this instance or the leader thinks there would have been a verbal fight. Rose's eyes looked daggers but she kept quiet and soon the feeling blew over.

"We decided to sing Christmas carols as a conclusion to the meeting and it was Rose who dashed out to her locker to get us a song book of carols. The meeting concluded on a happy note.

"The case worker said that in her conferences on December 10th, Rose had not brought up problems relating to the girls but rather had shown enthusiasm over the good time she was having with them.

"Her attitude toward adults has become more normal. She still rebels against their authority at times but does not need to seek their attention and approval so much. The housemothers say they just 'don't notice' her so much. The leader interprets this to mean that her need to aggravate them is lessened.

"The December 16 meeting was the Christmas party of the Sub

Deb Club. When the girls got home from school in the late afternoon, we all went to the living room where the leader had the materials available for trimming the Christmas tree, and arranging the tables.

"Everyone enjoyed getting ready. Finally everything was finished and we had fifteen minutes left before dinnertime. The girls sat on the floor near the tree and enjoyed the intimacy of the group while they sang Christmas songs softly. One of the girls, who had been most opposed to Rose earlier, took charge of selecting the songs. She proposed that two of the girls, whom she selected, sing a duet 'Silent Night' while the rest of us hummed it. Then she suggested that Rose sing as a solo 'Joy to the World' while we hummed a background. Rose was thrilled and responded very nicely. As we got up to go to the dining room, Rose threw her arms about the leader and said, 'This is the happiest day of my life!'

"After dinner we went out in the snow and carolled through the neighborhood for about an hour. Rose sang her solo and the other girls their duet several times. Part of the time Rose walked with her arm tucked in the leader's and part of the time with various of the others.

"When we came home for a story and refreshments, all of the girls were in the Christmas spirit. They had obtained some mistletoe and there was much kissing, especially of the adults. The club had four guests—the superintendent, the nurse, the secretary, and a guest who was our story teller. Rose helped three other girls serve the food. Everyone was gracious and kindly toward each other. As the party concluded and all the girls were kissing everyone goodnight, Rose whispered in the leader's ear, 'It has been a wonderful day!'

"In her next conference with the case worker, Rose made a significant statement: 'Mrs. S., I have a feeling that something terrible may happen. I'm getting along wonderfully with the girls!'

"In evaluating Rose's progress over the three months period, both the case worker and the group leader feel that their combined and concentrated efforts in her behalf have been well worthwhile. While Rose could probably say only that she is happier and is getting along better with everyone, some positive values have emerged for her.

Her more conforming behavior has brought forth a desirable response from the children and the staff. Her pleasure in that response helps to stimulate her effort to conform. Using her abilities for the good of the group has brought a more satisfactory response than her former 'showing off' ever did. She does feel the gradual acceptance of the group through her own contributions to it. By the use of her skills she is gaining group recognition. She is experiencing acceptance by non-aggressive, non-punitive adults. A sense of 'belonging' to the institution and to the club group is being born. Heretofore, Rose has never fully accepted being a member of the Home. Rose's parents have a deep sense of guilt over placing her at the Home. If Rose's behavior continues to improve and she can be happy at the Home, her parents' guilt will be lessened and they will feel that they are doing something constructive for her, through the placement.

"Both the case worker and the group leader feel that some regression in Rose's behavior with the group is likely. However, these two months of positive experience will provide a sort of cushion. Through this much of a repetition of constructive group experience, a foundation is laid and if a regression occurs, there is a foundation on which to fall back."

We cannot follow Rose through her subsequent progress toward more acceptable behavior. However, it is indicative of her changing position to note the increasing number of positive responses the group worker depicts in the sociograms given in Chapter VI, which describe interpersonal relations during the spring of the next year. Her increasing ability to adjust to others had its ups and downs as expected. At one meeting in the early spring when she was dancing with the leader she confided to her that she was "going to stop trying to be good." This slump in intentions was brought on by her father's attempt to remove her from the Home before the case worker felt either she or the family were ready for it. As this was worked out into a plan for her returning home in June she resumed her improvement. At the last meeting of the year, the leader reports the following conversation as she sat with Rose on a streetcar going to a picnic: "Our conversation touched on my leaving and the club's breaking up. Rose said that this club and I had taught her a very helpful thing—how to be friends with people. She said she had learned not to be sarcastic and how to laugh most of the time when the girls made her mad. I have been sure that Rose's adjustment had been through conscious effort even though she needed guidance and support from both Mrs. S. [the case worker] and me."

The process of referral to agencies outside the recreation-education agency requires of the group worker an ability to recognize need through symptomatic behavior, a sympathetic skill in dealing with the individual and a thorough knowledge of available resources. Such referral when it is needed is, in fact, one of the most expert aspects of the group worker's job. He must know how to get sufficient rapport to understand what the difficulty may involve, but he must avoid opening up problems too complex or too deep for him to deal with. He must know how to bring in the doctor, case worker or psychiatrist, as the situation may require, without seeming to reject or desert the member who may wish to maintain the relation with him. If the member wants and is able to establish the new relation the group worker must step back to a supportive role and return primarily to his position as leader.

The group worker is likely occasionally to receive referrals, from family or children's agencies, hospitals, churches, or other recreation agencies. The introduction of such people into the group situations available within his agency requires not only the understanding of the individual's needs and interests but the diagnosis of the types of groups available, the interpersonal relations into which he would need to fit and the program that suited his interests. The discovery of what Fritz Redl has called "group relevant" factors must be the joint responsibility of the case worker making the referral and the group worker who receives it.

In an agency or group established for recreational or educational purposes, the leader needs to keep this function clearly in mind. As the previous instances have illustrated, some people will appear within the agency who cannot enjoy themselves, establish the relations they want, or learn what they may set out to, until personal problems which are troubling them can be straightened out. There are invariably others who seek from a friendly and understanding leader assistance with difficulties that are disturbing them. To slip over treatment upon people who do not desire it nor understand that it is being done would be manipulation. But to help in meeting needs of group members for individualized assistance when wanted or required is an essential part of group leadership.

From the illustrative material presented in this chapter it is clear that the leaders of groups have a particular kind of relationship to group members which at times may prove of special value. The group leader needs to understand the nature of that relationship and how to use it for the assistance of individuals when it is needed. It has several facets. Within the group itself the group leader may be aware of the special needs of individuals as illustrated in the excerpt from the Sub Debs in this chapter. He may never see them by themselves, no words may pass between them and yet with this awareness within the context of the group itself the group leader may help to see that a person finds the stimulus, the recognition, the affection he is seeking. We can see this in Tony at the microphone or Ruth attending the City Council as clearly as we can with Art, the deaf boy, in his more obvious need for help in adjustment. In such adjustments the group leader can, within the flow of program and of the relationships, set the stage for many to play their parts with deeper satisfaction. The very diffusion and indirectness of such assistance provides the needed support and encouragement for many who would be threatened by any more individualized approach which broke into their reserve.

The group leader is likely to have many contacts with individuals outside the group. These may run all the way from requests for vocational guidance or medical care to the request for help with individual adjustment problems. In these instances, while the group leader is always a sympathetic listener, he cannot if he is to continue his function as a group leader enter upon a long-continued or deeply involved relationship with a member. This is not only because time will not permit, considering the usual work load of the group worker. It is not even because he may not be qualified to provide the service needed, which is in some instances certainly the case.

It is rather that his function as group leader requires him to keep a relation to all members and to the group-as-a-whole. This function is not superficial because he cannot enter upon such deep individual relationships. It is and must remain diffuse in order to be equally available for all. He can give essential but limited assistance like that provided for Art or Ray in getting into the group, or the support given Clarice in time of stress. Such assistance is a vital expression of the worker's warm relation to each member. Its limits are set by the worker's function for the group-as-a-whole. For many leaders who cannot bring about a referral even for those who need long-continued or deeper treatment and for the many leaders in communities where no resources for referral are accessible, this limited type of individual assistance is all they may be able to provide. They will do more harm than good if they attempt the expert service which only the psychiatrist, for example, should attempt. This in no way minimizes the value of the help they can render to boys like Art or girls like Clarice within the accepted limits of their function.

There are also those situations where the group leader works with another worker in a co-operative relation, as in the case of Rose. The other worker may be a psychiatrist, a doctor, a vocational counselor, a teacher, or some other professional person. The contribution of the group worker in such joint assistance may be of value in diagnosis and may through the relation in the group become, as with Rose, a part of treatment. Here the group worker needs to be aware both of the limitations and of the resources that lie within his function. The contribution of a trained and discerning person who sees and works with people in the spontaneous social interaction of the group is a unique and essential one when it can be fully utilized in co-operative effort to assist those who need and want it. Like all such assistance, any individualized help can be useful only when the person involved desires it and co-operates in it.

Some Guideposts for Leaders

IF THE READER HAS FOLLOWED thus far he has, we hope, been transferring into his own experience the problems and solutions discussed in the preceding chapters. It is to be hoped that such analysis of his familiar difficulties with his own club, class or committee will not have thrown him "distracted in the ditch considering how to run." As we shut the door upon the Bulldogs, the Jokerettes and their companions, it is well to cast these conclusions into a more generalized mold. In the second chapter we tried to set forth the assumptions that we believe to be now generally accepted as underlying group work. In this concluding chapter we would like to build upon those assumptions and the intervening presentation of the concrete problems of leadership in youth groups some guideposts for those who undertake such leadership.

These final considerations we shall center around two major questions: By what criteria does a leader test his own understanding of the group or, if he is in a supervisory position, the understanding of others? Secondly, by what basic objectives is he guided in the use of such knowledge and skill as he possesses?

The first question a leader might well ask himself is, How much do I really understand of what is going on here? Each of us inevitably brings to such situations his own needs and values, his own cultural traditions, his own predispositions determined by age, class position, and previous condition of servitude to all the molding forces of life. As we accept the role of club adviser, teacher, or executive secretary to the club, council, or committee the first requirement if we are to be of assistance is a sensitive awareness of the group as individuals, of what they are seeking from it, and of what they are bringing to it from their life experience. Where considerable differences of age, education, or social background exist this requires an especially sympathetic and nonjudgmental sensitivity to see life *as it appears to them.* Only as he can do this to some degree can any leader understand what growth is possible to them, what enjoyment in its deeper sense can be achieved, what effective part these persons can play upon the social stage of their generation.

Granted that he approaches his group with this kind of sympathetic insight, what does he look for if he is to understand what is going on about him? The previous chapters have, we hope, made concrete the essential elements by which he must be able to diagnose his group.

In such analysis of the group process, the first and most obvious step is the understanding of the bond that calls the group into existence. As we have indicated, the stated purposes give only a clue and sometimes a misleading one to a real insight into the mesh of needs and motives that create the group. The leader's approach to such understanding must lie rather in his ability to see through the surface behavior of the members, the fears and ambitions, the affection and hostility, the generous idealism, and the search for security that blend together into collective forms.

As the leader gets such insight into the dynamic forces that are creating the group he is then in a position to help the members find the appropriate form in which to clothe their collective needs. Group objectives, membership requirements, the structural form of club, class, or committee must be seen by the leader in terms of their ability to serve the needs and capacities with which members enter the group.

A second element in such analysis of the group process will consist of the understanding of the social structure of the group. As we have seen, this involves an insight into the evaluation that members constantly make of each other. The status each achieves and its basis in either the role of leadership or the attainment of some other pre-eminence are the first clues to such social structure. Underlying the rating process, however, the leader must seek for the scales of value that are being used spontaneously by the group. As he understands these bases for rating, he has discovered one aspect of the dynamic interplay within the group.

Intermingling with the rating process, the leader will learn to recognize the intricate pattern of interpersonal reactions in all its kaleidoscopic flux. The ties of friendship and of enmity, the flow of influence, the bonds that relate dominator and dependent, will assume a deeper significance as the leader sees them as significant expressions of personality unfolding in the interaction the group provides.

A third aspect of any evaluation of the group process will consist of the analysis of authority and government within the group. The various structural forms of the group government, its officers, committees, and constitution, which we have discussed in self-governing clubs, in interest groups, in representative councils and in many others, give only its skeleton. Such a skeleton is essential to a sound organism with clearly defined functions working in smooth co-ordination. The process of government consists also of that participation of the governed and that stimulus and guidance of leadership out of which the true authority of the group is born. This interaction, like the others, is at bottom an expression of the personalities of the participants and will bear the marks of their ability to lead, to select and evaluate appropriate leadership, to create a collective whole which subordinates impulse to the common goals.

A fourth element in the leader's evaluation will lie in the area of the development of program. Here he will want to examine how well rooted the program is in the vital interests of the group, whether it has provided satisfying outlets for emotional drives and expanding knowledge of increasingly valuable types. He will test the process by which the program was determined to see how much arose from the group itself, and whether his own contribution of skill and knowledge proved adequate to meet their needs.

One further aspect of the group's life it will be necessary for the leader to sense throughout all his dealings with it. He must be aware of the intangible but still obvious things by which the group indicates its esprit de corps. The intangible and permeating atmosphere of any group has its ups and downs of barometric pressure. It will, at times, be obviously high and clear, at others murky and overcast. Some flux in esprit de corps is to be expected but the leader will need to evaluate not only the pressure of the permeating atmosphere but its steadiness. He must watch the tendency it shows toward strength or weakness and the ability of the group to deal with crises or difficulties.

As he attempts to diagnose the group the leader will be aware also both of the individuals that make it up and of the surrounding community in which it is embedded. Inevitably these three—the individuals, the group, and the community—affect each other in constant interaction.

Any group leader who is attempting to see below the surface of his group will need, of course, to adopt some system of group recording, by which events can be evaluated, process discovered, and the meaning of the behavior understood. At least a minimum of narrative recording is essential if he is to have the basis for any well-considered understanding. As he adopts the practice of recording he will have the material by which his understanding can develop.

Any group worker is more than a passive observer or a sociological investigator of the group process. By the nature of his function he is an active agent. His understanding, therefore, is only the foundation upon which he acts. The feature that distinguishes the group-work process from the spontaneous social process of the gang on the street is the presence of a leader who takes a real part in making the group more valuable for its members and more productive for society. It is inevitable, therefore, that the group worker by his relationship to the group inserts a new and active ingredient in terms both of the function of the agency and of his own guiding values and objectives.

It is obvious that the understanding of group behavior can be used for many purposes. A skillful Nazi youth leader undoubtedly knew as well how to affect the control and morale of his group as any leader with democratic aims. The skillful politician has an expertness in such matters beyond the range of the average group worker.

This does not mean that group work as an approach is merely a body of technical knowledge about group behavior unrelated to social aims or unguided by any coherent philosophy. Group work, like all similar methods, must include both technical knowledge and the aims for which such knowledge will be used. All those who work with people, whether as case workers, educators, doctors, or group workers, must inevitably guide their skill by certain objectives. Such goals are there, functioning confusedly and implicitly when they do not function coherently and openly. To what ends, then, should the group worker put whatever skill and knowledge he may possess? Since guiding philosophies of this sort are only partially held in common it seems appropriate here to put these into more personal terms as the expression of the author's own convictions.

I believe that groups of this kind if properly understood and sympathetically led can provide for the participants a kind of social nourishment which will enhance life and encourage growth. If a group through the interaction of the members and the guidance of the leader is friendly, warm and accepting, it can give to its members a chance to experience mutual relationships and the diffused but significant securities that come from the sense of belonging. For different individuals, and at different age levels, this kind of acceptance will have varied meanings. For many it can contribute to emotional stability and security and can give acceptable guidance to both positive and negative feeling.

There are potentials in the way of education available in such leisure-time groups which can and should be developed. In the free and voluntary setting of such groups learning comes easily if program is wisely developed. Beginning with existing interests, learning can be expanded into wider and deeper forms of knowledge. Capacities can be brought to fruition, encouragement can be given to unused talents, and creative energies can find outlets that are both individually satisfying and socially valuable.

Within the life of such groups lie the occasions in which values can be remade. The standards that people bring to these groups reflect the community that has molded them. The issues that arise in the group give the opportunity to clarify what is at stake, to identify at points with more acceptable leadership, to guide through the pressures of the group toward the best we know in our contemporary culture.

One of the needs of our society is experience in more fruitful ways to occupy our expanding leisure. Some of what we now do with it is vicious or antisocial; much more is merely childish, futile, or trivial. It is only as our culture can discover avocations that have depth and meaning that we can take advantage of the time which technology presents us. The ancient human pursuits in art, in the pleasures of physical skill, in companionship, in philosophy and learning as an end in itself—these give us clues to what we might produce as a civilized people. Both the amount of leisure and its extension to larger proportions of the population make the manner of its use of greater importance. These groups should provide experimentation and example of what can be made out of time when it is "free" for our use.

We have in such groups also a chance to learn the art of democratic government, which is not afforded as well in many other settings. Democracy is not a form of government alone. It is also a habit of response to others, an ability to accommodate pressures, a respect for the uniqueness of each. These are social skills which are learned only through social experience. The small size and intimate character of many of these groups make them particularly useful for such experience.

We have also within our grasp one of the best means to bring about better understanding between differing and often hostile parts of our community. Through the program and activities of such leisure-time groups it is often possible to bring together people of differing racial and nationality groups, differing social classes, differing economic or political opinions. While we recognize the prejudice, intolerance and snobbishness with which we begin, we often can break through such barriers to produce an appreciation of people as they become known to each other. This is one of the most urgent needs at present and it is one to which the skill and understanding of group behavior can make a major contribution.

Such groups can provide for many a chance to work out their place as workers and consumers in our society. The selection of a job may be the concern of youth at the point of leaving school but for the experienced worker there are always questions which arise out of the work situation. While the major economic relations will be dealt with by the organized groups of labor and management, it is often true that in groups of other kinds, social clubs, discussion groups, consumer organizations, people can share their job experiences, thrash out their common difficulties, and at times make up their minds on their own and the community's economic problems.

It is essential that leaders in constant contact with groups of mature people should recognize their opportunity for the promotion of interest in current economic issues at the point where these issues have significance to them. This means a constant alertness to the problems they are confronting either as workers or as consumers, the stimulus to interest, and the provision of resources as needed for intelligent action.

The group worker has a similar responsibility to stimulate community participation as his groups can be interested in local and national issues. This, of course, does not involve propaganda for particular viewpoints. It does, however, involve the conviction essential in a democratic society that each individual should assume his social responsibilities as he has ability to do so.

In pointing to such objectives as guides for the group worker I am, of course, aware that not all will apply to every group. It is the very essence of this approach that program and relationships must be worked out in each instance to meet the specific needs of those particular persons. The common factor in them all is the concern of the group worker with individual growth combined always with an active participation in and responsibility for the social whole. These two basic aims are the warp and woof of the democratic philosophy.

It may seem to some that to point to such objectives is to lay claim to grandiose aims indeed. Such is not the intention. It is rather to indicate that here as elsewhere in our chaotic world we must build our defenses against destruction out of the frail but indestructible filaments of the human spirit. Against the renaissance of brutality and tyranny which our generation has seen, we must create a social fabric of emotionally stable personalities able to use their capacities to the full in ways which contribute fruitfully to the community that surrounds them.

This book has dealt largely with youth, in whose lives such group experience has great potentials. To prepare the young to function in such a world as ours is a significant undertaking. The "failure of nerve" that has foreshadowed the fall of civilizations comes when citizens no longer feel deeply and with conviction that they are worth saving. That is why it is so essential that the youth of America should understand in the roots of their being the nature of democracy and should develop the convictions that will cause them to assume the responsibilities of citizenship.

Here at the point of group leadership understanding adults have the opportunity to assist in such development. Such a leader must be concerned not only in the deep process of individual maturation but also in the awakening of youth to the broader meanings of the social scene. This is no call to propaganda, for by the very nature of what democracy requires youth must learn rather to think and act for themselves, intelligently and responsibly. But for all who serve as group leaders today, the final test of such leadership must be: In what ways can these youth be helped to face the real world in which they will mature? Are they ready to play their part in creating that free, abundant and unified society which the peoples of the world so earnestly seek? To ask less of ourselves as leaders is to fail youth in this crisis of world history. To ask this much is to call into action all the mature wisdom and creative courage of which we are individually capable.

Chapter I

1. A new realization of the significance of leisure led in the late 1920's and the early 1930's to a crop of both philosophical treatments and research studies. The following represent this period:

C. Delisle Burns, *Leisure in the Modern World*, New York, The Century Co., 1932.

E. C. Lindeman, *Leisure, a National Issue*, New York, Association Press, 1939.

George Andrew Lundberg, Mirra Komarowsky and Mary Alice McInerny, *Leisure, a Suburban Study*, New York, Columbia University Press, 1934.

National Recreation Association, *Leisure Hours of 5000 People*, New York, 1934.

Jessie Frederick Steiner, *Americans at Play*, New York, McGraw-Hill Co., 1933.

2. Commission on Implications of Armed Services Educational Programs of the American Council on Education, *The Armed Services and Adult Education*, Washington, D.C., 1947, p. 231.

3. For material on the development of recreation see the following:

Foster Rhea Dulles, *America Learns to Play*, New York, D. Appleton-Century Co., 1940.

Martin N. and Esther S. Newmeyer, *Leisure and Recreation*, New York, A. S. Barnes & Co., 1936.

Jessie F. Steiner, *Recreation and Morale*, Washington, D.C., National Education Association, 1942. Problems in American Life series, Unit No. 4.

4. For a recent formulation of this philosophy see Ott G. Romney, *Off the Job Living*, New York, A. S. Barnes & Co., 1945.

5. For material on the development of Adult Education see the following:

James Truslow Adams, *Frontiers of American Culture, a Study of*

Adult Education in a Democracy, New York, Charles Scribner's Sons, 1944.

American Association for Adult Education, *Handbook of Adult Education in the United States*, New York, 1936.

Lyman Bryson, *Adult Education*, New York, American Book Co., 1936.

Eduard C. Lindeman, *The Meaning of Adult Education*, New York, The New Republic, Inc., 1926.

6. For material on Workers Education see the following:

Theodore Brameld (ed.), Frank Baker and others, *Workers Education in the United States*, New York, Harper & Brothers, 1941.

Eleanor Coit, *Government Support of Workers Education*, New York, American Labor Education Service, 1940.

Ernest Edward Schwarztrauber, *Workers Education, a Wisconsin Experiment*, Madison, the University of Wisconsin Press, 1942.

Mark Starr, *Workers Education Today*, New York, League for Industrial Democracy, 1941.

7. For material on the Settlement Movement see the following:

Gaynell Hawkins, *Educational Experiments in Social Settlements*, New York, American Association for Adult Education, 1937.

Paul Kellogg, "Social Settlements" in *Encyclopedia of the Social Sciences*, New York, The Macmillan Co., 1935, Vol. XIV, pp. 157-162.

Mary Kingsbury Simkhovitch, *The Settlement Primer* (Revised Edition), New York, National Federation of Settlements, 1936.

Robert H. Woods and Albert J. Kennedy, *The Settlement Horizon*, New York, Russell Sage Foundation, 1922.

8. Lewis Mumford, *The Culture of Cities*, New York, Harcourt, Brace & Co., 1938, p. 298.

9. As an illustration of this type of development see

John McDowell, "A Neighbourhood is Born," *The Compass*, Vol. XXV, No. 6, pp. 8-11.

10. Youth Activities have received considerable attention from governmental authorities in England in recent years. See, for example

A. E. Morgan, *The Needs of Youth*, London & New York, Oxford University Press, 1939.

Teachers and Youth Leaders, Report of a committee appointed by the President of the Board of Education, London Board of Education, 1944.

Youth Service After the War, Report of the Youth Advisory Council appointed by the President of the Board of Education, London Board of Education, 1943.

11. For description of Nazi youth activities see the following:

Edward Y. Hartshorne, *German Youth and the Nazi Dream of Victory,* New York, Farrar and Rinehart, 1941.

Erika Mann, *School for Barbarians,* New York, Modern Age Books, 1938.

Marianne Welter, A Lost Generation, Master's Thesis, School of Applied Social Sciences, Western Reserve University, Cleveland, 1944.

12. For the studies of the American Youth Commission dealing especially with the leisure of youth see the following:

Howard M. Bell, *Youth Tell Their Story,* Washington, American Council on Education, 1938.

Gilbert Wrenn and D. L. Harley, *Time on Their Hands,* Washington, American Council on Education, 1941.

13. *Children in a Democracy,* General Conference Report of the White House Conference, Washington, Children's Bureau, United States Department of Labor, 1940.

14. For information on youth-serving agencies with dates of origin see M. M. Chambers, *Youth Serving Organizations,* Washington, American Council on Education, 1941.

15. See report by Oscar I. Janowski, *Summary of Jewish Welfare Board Survey Commission Report,* New York, Jewish Welfare Board, 1947.

16. For one illustration of such a change in policy see *Interracial Practices in Community Y.W.C.A.'s,* New York, National Board of the Y.W.C.A., 1944.

17. For one illustration of an agency attempting to work out such methods see Meyer Schwartz, *Toward an Interracial Policy in the Irene Kaufman Settlement, Pittsburgh, Pa.,* Master's Thesis, School of Applied Social Sciences, Western Reserve University, Cleveland, 1946.

18. A very extensive literature on recreational therapy and more recently on group therapy has developed. The following titles represent the major strands in this development:

John Eisele Davis, *Principles and Practices of Recreational Therapy for the Mentally Ill,* New York, A. S. Barnes & Co., 1936.

Jacob Klapman, *Group Psychotherapy Theory and Practice,* New York, Grune & Stratton, 1946.

Fritz Redl, "Clinical Group Work with Children" in *Group Work and the Social Scene*, New York, American Association for the Study of Group Work, 1943.

S. R. Slavson, *An Introduction to Group Therapy*, New York, The Commonwealth Fund, 1943.

See also S. R. Slavson and Gertrude Meyers, *Bibliography on Group Therapy*, New York, American Group Therapy Association, 1946.

19. See *Children in a Democracy*, p. 24.

Chapter II

1. For definitions of such positions see *Positions in Youth Serving Organizations*, New York, Associated Youth Serving Organizations, 1945.

In a number of communities studies of personnel including job definitions have been made under the auspices of Councils or Federations of Social Agencies.

2. See author's *Group Experience and Democratic Values*, New York, Woman's Press, 1947, ch. 4, "Changing Perspectives in Group Work."

3. See for example William Heard Kilpatrick, *Group Education for a Democracy*, New York, Association Press, 1940.

4. W. W. Charters and V. Fry, *The Ohio Study of Recreation Leadership Training*, Bureau of Educational Research Monographs, No. 2, Columbus, Ohio State University, 1942.

5. For other formulations of group work see the following:

Louis H. Blumenthal, *Group Work in Camping*, New York, Association Press, 1937.

Arthur Fink, *The Field of Social Work*, New York, Henry Holt & Co., 1942, ch. IX.

Clara Kaiser, *Objectives of Group Work*, New York, Association Press, 1936.

S. R. Slavson, *Creative Group Education*, New York, Association Press, 1937.

Social Work Year Book, New York, Russell Sage Foundation, articles in each year book from 1937 on.

Dorothea Sullivan (ed.), *The Practice of Group Work*, New York, Association Press, 1941.

6. Elton Mayo, *The Social Problems of an Industrial Civilization*, Cambridge, Harvard University Press, 1945.

7. For fuller expansion of this conception see author's *Group Experience and Democratic Values*, ch. 6, "On Becoming Professional."

Chapter III

1. For the definition of various social classes as used throughout this book see William Lloyd Warner and Paul S. Lunt, *The Social Life of a Modern Community*, New Haven, Yale University Press, 1941, pp. 81-91.

Chapter IV

1. For one of the best explanations of the psychological bases of play see Karl Menninger, *Love Against Hate*, New York, Harcourt, Brace & Co., 1942.

2. Robert Walder, "The Psycho-analytic Theory of Play," *The Psychoanalytic Quarterly*, Vol. II, No. 2, p. 222.

3. For a discussion of such face-to-face groups in the social structure of industry see

F. J. Roethlisberger, *Management and Morale*, Cambridge, Harvard University Press, 1942, pp. 46-66.

Maria Rogers, "Autonomous Groups in Industry," New York, *Autonomous Groups Bulletin*, Vol. III, Nos. 1 & 2.

4. Recognition of the place of such groups by labor leaders is evidenced in the following:

Clinton Golden and Harold J. Ruttenberg, *The Dynamics of Industrial Democracy*, New York, Harper & Brothers, 1942, pp. 181-186.

5. For sociometric analysis of such groups in institutions see

Helen Hall Jennings, *Leadership and Isolation*, New York, Longmans, Green & Co., 1943.

Jacob L. Moreno, *Who Shall Survive?*, Washington, Nervous and Mental Disease Publishing Co., 1934.

6. Warner and Lunt, *The Social Life of a Modern Community*, pp. 110, 350-355.

7. For one of the most discerning descriptions of this type of group see Helen Hall Jennings, "Sociometric Differentiation of the Psyche Group and the Socio-group," New York, *Autonomous Groups Bulletin*, Vol. II, No. 4.

8. Three studies of the same canteen describe this situation. See

Naomi Maise, *The Friendly Inn Canteen*.

William Simmons and Catherine Clement, *Youth Experience in a Canteen Hangout*.

These were Masters' Theses in the School of Applied Social Sciences, Western Reserve University, Cleveland, 1947.

9. For a discussion of the psychological basis for avocational activities see the following:

W. C. Menninger, "Psychological Aspects of Hobbies," *American Journal of Psychiatry*, Vol. 99, pp. 122-129.

"Recreation and Morale," *Bulletin of the Menninger Clinic*, Vol. 6, No. 3, Topeka.

10. James W. Mower, "A Comparative Study of Hobby Activities," *Bulletin of the Menninger Clinic*, Vol. 7, No. 3, Topeka, pp. 82-87.

11. *Ibid.*, p. 102.

Chapter V

1. For discussion of the role of the executive secretary see author's *Group Experience and Democratic Values*, ch. 3, "The Executive Director as Leader."

2. For material useful in such discussion see Joseph Samler, *Vocational Guidance Through Groups*, Washington, B'nai B'rith Vocational Service Bureau, 1943.

3. Edith Buxbaum, "Transference and Gang Formation in Children and Adolescence," in *The Psycho-analytic Study of the Child*, New York, International Universities Press, 1945, Vol. 1, pp. 351-365.

4. *Ibid.*, p. 351.

5. Helene Deutsche, *The Psychology of Women*, New York, Grune & Stratton, 1944, Vol. 1, p. 36.

6. See Peter Blos, *The Adolescent Personality*, New York, D. Appleton-Century Co., 1941, pp. 254-266.

7. Roy R. Grinker and John P. Spiegel, *Men under Stress*, Philadelphia, The Blakiston Co., 1946, p. 40.

8. Mayo, *The Social Problems of an Industrial Civilization*, pp. 7-8.

9. Warner and Lunt, *Social Life of a Modern Community*, pp. 81-91.

10. John Dollard, *Caste and Class in a Southern Town*, New Haven, Yale University Press, 1937.

11. For the place of age and sex in creating the social structure see the following:

Ralph Linton, "Age and Sex Categories," *American Sociological Review*, Vol. VII, pp. 589-603.

Talcott Parsons, "Age and Sex in the Social Structure of the United States," *American Sociological Review*, Vol. 7, pp. 604-620.

12. Blos, *The Adolescent Personality*, pp. 248-254.

13. For studies showing social factors affecting the amount of group participation see the following:

Gordon W. Allport, "The Psychology of Participation," *Psychological Review*, Vol. 53, No. 3, pp. 117-132.

C. Arnold Anderson, "The Pattern of Social Activities in a High Participation Group," *Rural Sociology*, Vol. IV, pp. 463-464.

W. A. Anderson, "The Family and Individual Participation," *American Sociological Review*, Vol. 8, pp. 420-424.

Stuart Chapin, "Social Participation and Social Intelligence," *American Sociological Review*, Vol. 4, pp. 157-166.

Warner and Lunt, *Social Life of an American Community*, pp. 301-355.

14. For effect of nationality background on club affiliation and recreational interests see Welfare Council of New York, *Survey of Boys Work in Brooklyn*, New York, 1931, pp. 180-221.

15. For relation of type of participation to ethnic factors see, for example, Gunnar Myrdal, *The American Dilemma*, New York, Harper & Brothers, 1944, pp. 810-857.

16. For studies showing distribution of participants in youth serving agencies by economic status see the following:

Howard Whipple Green, *Persons Participating in Leisure Time Activities by Economic Status in Greater Cleveland*, Cleveland, Health Council, 1938.

Ellery F. Reed, *Relation of Group Work and Case Work Agencies, a Comparative Study of Juvenile Court versus Group Work Youths*, Cincinnati, Community Chest, 1944.

17. Frederick Milton Thrasher, *The Gang*, Chicago, University of Chicago Press, 1927.

18. Henry Street Settlement, *Rooms of Their Own, a Survey of 28 Lower East Side Social Clubs*, New York, 1939.

19. Welfare Federation of Cleveland, *A Study of Non-affiliated Youth in the Glenville Area*, Cleveland, 1947.

20. Sanoma Nixon, *The Unattached Club, a study of unaffiliated clubs of Negro boys and girls in the Lower Woodland Area, Cleveland, Ohio*, Master's Thesis, School of Applied Social Sciences, Western Reserve University, Cleveland, 1942.

21. As illustration of this see *The Greek and the Independent*, Department of Sociology, Southern Methodist University, Dallas, 1938.

22. This situation was reported as quite usual among certain cellar clubs in New York by a student who had worked with them in a WPA project. Evidence of a similar relation of a boys gang to two sets of girls has appeared in one of the Cleveland canteens.

23. Welfare Federation of Cleveland, *Study of Non-affiliated Youth in the Glenville Area.* In one high school studied it was found that 46 per cent of the boys and 49 per cent of the girls belonged to non-affiliated groups not related to school, church or social agency. Of these people, 76 per cent of the girls and 45 per cent of the boys also belong to recognized organizations and 31 per cent of both boys and girls belong to clubs in such organizations.

24. For recent attempts to deal constructively with autonomous youth groups see the following:

Frank Caplin, "Extending Educational Services to Autonomous Groups of Unemployed Youth," New York, *Autonomous Groups Bulletin*, Vol. II, No. 1.

John B. Martin, "A New Attack on Delinquency," *Harper's Magazine*, Vol. 188, pp. 502-512.

R. J. Pulling, "A Public School Service for Autonomous Groups," New York, *Autonomous Groups Bulletin*, Vol. II, No. 2.

25. For effect of class position on intimate clique relations see Warner and Lunt, *Social Life of An American Community*, pp. 111-112.

26. See for example William Foote Whyte, *Street Corner Society*, Chicago, University of Chicago Press, 1943.

Chapter VI

1. For the use of sociometric measurement in youth groups see for example,

Merle Elliott, "Patterns of Friendship in the Class Room," *Progressive Education*, Vol. XVIII, No. 7, pp. 383-390.

Moreno, *Who Shall Survive?*

E. de A. Partridge, "The Sociometric Approach to Adolescent Grouping," *Sociometry*, Vol. VI, No. 3, pp. 258-263.

2. Jennings, *Leadership and Isolation.*

3. For descriptions of the rating process see Charlotte Bühler, "Social

Behavior of Children" in C. Murchison, *Handbook of Child Psychology*, Worcester, Clark University, 1933, pp. 385-386.

Wilbur I. Newstetter and Research Associates, *Group Adjustment*, Cleveland, Western Reserve University, 1938.

Caroline McCann Tryon, *Evaluations of Adolescent Personality by Adolescents*, Washington, Society for Research in Child Development, National Research Council, 1939.

Chapter VII

1. Mary L. Northway, "Outsiders," *Sociometry*, Vol. VII, No. 1, pp. 10-25.

2. See H. Meltzer, "Group Differences in Nationality and Race Preferences in Children," *Sociometry*, Vol. II, pp. 86-105.

——, "Hostility and Tolerance in Children's Nationality and Race Attitudes," *American Journal of Ortho-psychiatry*, Vol. II, pp. 662-675.

Chapter VIII

1. For discussion of problems of government in such groups see Charles Merriam, *Public and Private Government*, New Haven, Yale University Press, 1944.

2. For discussion of the relation of group experience to attitudes toward authority and social responsibility see Karl Mannheim, *Diagnosis of Our Time*, New York & London, Oxford University Press, 1944, pp. 51-58.

3. For discussion of the emotional bases of discipline problems see the following:

Fritz Redl, "Group Psychological Elements in Discipline Problems," *American Journal of Orthopsychiatry*, Vol. 13, pp. 77-81.

G. V. Sheviakov and Fritz Redl, *Discipline for Today's Children and Youth*, Washington, National Education Association, 1944.

4. An interesting discussion of the unique value of recreation activities as providing opportunity for youth to learn self-government is found in *The Civilian Conservation Corps*, Recommendations of the American Youth Commission of the American Council on Education, Washington, 1940.

5. See author's *Group Experience and Democratic Values*, ch. 8, "The Value of Group Life for Teen Age Youth."

6. The attitudes toward authority found in this group are much the

same as those produced in an artificially created "autocratic social climate." See Kurt Lewin and Donald Lippett, "Patterns of Aggressive Behavior in Experimentally Created Social Climates," *Journal of Social Psychology*, Vol. 10, pp. 271-299.

7. See Frederick J. Hacker and Elizabeth Geleerd, "Freedom and Authority in Adolescence," *American Journal of Orthopsychiatry*, Vol. 15, pp. 621-630.

8. See Hazel Osborne, "Problems in Teen Age Hangouts," *Proceedings National Conference of Social Work*, New York, Columbia University Press, 1944, pp. 148-159.

9. For a simple condensed statement of these procedures see *Democracy in Trade Unions*, New York, American Civil Liberties Union, 1943.

10. See author's *Social Process in Organized Groups*, New York, Richard R. Smith, 1930, ch. 5, "The Functions of Leadership."

11. Emily Alice Cleaveland, *Senior Girls Leaders Groups*, a study of six senior girls' leaders groups in the Cleveland Settlements, Master's Thesis, School of Applied Social Sciences, Western Reserve University, Cleveland, 1939.

12. See Ordway Tead, *Creative Management*, New York, Association Press, 1935.

Chapter IX

1. Herbert Read, *Education Through Art*, London, Faber and Faber, 1943, p. 5.

2. Ruth Anderson Radir, *Modern Dance for the Youth of America*, New York, A. S. Barnes & Co., 1944, p. 13.

3. For description of the characteristics of the so-called "character building" youth programs see Hugh Hartshorne, *Character in Human Relations*, New York, Charles Scribner's Sons, 1932, pp. 34-43.

4. See Dorothy Height, *Step by Step with Interracial Groups*, New York, Woman's Press, 1946.

5. There is considerable evidence of an apathy and lack of interest in social issues among youth. See for example

Nellie Pauline McGill and Ellen Nathalie Matthews, *The Youth of New York City*, New York, The Macmillan Co., 1940, pp. 225, 338.

Homer Rainey, *How Fare American Youth*, New York, D. Appleton-Century Co., pp. 153-178.

6. For illustrations of successful projects used in stimulating social

interest see Paul Robert Hanna, *Youth Serves the Community*, New York, D. Appleton-Century Co., 1936.

7. See author's *Group Experience and Democratic Values*, ch. 10, "Group Work and Social Change," and ch. 11, "Group Work and Social Action."

Chapter X

1. Helen Hall Jennings, *Leadership and Isolation*, pp. 42-43.

2. This type of relationship seems to have been openly and consciously promoted within Nazi and certain pre-Nazi youth groups in Germany. Within the Männerbund or Bundisch organizations characteristic of Nazi youth activities the tie between leader and group was used to create groups pervaded by an erotic bond and this form of social life was regarded as superior preparation for citizenship in the Nazi state. This is undoubtedly related to the psychological immaturity essential to maintaining a dictatorship. See Aurel Kolnai, *The War Against the West*, New York, The Viking Press, 1938, pp. 79-84.

3. An extensive literature on the relation between case work and group work has already developed. The following represent the major strands of thinking in this area:

American Association of Group Workers, *Group Work-Case Work Cooperation, a Symposium*, New York, Association Press, 1946.

Children in the Community, the St. Paul Experiment in Child Welfare, United States Children's Bureau Publication 317, Washington, 1946.

Merrill Conover, "The Joint Use of Group Work and Case Work Techniques," *The Family*, Vol. XXIII, No. 7, pp. 264-273.

Gordon Hamilton, *Theory and Practice of Case Work*, New York, Columbia University Press, 1940, ch. 10.

Clara Kaiser, "The Dynamic Integration of Case Work and Group Work Agencies," *Proceedings New York State Conference of Social Work, 1944*.

Susanne Schultze, "Re-thinking Institutional Services for Dependent Children," *Proceedings, National Conference of Social Work*, New York, Columbia University Press, 1946.

Margaret Svendson, Dorothy Spiker, *et al, An Experimental Project in the Integration of Case Work and Group Work Services*, Chicago Institute for Juvenile Research, Jewish Children's Bureau and Jewish Social Service Bureau (no date).

Anne Tyler, *Case Work and Group Work. Similarities and Differences*, New York, New York Welfare Council (no date).

Gertrude Wilson, *Group Work and Case Work Their Relationship and Practice*, New York, Family Welfare Association of America, 1941.

I N D E X